Arab *and* Christian?

Christians in the Middle East

For Johannes Blauw
guru and friend

A. Wessels

Arab *and* Christian?

Christians in the Middle East

Kok Pharos Publishing House
Kampen – the Netherlands

CIP-GEGEVENS KONINKLIJKE BIBLIOTHEEK, DEN HAAG

© 1995, Kok Pharos Publishing House
P.O. Box 5016, 8260 GA Kampen, the Netherlands
ISBN 90 390 0071 9
Cover design by Dik Hendriks
Further information on cover see page 209
Translation by John Medendorp and Henry Jansen

Contents

INTRODUCTION

"Arabic cannot be Christianized."

Arab and Christian

Arabs are not currently 'in' in the West. They are usually equated with Moslems. There is, however, in the West, an anti-Islamism, negative feelings toward all things Arabic and Islamic, which is analogous to the anti-Semitism directed against the Jews. This is sometimes even true of the scholars who study the culture and world of the Arabs. The Moroccan historian Abdallah Laroui has shown that there are scholars in the West who focus exclusively on 'dead Arabs' in order to avoid dealing with the living. Some of them take great pleasure in exaggerating the gulf between the illustrious ancients and their unworthy descendants.[1]

Arab and Christian—this title expresses a certain ambivalence. It could mean Arab as opposed to Christian, as in the expression Moslem and Christian; or it could mean both Arab *and* Christian.

There are many people in the West who think of Arabs only as Moslems. Such an association appears obvious. After all, the overwhelming majority of Arabs from Morocco to the Sudan, from the borders of Turkey to those of Iran, are indeed Moslems. Nevertheless, there are Christians in the Arab world, and there are even Arab Christians, although they are a continually diminished, and perhaps also diminishing, minority. Not only is this unknown to many in the West, it is also denied by many Arabs. In August 1980, the Libyan president, Colonel Qadhafi, declared that Arab Christians simply had to convert, since "it is a contradiction to be both Arab and Christian." When he was questioned in an interview with a Lebanese newspaper concerning the fate of the ten million Christians who were estimated to live in the Arab world at that time, he declared that if Christian Arabs were to be authentic Arabs, they would have to accept the Islamic faith. He explained the Lebanese conflict as a problem of split-personality, resulting from the fact that there were those who were attempting to be both Arab and Christian. "Christians who live in the Arab world," he stated, "have closer links to the Vatican than to Mecca. They have a European spirit in an Arab body."[2] Qadhafi does, therefore, acknowledge the existence of Arab Christians,

1

but apparently thinks that they should not exist, or at least not exist any longer. One is immediately reminded of the Arabic saying quoted above: "Arabic cannot be Christianized."

It cannot be denied, however, that ever since the beginning of the Christian era, there have been 'Arab Christians'. Already in the book of Acts of the Apostles (New Testament) we read that on the day of Pentecost, the Arabs also heard the apostles proclaim the great deeds of God in their own language (Acts 2:11). Paul also went to Arabia after his conversion (Galatians 1:17). At the first ecumenical councils of the ancient Church, there were Arab archbishops present. In the pre-Islamic period, the Christian faith grew among the Arabs.[3]

On the northern border of what is now called Saudi Arabia, just as in the south of the Arabian peninsula, Christian churches could at one time be found. The city of Najran, in Yemen, was for many years an important Christian center. During the life of the prophet Mohammad (570-632), he received a delegation of Christians from Najran, with whom he had a dialogue concerning the understanding of Jesus Christ. Although it is true that the Arabian peninsula was never completely Christianized, Christians and Christian churches were found there. In the Yemen capital, Sana'a, there once stood a Christian church which had to function as a type of competitor to the Ka'bah, the holy shrine for Islam which already existed at Mecca prior to the emergence of Islam. It is also said that Mohammed, who rose as a prophet in the seventh century, met a certain Christian monk named Bahira in his home town. There is also a story about the cousin of his wife, Khadija, a certain Waraqah ibn Nawfal, who was purported to have been a Christian. Whatever the case may have been, there can be no doubt that the new Islamic religion immediately encountered 'Arab Christians' along its way.

Christians were regarded by Mohammed as 'people of the book'. That meant that they were to be respected and tolerated, and not forced to convert to Islam, even though conversion was considered desirable. Soon after the death of Mohammed (632), however, it appears that a second faith was no longer tolerated, especially in the heartland of Arabia. Under one of Mohammed's successors, Caliph 'Umar ibn al-Khattab (ca. 590-644), the Christians of Najran were exiled to Iraq. Under another caliph, 'Umar ibn 'Abd al Aziz (mostly indicated as 'Umar II. 717-720), the command was given to deal with a certain Arab Christian tribe. Not unlike the contention of Qadhafi, he is reported to have

2

said: "This is an Arab tribe, and therefore cannot confess Christianity."
Because they were Arabs, however, this consciously Arab tribe refused
to undergo the humiliation of having to pay tribute (*jizya*)—the poll-tax
which was soon imposed on Christian subjects of Muslim rule—like the
other non-Arab and non-Islamic tribes. 'Umar II permitted them to pay
the poor tax required from Moslems, although he doubled the amount for
Christians. He did, however, require that their children not be baptized,
but be raised as Moslems.[4]

Shortly after the Islamic conquest, the Christian Arab tribes appealed
to the Byzantine emperor for help. He, in turn, sent a fleet of ships to
Antioch, which landed in 638. Christian tribes, among whom were the
Arab tribe named Banu Tanukh, who lived south of Aleppo (Syria), rebelled and allied themselves with the Greeks. When the Moslem general
heard this, he called upon them, after their defeat, to accept Islam. Some
of them complied, but part of the tribe refused. A century and a half
later, another caliph forced some of the remainder to become Moslems.[5]

From various indications it appears that many caliphs were sympathetic to the desire of certain Arab tribes to become, but especially to
remain, Christian. Although tolerance toward others was practiced, and
religious force was, as a rule, avoided, pressure was brought to bear on
Christian Arabs to convert to Islam. Qadhafi, who rose to power in a
country (Libya) which is thoroughly Islamic, represents an Islamic point
of view which, with the exception of the western part of the Arab world
(the *Maghreb*), is not shared by Moslems in other countries, especially
not where Arab, Arabized, and non-Arab Christian communities—the Armenians are a good example of the latter—continue to exist in the midst
of a world which has for the most part embraced Islam.

The statements of Qadhafi illustrate the contemporary problems of
being both Arab *and* Christian. There is a tension among Christians in
the Arab world, and among Arab Christians, with respect to their own
identity. Can Arab Christians in an Arab world be and remain Christians? Has not the historical process of Arabization been synonymous
with that of Islamization? Are they, and do they feel, part of the Arab
world, and are they considered to be an integral part of that world by
Moslems, or are they foreigners, aliens, or to use the words of Qadhafi,
a "European spirit in an Arab body?"

It is no coincidence that Lebanese Christians were mentioned in this
connection. When one refers to Lebanese Christians, one usually means

3

the Maronites. A division appears among the various churches in the Middle East, and among the Christians within those churches, when it comes to their attitude toward Moslems. Very generally speaking, in addition to an attitude of neutrality, there is an antithetical attitude which can all too quickly lead to a self-sought and self-imposed *isolation*, a type of ghetto existence. A much more *open* attitude can also be found among Christians, directed instead toward fruitful coexistence and interaction. The Maronites felt themselves very threatened by the rise and spread of Islam in the seventh century, and over the course of the centuries they have been able to put up a certain degree of resistance, protected as they were by the mountains of Lebanon. Their self-sufficiency and independence was not left uncontested. On the contrary, all through the centuries, bloody confrontations took place. Yet the Maronites have been able, more than any other group of Christians—with exception of the Armenians—to obtain and maintain a certain degree of political independence.

Throughout the course of history, European and western 'Christian' powers have continually been concerned themselves with the fate of the peoples of the Middle East. That has especially been the case since the crusades. The European powers of the time actively sought an alliance with Christian minorities, which they often exploited for their own interests. In the age of the crusades (1095-1291), the Maronites, like the Armenians, lent a helping had to the crusaders. Lebanon was at that time, and also later, seen not no much "as the western front of the Arab East, but as the eastern front of the Christian West."[6] In the First World War, Assyrian conscripts fought alongside the British in the battle for the Middle East. That cooperation of local Christians with foreign 'Christian' powers, often at the expense of their Islamic neighbors, was viewed by Moslems as collaboration. Local Christians usually had to pay for this when the political tide turned.

There are still Maronites who claim that they are not Arabs, but Phoenicians.[7] In this way they express their distance from the Arab world. This suggest a polar relationship: Moslems on the one side and Christians on the other. Thus, the civil war which has been fought in Lebanon since 1975 until about 1990 can be conceived of as a religious war between Christians and Moslems, and the threat to the Lebanese state can be regarded as a threat to continued Christian existence.

In a novel by Ethel Adnan, *Sitt Marie-Rose*, a true story about a Greek-Catholic woman is related who proved to be sympathetic to the Palestinians and their cause. Her position was not acceptable, however,

4

to certain 'right-wing' Christian groups during the Lebanese civil war. She was kidnapped, purportedly by a group called Defenders of the Cedars, and was killed in April 1976.

The story clearly depicts how certain Christians view their existence, a view which immediately calls to mind the young men of the Christian militias, such as the Falangist, or those who filled out the ranks of the militia of the Lebanese president-elect at the time, Bashir Jemayyil, who was killed in September 1982 before he could take office. In the novel a Christian youth says:

My name is Tony, and I will never be called Mohammed. That is as clear and inevitable as the succession of the hours .... We are the young people of the Christian quarter and our militia is at war with the Palestinians. They are Moslems. So we are at war with islam, especially when it tries to stand in our way ....

"These youth idolized the crusaders," the writer continues. Concerning one of the youths she adds:

... He identified himself with Frederik Barbarossa (ca. 1123-1190, the leader of the third crusade), since his hair was slightly red. He bitterly lamented the fact that Saladin had conquered Jerusalem, as though it had happened recently. They all extolled the crusades. The French priests [who were teaching at many Lebanese schools] lead a procession every year in which the students from the Christian schools dressed in white tunics with a piece of red cloth sewed to the front and the back .... They sang in the streets of Beirut that day, "I am a Christian. Behold my glory, my hope and strength." The following day at school they were proud of the fact that they had challenged the unbelievers. They are accustomed to dreaming of a mounted Christianity, striding out with helmet, boots, and rattling sabres, a Christianity which impales the Islamic infantrymen like Saint George impaled the dragon.

The writer, who represents an opposing Christian view, continues:

I remember that I said to him that walking in a procession dressed like a crusader was the most ridiculous thing in the world. He laughed at me, and his laugh still rings in my ears. You are a girl, you do not know what it is like to be a young man of twelve. I remember that I had answered him, "Are you sure?" he asked me, with a sadness which misted his eyes. "What will happen to me then?[8]

The first attitude described is typical of some Christians, for example, some Maronites, but definitely not all of them. It stands in contrast to another, more open attitude towards the Moslems, which can be found more frequently among the Greek Orthodox. Of all the Christians, they most feel and act like Arabs.

The 'Orthodox' Churches of the Middle East

This book will describe the positions and backgrounds of the various Christian churches in the Middle East. The churches will be discussed separately. Some of the churches are found mainly in certain countries, such as the Coptic Church of Egypt and the Maronites of Lebanon. Therefore something of their predicament in their countries is discussed. Others can be found except for Armenia in several countries in the Middle East, the Syrian Orthodox, Greek Orthodox, and the Armenians are spread over Lebanon, Jordan, Syria, Turkey, and Iran. The area under consideration, therefore, extends over nearly the entire Eastern Arab world (*Mashriq*), from Turkey to Iran, better known as Middle East.

The qualification 'Orthodox' means for most people in the West adherence to true doctrine. The Roman Catholic Church, as well as many Protestant churches claim to be 'orthodox' in that sense, since they accept, for example, the decisions of the Ecumenical Council of Chalcedon (451). But that does not in any way mean that other churches would have relinquished this claim. Several designations have come into use, such as Chalcedonian or pre- or non-Chalcedonian, depending on the position of the churches with respect to this important ecumenical council. These designations are often considered unacceptable by the churches concerned. But also names like Monophysite are rejected, since they are considered denigrating.[9]

For the sake of clarity, it is perhaps good to give already at this juncture an overview of the various names that the churches in the Middle East have been given, as well as those they themselves.

First there is the Byzantine or Greek Orthodox or, in Arabic, *Rum* (which is Arabic for Byzantium) Church. It is frequently simply called the *Orthodox* Church. The spiritual head of the church is the Patriarch of Antioch, whose see is now in Damascus. The Greek Orthodox also have a Patriarch in Jerusalem. The Church is *autocephalous*, i.e., it has its own head. They locate themselves under the Ecumenical Patriarchate of Constantinople, the church with which the Western church was joined until the great schism of 1054. The Patriarch of Constantinople is considered the first among equals.

Secondly, there is the 'Syrian' Church. Three churches claim unity with the Syrian tradition:

6

A. The West Syrian, Jacobite (Monophysite), now usually referred to as the *Syrian Orthodox Church*. The seat of the Patriarch was originally that of Antioch, but now is Damascus.

B. The East Syrian, Nestorian (Dyophysite), now called the *Assyrian* Church. The see of the Patriarchate was originally in Antioch, for several centuries was located in Baghdad, but since 1940 has been in Chicago.

C. The *Maronite* Church, now unified with Rome. The see of the Patriarch was originally located in Antioch but is now in Bkirki (Lebanon).

A third church is the *Armenian* Orthodox or *Gregorian* (Monophysite) Church, headed by the Catholicos of Echmiadzin (in Armenia) and of Cilicia (Sis) now in Antilias (Lebanon). In addition, there are Patriarchs of Jerusalem and Istanbul.

There is also, fourthly, the *Coptic* Church (Monophysite). The Patriarch, originally seated in Alexandria, is now in Cairo.

Moreover, there are churches that are associated with Rome (aside from the Maronite Church already mentioned above):
- the *Greek Catholic*, now usually referred to as the *Melchite*, Church, under the Patriarch of Antioch, now in Damascus;
- the *Syrian Catholic* Church under the Patriarch of Antioch;
- the *Armenian Catholic* Church under the Patriarch of Cilicia;
- the *Chaldean* Catholic Church (formed by former Nestorians) under the Patriarch of Babylon, now in Baghdad.
- *Latin* churches under the Latin Patriarch of Jerusalem.

There are also various Protestant churches in the Middle East. These are primarily Episcopalians or Anglicans, Presbyterians and Congregationalists, as well as Armenian Protestants. There are also small groups of Protestants from other denominations (such as the Baptists).

In 1974 the *Near East Council of Churches*, which had been primarily a council of Protestant churches (except for the Syrian Orthodox Church), changed its name and composition. It became the *Middle East Council of Churches (M.E.C.C.)*. This organization represents three families of churches: the Chalcedonian, non-Chalcedonian, and Protestant churches in the Middle East (including the Sudan, Cyprus, and Iran). The Roman Catholic Church (including the Maronites) also became a member as of the fifth general assembly held in January of 1990 in Nicosia, Cyprus (the Nestorians or Assyrians are so far not represented in this body) and thus represents four families now. The event was by many described as 'a new Pentecost'.[10]

With each church, the historical background will be considered, from earliest times until the present. These churches have stood in a living tradition since the 'ancient church'. Some of these churches are known to Western Christians only as theological views in textbooks on dogmatics, or as the names of heretics (Monophysites, Nestorians) who have been condemned for once and for all by the major church councils.

In the first chapter we will in order to set the scene give a description of the history of the interaction of Christians and Jews in the Islamic environment throughout history (I). In light of the fact that these churches also have a great deal in common, however, the doctrinal background and especially the individual liturgies will be discussed (II).

We will begin our overview of the individual churches—whereby we will have a particular interest in their relations to the Moslem environment throughout history until the present—with the Greek Orthodox, Byzantine (*Rum*) or simply the Orthodox Church. This is the church with which the Western church was directly united through the ecumenical Patriarch of Constantinople until the great schism of 1054 (III). The 'Syrian' Church will then be presented in two chapters: the Syrian Orthodox or the Monophysite church, and the Assyrian or the Nestorian Church (IV). The third Church which belongs to the 'Syrian' tradition is the Maronite Church of Lebanon (V). Finally, the Coptic Church will be examined (VI).

After the break of 1054, the Roman Catholic Church attempted to make contact with the Eastern Orthodox Church and with other churches of the East as well. In a number of cases that led to a unification or to the establishment of the so-called 'uniate' (i.e. united with Rome) churches, although this name is not used by themselves (and will be therefore avoided). In each chapter, these separate churches will also be taken up and briefly discussed. The Armenians, who compose the oldest Christian Kingdom, will then be discussed (VII).

In the chapter "Aliens at Home," the role of mission, especially that of Britain and the United States, since the last century and of the present Protestant churches in the region will be considered in order to evaluate the question of Christian identity in the context of Western involvement in the Middle East (VIII).

In the conclusion of the book, the question will be asked whether the churches still have a future in the Middle East. In so doing, we will reexamine the position of the churches in the western part of the Arab world, formerly *Maghreb*, to see what light they may shed on future development in the eastern part of the Arab world (the *Mashrik*). We will also inquire as to the consequences of the phenomenon of the so-called 'renaissance' of Islam, or Islamic fundamentalism, for the relationship between Jews Moslems and Christians (IX). The purpose of this last chapter is to give insight into the decisive phase of history in which these churches are now living, in which they face the challenge of "constructing a new paradigm for a spiritual and political society or allowing themselves to be driven further from the world which is 'the house of Islam' for millions (*dar al-islam*)." As Jean Corbon states,

They are confronting the dilemma of either leading a type of ghetto existence or of being or becoming a true Arab church. In each of the nations of the area under consideration, Christians share the same fundamental problems, whether they are of an economic, civil, ideological, cultural, spiritual, or pastoral nature. They also share the paths down which they as Christians strive to follow Christ.[11]

NOTES

1. Laroui, 18.

2. *Le Monde*, 17, 18 August 1980. During a visit to Rwanda in 1985 he declared: "Islam is the religion of Africa, Christianity the one of the agents of colonialism, the French, Belgians, German and American enemies, and the one of the Jews as well." *Le Monde*, 25 May 1985.

3. Trimingham, 1979.

4. Browne, 34; Betts, 12.

5. Browne, 58, 59.

6. Yamak, 36.

7. Cf. Corm, 1966, XXXIX.

8. Adnan, 44, 55, 56.

9. Atiyah, 179.

10. *Het christelijk Oosten*, XLIII (October 1991), 271.

11. Corbon, 1977, 61.

I. JEWS AND CHRISTIANS IN THE ARAB/ ISLAMIC ENVIRONMENT

The toleration which the present day Moslems professes for Christians and Jews is too often not that of a humble believer for those whom he recognizes as serious seekers of the same truth, but the contemptuous tolerance of the strong for the weak.

A. Hourani[1]

Introduction

The churches of the Middle East have during the last fourteen centuries, like no other churches in the course of history, viewed their past in contrast to and at the same time as part of the world of Islam. In order to understand properly the relation of Christians and the church toward Moslems, a relation which will be discussed time and again in the following chapters, it would be helpful to give a separate overview of those relations over the course of the last fourteen centuries. Because Jews, like the Christians, are a minority in the Islamic world it is also important to describe their position as well. In this way, insight can be gained into the contemporary situation—after the foundation of the state of Israel for instance—which will be dealt with again in more detail in the last chapter.

The Prophet Mohammed and the Jews

In order to understand the contemporary Arab/Islamic attitude toward the Jews (including the state of Israel), it is important to examine the position of the prophet Mohammed with respect to the Jews, since the position that he assumed toward the Jews and Judaism during his lifetime is in part determinative for the position of the later Moslem Arabs.

Mohammed originally regarded the Jews as *ahl al-kitab*, or 'people of the book', the book being *Tawra* (Torah). They adhered to the book of Moses, just as the Christians adhered to the *Injil*, the gospel, 'the book of Jesus'. One could even say that Mohammed was to a certain extent oriented toward Judaism, since, when in Mecca, he prayed toward Jerusalem, just as Daniel did, when in a foreign land (Daniel 6:11). The ritual prayer itself, the *salat*, may have been taken over by Mohammed from a Jewish (or Christian?) ritual prayer. When Mohammed was in

Medina, where Jewish tribes lived (the Banu al-Nadir, the Banu Qaynuqa' and the Banu Qurayzah) he followed their custom of fasting on the Day of Atonement, the *Ashura*, a custom which he chose to continue for Moslems even after he broke with Judaism. From then on, however, Moslems were required to fast during the month of Ramadan.[2]

Mohammed believed that what he preached was in accord with what God had revealed to Moses. The Koran says with regard to the Banu Isra'il (Israelites) that they had been chosen and blessed above all others.[3] They were characterized as those with whom God had made a covenant,[4] to whom God had given the scriptures and prophecy,[5] to whom the east and west of the land (of Palestine!) had been given as an inheritance.[6] It was Mohammed's hope to convert them to his own views, since he recognized in them a people who studied the scriptures.[7] When Mohammed's preaching met with little success in his home town of Mecca and he experienced persecution, he decided to flee to Medina (Yathrib), in part with the hope that he would receive a hearing from the above-mentioned Jewish tribes living there. Mohammed even hoped to meet the expectation that apparently prevailed among the Jews of Medina of a coming prophet or Messiah. In Medina Mohammed came into regular contact with the Jews for the first time. According to the Arab historian al-Baladhuri (died 892), these were Jews whose ancestors had fled to Arabia as a result of the destruction of the temple by Nebuchadnezzar.[8]

Mohammed experienced conflict between his own deep respect for the scriptures of the Jews and Christians *and* the possessors of those scriptures for the first time in Medina. Mohammed made attempts to win the Jews over to his own religion (Koran 2:41). Originally, after his arrival in Medina, Mohammed forged a covenant of coexistence, sometimes broadly referred to as 'the constitution of Medina', whereby the Jews attached to various Arab tribes, the al-Aws and al-Khazraj, were integrated into the city-state and were assured by him of help against internal and external enemies and were permitted freedom of religion: "The Jews their religion and the Moslems their religion."[9] In an effort to defend and legitimate the Camp-David agreement between Israel and Egypt after 1979 reference was made at the time in the Egyptian press to this covenant of Medina.

Mohammed's attempts to approach the Jews met with disappointment, however. The Jews did not recognize him as either prophet or messiah.[10] After all, according to them the one to come could not be an Arab. With but few exceptions, the Jews did not take him seriously and

11

withheld from him, so the accusation goes, information regarding the content of the Torah. Mohammed's religious claims were rejected. Although in the latter part of his stay in Mecca—thus before the *hijra*, i.e. the emigration of Mecca and his close companions from Mecca to Medina in the year 622—Mohammed still viewed Israel approvingly because of the revelation given to them by Moses (32:23; 45:16), his approval soon turned to rebuke. He called on them to keep their covenant with God (2:40 (38)), to remember their election and how they had been delivered from the hand of Pharaoh (2:47 (44); 2:50 (47)). He reproached them for keeping part of scripture concealed (2:174 (169)), for having kept the revelation secret (2:77 (72)), and accused them of having twisted the scriptures or having changed God's words (2:75-79 (70-73), 3:78 (72); 5:13 (16),41 (45))—*tahrif*—and having broken the covenant with God (2:100 (94); 3:187 (184)). At this point the Koran begins to speak of Jews (*yahud*) instead of the Banu Isra'il, and the latter term is reserved for their Old Testament ancestors.

During this period, the Koran ascribes to the Jews all kinds of despicable things: that they worshipped 'Uzayr (Ezra) as God's son (9:30), and wanted to blow out God's light (9:32), that they had declared some of the prophets liars and had killed others (5:70 (74)). They were charged with having mocked Mary, the mother of Jesus, and having said that she had crucified him (4:157 (156)). They were the enemies of God (2:98 (92)), and of believers (= Moslems) (5:82 (85)). They are called disobedient, blind and deaf (5:71 (75)), and are said to be those who sought to bring ruin upon the earth (5:64 (69)), and to extract usury (4:161 (159)). Therefore believing Moslems should not accept Jews or Christians as friends (5:51 (56)). The Jews wrongly believed that the hand of God was clenched shut, when it was in fact wide open (5:64 (69)). The Koran protested against specific Jewish dietary laws and against their view of the Sabbath as well. Finally, the Koran found that Jews and idol worshipers were the worst enemies of believers (5:51 (56)), while Christians were viewed with more sympathy *vis à vis* Moslems (5:82 (85)).

In spite of the obvious development in the attitude of Mohammed from his Mecca period (610-622) to his Medina period (622-632), and the increasing severity of his critique of and opposition to the Jews, the authenticity of God's covenant and his revelation to them were never as such denied, even though the Jews were accused of having broken the conditions of the covenant and having twisted the scriptures. Not even in the Medina period was it denied that the way of salvation was given to the Jews: "Those who believe and who confess Judaism, and the Christians and the Christians and the Sabians, who believe in God, the last day, and do good works, for them their reward is with their Lord" (2:62 (59)). Also in the Medina period, the Koran did not paint all the Jews with the same brush, but rather acknowledged that a portion of them had become unfaithful while others had kept the covenant and would receive their reward from God (2:146 (141)).[11]

The definitive break with Judaism was symbolized by the change of orientation in prayer (qiblah). The place where this change occurred is marked by the 'mosque of the two qiblahs.[12] From that moment on, Islam separated itself from Judaism, as it were, and developed as a separate religion.

In Medina, unlike in Mecca, Mohammed was a political as well as a religious leader of a community. The Arab tribes living there had invited him to act as a mediator of sorts. The three Jewish tribes were allied with various Arab tribes, and so it was not simply a question of Jew versus Arab. During the first year and a half after Mohammed's emigration from Mecca to Medina in 622, the political agreement between the Arab and Jewish tribes under Mohammed's leading, in which the religious discrepancy was tolerated, remained intact. But after the rejection of Mohammed's spiritual claims and the less than enthusiastic support of and even antipathy toward his struggle against the people of Mecca, Mohammed thought it necessary to divest himself of his spiritual and political opponents. After some provocations and conflicts, two tribes were banned from the city of Medina. One of the tribes, however, the Banu Qurayzah, which had betrayed Mohammed in a militarily precarious situation, was liquidated by Mohammed, or at least the approximately eight hundred male members of the tribe. Only four managed to save their lives by converting to Islam. Even the Moslem sources cannot help but speak with respect and marvel at the way in which these Jews met their fate.[13] As soon as the Jewish question had been politically and militarily resolved in this way (with the exception of a few later conflicts with the Jews in other parts of the Arabian peninsula), the relationship between Jews and Moslem improved, and some Jews even returned to Medina.

The Prophet Mohammed and the Christians

At the beginning of the rise of Islam in the seventh century after Christ, Christianity had spread in the Middle East beyond the Tigris river and in Europe, until the Rhine. Islam came into existence in part through contact with the Eastern churches, and the Christianity that Mohammed

13

came to know was Eastern Christianity, primarily in its Syrian Orthodox and Nestorian form. Mohammed was apparently aware of the various schools of thought and divisions that existed among Christians.[14] Not long after Mohammed, Moslems no longer spoke of the church in the singular (*millet*) but of communities in the plural (*milal*), and appeared to be well aware of the various names of the churches and their respective beliefs.[15] A work attributed to the renowned Islamic theologian, Abu Hamid al-Ghazzali (died 1111), displays, for instance, a rather detailed knowledge of the various christological views and the different Christian churches.[16]

Although the question regarding Mohammed's knowledge of Christianity before his prophetic activity can never be answered with complete precision, his contact with, knowledge of and kinship with the Syrian Church, in its Jacobite or Nestorian form, would have been the greatest. It has been maintained that Mohammed's emphasis, at the beginning of his work on the fear of hell, is closely related to monastic views, espoused in various parts of the Syrian Church.[17] In spite of the differing opinions Mohammed encountered among Christians, it is clear that he recognized his link with the Christian faith.

Certain statements in the Koran with respect to Christianity would later, under Caliph 'Umar II, form the basis for rules governing the conduct of Islamic governments and common Moslems toward Christians. One of the harshest statements in the Koran regarding Christians reads:

Fight those who do not believe in God, until the last day, and forbid them that which God and his messengers have forbidden, and those who do not adhere to the true religion among those to whom the Scripture has been given (Jews and Christians), until they bring tribute (*jizya*) from their hand in submission (Koran 9:29).

Like the Jews, Christians are 'people of the book' (*ahl al-kitab*), or people of protection (*dhimma*). A forced conversion is considered illegal, based on the Koran: "There is no force in religion" (Koran 2:256). But a price (*jizya*) must be paid for 'protection' (*dhimma*). The *dhimmi* status as it later developed goes back in principle to the treaty made by Mohammed with the Christians of Najran in 632.

Mohammed and Jerusalem

For Mohammed, before Mecca became the place to which prayers were directed, it was Jerusalem towards which he prayed (Koran 2:136,

14

138). There is a tradition that says that in the last days prayer will again be directed toward Jerusalem.[18]

There is yet another reason why Jerusalem is so important for Mohammed and Moslems. The holy place with the Dome of the Rock (*Qubbat al-Sakhra*) and the *al-Aqsa* mosque (literally, 'the farthest mosque'), is honored as the place to where Mohammed made his nightly journey (*isra'*), and the place from which the ascension occurred (*mira'j*). The term 'the farthest mosque' refers not only to the current mosque that bears the name, but also to the temple square as a whole. The medieval traveller, Ibn Battuta (1304-1377), related how he found, under the Dome of the Rock, a cave where Mohammed supposedly dwelt before his ascension. This place was used by, among others, the theologian al-Ghazzali, mentioned above, as a place of meditation. The fire that was set in the *al-Aqsa* mosque on 21 August 1969 by an Australian, in which the pulpit (*minbar*) that had once been given as a gift by the well-known Saladin (1137-1193) was destroyed, at the time caused a great deal of unrest in the Arab and Islamic world .

Jerusalem assumes a special place in Arab piety. As it is said, "A prayer spoken in the *bayt al-maqdis* (the holy place, i.e., Jerusalem), is better than a thousand prayers in other holy places." And according to the Persian Arab author Ahmad al-Hamadani (968-1008), writing in the tenth century, "Whoever prays in Jerusalem, prays as though he were in heaven." Before the Six Day War of 1967 (in which East Jerusalem was occupied by Israel), Moslems who made the pilgrimage to Mecca were in the custom of combining it with a visit to Jerusalem either on the trip there or the trip back. The prophet Mohammed is said to have said: "Whoever makes a pilgrimage to Jerusalem and prays there in the same year that he makes a pilgrimage to Mecca, will be cleansed of his sins." In popular Moslem piety, the city is viewed as the place where the final judgment will take place.

In 636, four years after Mohammed's death, Palestine was conquered by the second successor of Mohammed, caliph 'Umar ibn al Khattab, who, as the story goes, accepted the surrender of the city from the hands of the Greek Orthodox Patriarch Sophronius of Jerusalem (ca. 560-638). 'Umar made the rounds of the captured city together with the patriarch and arrived at the Church of the Holy Sepulchre precisely at the hour of prayer. 'Umar was then said to have rejected the proposal of the patriarch to perform his prayer (*salat*) in the church because, as he is purported to have said, Moslems could then later use his example in order to change the church into a mosque. This tale is probably, however, fictional. It was told by a Christian in the tenth century for the apparent purpose of appealing to the authority of someone no less than an 'Umar in order to prove that Christians had and continue to have right to the Church of the Holy Sepulchre, or the Church of the Resurrection (*kanisat al- qiyâma* as the Arabs refer to it). Evidence that this is a tendentious tale can be found in the fact that this same author related that contrary to the purported command of 'Umar, Moslems had established a mosque on the steps of the Basilica of Constantine, called the *jami'a* of Umar, because 'Umar was said to have prayed there.

The actual circumstances were probably somewhat less idyllic. It is supposed that the patriarch suggested to the caliph, who sought a holy place for Moslems, that he take the Jewish temple square, which was at the time being used as a refuse dump, in order to forestall his taking the Church of the Holy Sepulchre. What appears certain, in any case, is that 'Umar established a place of prayer there. The 'rock' was not known from the Old Testament, but was mentioned in the Talmud. The Dome of the Rock, which was later built over the site, is not the so-called 'Umar mosque. The Dome of the Rock was not built by 'Umar, nor is it a mosque in the strict sense, even though prayers are performed there. The 'temple square' seems indeed to have been in a state of ruin at the time, before it was cleaned out by 'Umar. Christians in the East appear to have reasoned that the destruction of the holy city under Titus in A.D. 70 and the later deliberate desecration of the temple square was a confirmation of divine rejection of Israel. The ruin of the place was then a symbol of this fact.

Under the Ommajad dynasty (661-750) the importance of Jerusalem grew for Moslem Arabs. The first ruler in this dynasty, Mu'awiyya ibn Abu Sufyan (661-680), had himself declared caliph in Jerusalem. One of his successors, 'Abd al-Malik (685-705), commanded the Syrians to make their pilgrimage to the holy rock in Jerusalem instead of to Mecca. "This rock will be for you in the place of the Ka'bah [in Mecca]." There is even a tradition of Mohammed according to which he regards Mecca, Medina and Jerusalem as of great importance for pilgrimage, indeed, Jerusalem even ought to be placed above other holy sites. As an expression of his high regard for Jerusalem, 'Abd al-Malik had a dome built in 691 over the rock on which, it was believed, the hoofprint of the winged horse of Mohammed, Boraq, could still be seen. This dome was supposed to surpass the Church of the Holy Sepulchre in beauty in order to symbolize Islam's conquest of Christianity. Both holy places together are referred to by Arabs as *Al-Haram al-Sharif* ('The Noble Sanctuary').[19]

Jews and Christians as 'Protected Citizens'

Under Mohammed's successors the Jews and the Christians disappeared from Central Arabia. The Moslem tradition relates how under the second caliph, 'Umar ibn al Khattab, the Jews and Christians were driven out of the Arabian peninsula. This was seen and justified as the fulfillment of the wishes of Mohammed himself, who supposedly said that "no two religions should exist together in the Arabian peninsula."[20] To this very day, non-Moslims (Arab or non-Arab) may not enter the cities of Mecca and Medina. In present-day Saudi Arabia churches are not allowed. Christian worship services are not openly admitted and priests or pastors are not allowed into the country in any official capacity.

One can find both the negative and positive attitudes towards the Jews which appear in the Koran reflected in the history of the Jews in the Arab world.

In order to understand the situation of non-Moslems (both Jews and Christians) within the Arab and Islamic world in more recent history, it is helpful to consider the conventional Moslem view, which cannot be found as such in the Koran, but according to which the world is divided into the house of Islam (*dar al-islam*) and the house of war (*dar al-harb*). There is, in addition, a third realm mentioned, the *dar al-sulh*, or the house of 'truce', in which Islam is not sovereign, yet a treaty can be made with its inhabitants. Non-Moslems within the house of Islam, especially Jews and Christians, were under Moslem protection, or *dhimma*, and were for that reason called *dhimmi*s. The public and private rights of *dhimmi*s were regulated by treaty, while no political rights were granted. The *dhimmi* was required to pay a head tax, or *jizya* for the protection he received, and to submit to Moslem authority. The Moslem authorities, for their part, provided the *dhimmi* with protection against external attack. If the Moslem did not fulfill this obligation, the tax would not be required.[21] With payment of the head tax and property tax (*kharaj*), the free exercise of religion was guaranteed. That entailed, among other things, that no one would be forced to change religions. Those who enjoyed this status were, in addition to the Jews and Christians, the Sabians, the Samaritans, and the Zoroastrians. The following provisos were among those added for comportment:

1. the obligation to wear distinctive clothing;

2. the prohibition against building buildings that were higher than those of the Moslems;
3. the prohibition of the public consumption of wine or the public display of crosses or pigs;
4. the obligation to bury the dead without crying or wailing;
5. the prohibition against riding a horse.[22]

Over the course of time, certain colors were prescribed for clothing: blue for Christians, yellow for Jews and red for Samaritans. White was the color of the Umayyads (the rulers in Damascus 661-750) and black that of the 'Abbasids (the rulers in Baghdad from 754 until 1258). Originally, such regulations regarding clothing would have been superfluous, since these distinctions were already practiced.[23] It is, however, understandable that the difference in clothing, originally perhaps required for the purpose of distinguishing one group from another, had discriminatory consequences, and that ultimately was its aim.

In practice, these and similar regulations have functioned with varying intensity. The head tax (also not practiced everywhere and at all times), was in fact one of the heaviest burdens weighing on the *dhimmi*. Although the position of the Jews in the Islamic world was better than that of Jews in 'Christian' Europe during the Middle Ages and the Jews welcomed the Moslem conquest of Spain and preferred Arab rulers to Byzantine, the Islamic world was still host to pogroms (for example, in Spain in 1066), banishment (for example, in Yemen in 1679),[24] and forced conversions (for example, under the Almohads, a Moorish/Spanish dynasty 1147-1269 in Spain).[25] In fact, the well-known Spanish Moslem theologian, Ibn Hazm (died 1064), who also berated Christians, wrote a book against the Jews entitled: *ifham al-yahud*, "The Silencing of the Jews."

Moslems as Liberators?

Initially several 'national' churches, such as the Syrian and Coptic Churches, which were in continual conflict with Byzantium, viewed the arrival of the Islamic Arabs as a liberation from the 'imperialistic' Byzantine yoke. The Jacobites, for example, enjoyed more religious freedom under the Moslems than they had under their fellow Christians of Byzantium.[26] Although is was little more than the exchange of one ruler for another, the preference was given, at least at first, to the new. The 'advantage' of the new authorities was, however strange this might sound, the fact that they were not Christians, for the Byzantines exerted

18

pressure on their fellow Christians in religious as well as political matters. While some Copts may have viewed the Arab conquest as a liberation from their Byzantine oppressors, others soon were of the mind that the new rulers were no better. John, Bishop of Nikion (around 700), said with respect to the Arab conquest: "The yoke they laid on the Egyptians was heavier than the yoke laid upon the Israelites by Pharaoh."[27] The fiercest resistance against the invasion of the Arab Moslems was offered by the Armenians and the Mardaites, who were later absorbed by the Maronites, and they were "the most persistent in believing that some concerted Christian resistance could and should be maintained."[28]

The Umayyad Era (661-750)

Christians played an important role in the formative period of early Islam in Damascus and later in Baghdad. They were involved with the work of translation and transmission of Hellenistic culture and philosophy and were active in the medical sciences. Although the process of Arabization existed before the Moslem conquest of Syria and Iraq, it began to spread in earnest in the urban areas during the rule of the Umayyads and gradually displaced the Greek language. In rural areas Syriac continued to be used.[29]

In 661, the rule of the Umayyads began in Damascus under the leadership of Mu'awiyya ibn Abu Sufyan (661-680). He was married to an Arab Monophysite, Jacobite wife. Already before 661 he was governor of the city. The Mansur family, to which the later famous 'Greek' Orthodox Father, John of Damascus (676-749/753), belonged, is said to have been involved in 635 with the opening of the gates of Damascus for the Moslem armies of Khalid ibn al-Walid (died 641/642). A contemporary Lebanese historian accordingly accused them of betraying Eastern Christianity.[30] For many years, John of Damascus, who was not Greek but Syrian, served as secretary to the caliph, but later withdrew to the Saint Sabas monastery south of Bethlehem, which may indicate that he had fallen into disfavor.[31] He wrote a dialogue of sorts with a Saracen, which could serve as a primer for discussion with Moslems on questions such as the divinity of Christ and the freedom of the human will. John viewed Islam as the latest of the Christian heresies.[32]

From time to time in the Umayyad era, Jacobites and Nestorians held high positions at court. As an example one could mention, in addition to John of Damascus, the renowned Jacobite poet Akhtal (died 710), who came from the Monophysite Christian Arab tribe of the Banu Taghlib of northern Syria, whose poetry still appears in Arab school books. He held the favor of caliph Yazid (680-683) and 'Abd al-Malik (685-705), even though he was ostentatiously Christian. He had the custom of wearing a large gold cross around his neck in public. Around 649, a Nestorian bishop described these Arabs as those who did not strive against the Christian religion, but rather defended it and held respect for priests and saints making contributions to churches and monasteries.[33]

This does not, however, mean that Christians (and Jews) were not already then exposed to various restrictive regulations and ridicule. Tolerance was not the same thing as complete freedom. According to the regulations traced back to 'Umar ibn 'Abd al-Khattab, but probably deriving instead from 'Umar ibn 'Abd al-'Aziz, Christians were required to dress distinctly, were not permitted to ride horses, carry weapons, or build new churches, were restricted by rules governing the restoration of existing church buildings, could not ring any church bells, hold any processions, nor wear the cross in public. There were also personal restrictions. An Islamic man could marry a Christian wife, but a Christian man could not marry an Islamic woman unless he converted to Islam and raised the offspring of the mixed marriage in the Islamic faith, a regulation that continues almost universally in the Islamic world to the present day.[34] Christians have at times called this 'Umar II the 'antichrist', because he extended the head tax to those who originally were exempt.[35] Sporadic persecutions took place at the whim of the respective princes, for example, under 'Abd al-Malik. Monks who before his time were not required to pay taxes, were now forced to do so. In 705, during his reign, the basilica of John the Baptist was turned into a mosque, the Umayyad mosque.[36] Al-Walid (705-715) has the reputation of having been a hater of Christians and having destroyed churches. He had initially promised Christians that they could keep their churches, but he is thought to have been the one who destroyed the Church of John the Baptist, one of the many churches that claimed to have the head of John the Baptist. This mosque is viewed by Moslems as the most important 'holy place' after Mecca, Medina, and the Dome of the Rock in Jerusalem.[37] In spite of the persecution under 'Abd al-Malik and the discriminating regulations of 'Umar II, Christians remained loyal to the Umayyads.

It is important to keep in mind, however, that the pressure exerted on the Christians frequently was not primarily religious, but economic in nature. That was also the case, for example, during the reign of 'Umar

20

II.[38] Economic factors are primarily to blame, for example, for the sudden disappearance of the now so-called 'dead cities' of northern Syria - east of Antioch in the direction of Edessa. These cities had increased in importance before the Arab conquest as a result of trade between East and West. This trade came to an end, however, when the Arab empire gained the upper hand. Since the commercial ties were no longer possible, the cities were depopulated.[39]

In the middle of the eight century, the Umayyad regime came to an end. It is claimed that at this decisive moment in Islamic history, prayers from the desert monasteries in Egypt—Dayr Abu Maqar—brought about the fall of the Umayyads.[40]

The 'Abbasid Era (750-1256)

With the ascent to power of the new dynasty of the 'Abbasids, the center of the Islamic kingdom shifted from Damascus to the newly established (754) capital city of Baghdad. Christians under the 'Abbasids were required to pay for their loyalty to the Umayyads. Because of their loyalty, they were viewed as a sort of 'fifth column'.[41] Around 760, the taxes on all Christians were doubled. This led to a steady stream of conversions as a form of 'tax evasion'. This also gave impetus to the ninth-century flight of Christians to Cyprus, including a large group of Maronites. Members of Arab Christian tribes, who had previously refused to pay the head tax, because they were Arabs, were required to pay the poor tax, which now was also obligatory for Moslems, although Christians were required to pay double. Around 780, the last Arab Christian tribes, the Banu Tanukh, were forced by the caliph to convert to Islam. The celebrated blind poet, Abu al-Ala al-Ma'arri, is a descendent from this tribe. At the request of al-Mahdi (775-785), who was of the opinion that Byzantines were politically exploiting their fellow Christians, 5,000 members of this tribe near the city of Aleppo in northern Syria converted to Islam.[42] During the patriarchate of Michael I (744-768), 24,000 Copts in Cairo and the vicinity accepted Islam and so were exempted from taxation. This method of dangling before Christians various incentives was responsible for numerous conversions.[43] The social handicaps also induced more and more Christians to embrace Islam, a movement to which the churches could offer little resistance. The church also had little attractions to offer, as was the case with the Nestorians who for a time remained outside the realm of the caliphs.

The attitude of the 'Abbasid caliphs toward Christians hardened with time. Harun al-Rashid (786-809) commanded both Jews and Christians to

21

assume certain Moslem customs. In 806 he had the churches along the Byzantine border destroyed. When a courtier informed Harun al-Rashid that Christians in certain churches worshipped the bones of the dead, he ordered the churches razed. Although, when he later learned the truth regarding these relics, he had the churches rebuilt.[44] The *dhimmi*s in Baghdad were required to wear clothing different from that of Moslems and to ride on different animals. The Christians in the vicinity of the Byzantine border suffered much from the military campaigns of Harun al-Rashid, which were advertised as *jihad* against the Byzantine emperor, Nicephorus I (802-811). As a result of the suffering, 12,000 Armenians crossed the border into the Byzantine empire. The same occurred during the reign of al-Ma'mun (813- 833).[45] Destructive to the Christian cause was the fact that in cases of internal ecclesiastical disputes, appeal would occasionally be made to the Islamic governor. Bribes were sometimes used to secure the appointment of patriarchs, as was the case in the appointment of the Nestorian Patriarch Timothy I (780- 819).[46]

During the reign of al-Mutawakkil (847-861), the regulations of Umar II regarding special clothing for Jews and Christians was again enforced and certain churches and synagogues that had recently been built in Baghdad were demolished.[47] During the regime of al-Mutawakkil, many Christians denied Jesus "on account of their love for their possessions or on account of the poverty they endured."[48]

Jews, Christians and Science in the 'Abbasid Era

Jews and Arabs (Moslems and Christians) have lived together for centuries in the Arab-Islamic world. It is frequently forgotten today that for centuries the vast majority of Jews lived not in Europe or the West, but among the Moslems. Judaism in the Arab world has frequently flourished, not only in Moorish Spain (*al-Andalus*), but also in Iraq. Jews were in a position to contribute and in fact did contribute to the development of culture, poetry and philosophy in the Arab world.

For centuries the central leadership of the Jewish community lay in the Arab world, because whatever persecutions or abuses they may have encountered there in the Middle Ages, they were relatively better off there than in the Western Christian world of the day. When the Jews were persecuted and expelled during the *reconquista* of Spain, many of them sought refuge in North Africa and in Arab Palestine! Maimonides himself fled via Palestine to Cairo. The incidental persecution or expression of anti-Jewish sentiments that were manifest in the Arab world were generally not accompanied by the same religious anti-Semitism that was so characteristic of Christian Europe. Moreover, the position of the Jewish community must not be viewed apart from that of other minorities, including Christians, in the Middle East. While Christians were sometimes able to advance far and to attain important positions, they too had experienced persecution, at times more severe than that of the Jews.

In spite of these circumstances, Christians played an important role in the area of science during the period of 'Abbasid control. They performed the important function of translating and transmitting Hellenistic culture to Moslems—from Greek and Syriac into Arabic—a heritage which Moslems would later 'return' to Western Christianity, as it were, via Spain. There existed in this period many opportunities for travel between the intellectual centers of Spain, Damascus and Baghdad.[49]

Husayn ibn Ishaq (808-873) belonged to an Arab tribe in Hira, which remained loyal to the Nestorian Church after the arrival of Islam. He was most probably bilingual already in his youth: Arabic as his native tongue and Syriac as the language of liturgy and Christian higher education. He studied medicine and became the court doctor of al-Mutawakkil. He has been called the "sheik of translators" and "source of science and a mine of virtue."[50] He was affiliated as a scholar with the 'Abbasid academy *Dar al-Hikma* (House of Wisdom), which was established by al-Ma'mun in 830, and surrounded himself with well-trained disciples. He is the most important transmitter of Greek science to the Arabs. He translated works of Hippocrates, Galenus and Plato (e.g. the *Republic*).

Once, when asked by the caliph to compose a lethal poison for one of his enemies, he refused, and when asked why, he replied: Two things: my religion and my profession. My religion decrees that we should do good even to our enemies, how much more to our friends. And my profession is instituted for the benefit of humanity and limited to their relief and cure. Besides, every physician is under oath never to give anyone a deadly medicine.[51]

Nestorian and Jacobite clergy were usually trained in medicine even before they were trained in the humanities. While during the Byzantine period much energy was expended in theological rebuttal of the Chalcedonian doctrines, under Arab rule Jacobites and Nestorians could apply their energy to other subjects. Consequently, they wrote hagiographies and produced works in the area of history, astronomy, the natural sciences and medicine.[52]

The Seljuks (From the Eleventh Century)

The nomadic Seljuks originally came from central Asia. In the eleventh century they extended their control over Khorazan, Persia, Iraq, Armenia and Asia Minor. In 1055 they were able to establish their sultanate in Baghdad to which the 'Abbasid caliphate was made subject.[53]

There are primarily two reasons cited for the gradual change which came about in the attitude of Moslems toward the Christian community. In the first place, an increasingly better education of Moslems made them less dependent on the services of Christian functionaries. Many Christians lost their positions simply due to the fact that they were Christians. In the second place, the non- Arab element in the 'Abbasid empire began to grow. Over the course of time, these Turkish, or Turkoman sultans took over de facto power from the caliphs. At the end of the eleventh century the 'Abbasid caliphs were little more than puppets. This led to an increasingly fanatical opposition to Christians.[54]

As soon as the hegemony of the Seljuks began, a Turkish dynasty gained for the first time a leading role in the Islamic world. They may have originally appeared as the protectors of the 'Abbasid caliphs, but soon enough they became the actual rulers of most of the eastern and central provinces of the 'Abbasid kingdom. They declared holy war against the Fatimids (909-1171), a Shi'ite dynasty that reigned for many years in Egypt and other parts of North Africa. They did not succeed in conquering Egypt, but they did manage to wrestle Palestine and Syria from Fatimid control. In 1070, they conquered Jerusalem. Their treatment of Christians and their conduct in the holy places in Palestine may have in part been the reason for the unleashing of the crusades.

In the border region with Byzantium they booked several military successes. Antioch and Edessa were won from the Byzantine empire. In 1071 the Byzantines were dealt an overwhelming defeat, opening the way for the Seljuks to the heart of Asia Minor. In 1075 an independent Turkish state was formed which produced several dynasties. The extent to which the Byzantines had been weakened became apparent when Iznik (Nicea)—near Constantinople—was made the capital of the Seljuk state, although the city was soon lost in the first crusade (1096-1099). Soon thereafter (1097), Konya (biblical Iconium) was made the new capital. Later at the court there, the banished poet and mystic Jalal al-Din Rumi (1207-73), who was also much appreciated by the Christians of his day, took refuge.[55] The nomadic Seljuks were therefore the first Moslems able to gain a foothold in Asia Minor and also those who initiated the Turkanization of the region.

The dynasty of the Seljuks was known for its intolerance and oppression, and these were only strengthened by the crusades. These and other factors worked to the extreme disadvantage of the Jacobite Church in upper Mesopotamia (Iraq).[56]

The Fatimids (909-1171)

The Shi'ite dynasty of the Fatimids that arose in North Africa carried on opposition to the Sunni 'Abbasids. In 969 they came to power in Egypt, where they established in that same year the city of Cairo. In spite of the strongly Shi'ite population there, their power remained restricted.

Especially during the decline of the Fatimid regime in Egypt (909-1171), it came to the point of outright persecution under the infamous caliph al-Hakim bi Amr Allah ('disappeared' in 1021). He did not, however, persecute Jews alone or even primarily. He also persecuted Christians. It is striking that Christians often fared worse and were more bitterly hated than the Jews,[57] and Christian communities were gradually uprooted or disappeared, while Jewish communities were able to maintain themselves.[58] It is even said that Christians sometimes made use of the yellow Jewish turban in order to gain safe conduct on the streets.[59] It is also striking that the spiritual descendants of the Fatimid caliph Hakim bi Amr Allah, the Druzes, who view him as a divine figure of sorts and await his return, are the only minority in Israel who are viewed as loyal enough to make up part of the Israeli army. This can also be connected with the fact that the Druze have been able over the course of time to survive under the most diverse regimes, in part due to a Shi'ite perspective according to which the deepest feelings and convictions are kept hidden (taqiyya).

The Fatimids exercised only mild opposition to the crusades, due to their enmity with the Sunni Seljuks and their trade relations with Italy, southern France and Byzantium.[60] Christians (and Jews) repeatedly occupied important civil positions during the regime of the Fatimids. In general, exceptions excluded, the Fatimids were kindly disposed toward the Christians. That was the case, for example, with the Fatimid caliph al-Mu'iz (952-975). A legend relates that a certain Ibn Killis, in an attempt to embarrass the Copts, pointed out to this caliph the verse in Matthew 17:20 where Jesus says: "If you have faith as a grain of mustard seed, you will say to this mountain, 'move from here to there', and it will move; and nothing will be impossible to you." The caliph then summoned the patriarch and commanded him to perform the same mira-

25

cle in order to show the truth of his religion. The patriarch and the congregation together maintained a vigil of prayer for three days and nights. When he dozed off in the church, the virgin Mary directed him to a humble and illiterate tanner, who was of great piety. In this way he found a man of faith and in a picturesque account the Muqattam hill near Cairo moved slightly, while the clergy and the congregation sang a hymn of mercy behind the poor yet distinguished tanner.[61]

Another Fatimid caliph, Nizar al-'Aziz (975-996) married a Christian woman whose two brothers he himself appointed as Patriarchs of Jerusalem and Alexandria.[62] The situation for Christians changed dramatically for the worse under the government of Hakim bi 'Amr Allah. In 1009 he destroyed the Church of the Holy Sepulchre in Jerusalem.[63] The Fatimid territory in Palestine, southern Lebanon, and southern Syria ultimately fell into the hands of the crusaders. The last caliph of the Fatimids was removed in 1171 by the last minister (vizier) of Saladin (1137-1193), who established the house of the Ayyubids.

The Crusades and the Christians of the East

It is important to spend some time looking at the period of the crusades, since they had grave consequences for the Christian churches and communities in the Middle East. In 1071, the Seljuks succeeded in defeating the main army of the Byzantines in Armenia. In the course of 1074, the Seljuks pressed on into Asia Minor and caused pope Gregory VII (1072- 1085) to call for an armed expedition to the East, which already bore the features of a crusade. In 1095, however, Pope Urbanus II (1089-1099) issued the call in Clermont Ferrant (France) for what would become the first crusade. He saw in the treaty with the Byzantine emperor a means of driving back the advance of Islam. He had already received from the Byzantine emperor, Alexius Commenus (1081-1118), who was in desperate need of Western mercenaries to protect his long border, a request for military support.[64] The cry of the crusaders was "*Deus le volt*" ("God desires it"). The crusades were referred to as pilgrimages and the events which accompanied them were called *magnalia Dei*, the great acts of God. It was viewed as a new period of salvation history, described by the title of a book from that era as *The Acts of God by the Hands of the Franks* (Guibert de Nogent, died 1124). God was seen as the One who through the Holy Spirit had unambiguously designated the Franks as the people chosen to lead the expedition. The crusader was both soldier and pilgrim.[65]

In 1098 the crusaders occupied Antioch, and instituted a Latin hierarchy there. The consequences of the great schism of 1054 were just becoming visible. The break between East and West was definitively fixed in the fourth crusade (1202-1204), when Constantinople was occupied by the crusaders and plundered. The subjection of the church of the East was in line with the wish of the pope.

In the closed worldview of the crusaders, there was no room for the heterodox. That applied equally to the Jews, the Byzantines and the Moslems. The Byzantines, who were depicted as morally corrupt, were sometimes viewed as not being fellow-believers at all. Other Eastern Christians too were regarded by the crusaders as unreliable.[66]

For the Eastern Christians, Jerusalem played an important role, being a center of Christian pilgrimage. The crusaders also saw themselves as pilgrims. When in 1099 Jerusalem was conquered by the crusaders, both Jews and Moslems were slaughtered, regardless of age or gender. It is told of one of the combatants that when he "later that morning went to visit the Temple area he had to pick his way through corpses and blood that reached up to his knees."[67] After the victory, they went to the Church of the Holy Sepulchre to give thanks to God for the success. The massacre that occurred in Jerusalem caused great shock. The Jews were accused of having helped the Moslems and Jerusalem was cleansed of its Jewish and Moslem inhabitants. It was this bloodthirsty proof of Christian fanaticism that recreated the fanaticism of Islam. When, later, wiser Latins in the East sought to find some basis on which Christian and Moslem could work together, the memory of the massacre stood always in their way.[68]

Christians in the East took an ambivalent approach to the crusades. In Cilicia and other places, the Armenians were prepared to provide troops to assist the effort against both Greeks and Turks. In spite of everything, the Armenians remained the only troops on which the Frankish princes could rely.[69]

The Maronites, who already long before had joined the fight against the Arab Moslems, assisted the crusaders as archers and guides. This was the case during the campaign of Raymond of Toulouse (1042-1115) one of the most important leaders of the first crusade. He participated in the conquest of Jerusalem and founded the county of Tripoli. He died while storming that city.[70] The Syrian Orthodox openly displayed their satisfaction at the victory of the crusaders. With respect to Palestine it is said that the Greek Orthodox and Syrian Christians there originally welcomed the crusaders as friends, but gradually began to see them as conquering oppressors.[71] It is said that the *dhimmi*s showed great indifference toward their so-called liberators. There was even talk of enmity due to the serious attacks by the Franks against the non-Latin rites.[72] But regardless of whether the Christians in the East had assumed a positive or negative position toward the crusaders, none of them escaped the consequences of the fall of the Latin kingdom. The Melchites prayed openly in Jerusalem for an Islamic victory while the rest were still fighting against the siege of Saladin in 1187.[73] A Cypriot monk wrote shortly after Richard the Lionhearted's (1175-1199) failure to conquer Jerusalem in 1191 in the third crusade: "No, it did not please Divine Providence to chase out the dogs from the Holy City in order to put the wolves in their place."[74]

The crusades contributed greatly to the alienation between Moslems and Christians in the East. Since that time, the position of the Eastern churches and communities worsened in the Islamic world, even though the Christians of Syria and Egypt were not responsible for the conflict with the Frankish conquerors (1097-1144). "The crusades left them disillusioned and enfeebled; the aftermath decimated them. Ironically, the venture which had its inception in the urge to defend Christendom came near to destroying its Eastern wing."[75] Although in the centuries prior to the crusades Syrian Christians had functioned as 'intellectual liaison officers' between Christian Europe and Moslem Asia, they saw their usefulness die in the crusades.

The Ayyubids (1174-1250)

From the middle of the twelfth until the middle of the thirteenth century, a dynasty of Kurdish descent (the Ayyubids) ruled in Egypt, Syria, Palestine, Iraq and Arabia (Yemen) and was to play an important role in the history of the crusades. The most renowned Kurdish Ayyubid prince was without a doubt Salah al-Din, otherwise known as Saladin (1137-1193). His hegemony extended at its peak from the Tripolitan border in North Africa to the Tigris, and from the southern Arabian coast of the Indian Ocean to the Armenian mountains. He ended the Shi'ite Fatimid caliphate in Egypt in 1171 and led that land back to Sunni Islam. During the crusades he led the 'holy war' against the crusaders. His great ambition was to vanquish Jerusalem and the crusader holdings in Palestine, Syria and Lebanon. On 2 October 1187, he succeeded in taking Jerusalem. There was a vast difference between the conquest of Jerusalem by Saladin and the previous conquest by the crusaders. "His mercy and kindness were in strange contrast to the deeds of the Christian conquerors of the first crusade."[76] For example, he encouraged the Jews to settle in Jerusalem once again.[77] The cross that had been placed on the Dome of the Rock was sent by the sultan to the caliph of Baghdad and was there buried on the threshold of the gate called Bab al-Nabi al-Sharif in such a way that the bronze and gold cross remained visible.[78] Before he died, Saladin had achieved his ambition with the exception of Antioch, Tripoli, Tyre and the fort at Acco, which had been regained by the English king Richard the Lionhearted and the French king Philip August in the third crusade (1189-1192).

In 1218, the prince al-Malik al-Kamil (1218-1238), the nephew of Saladin, was confronted with the crusaders of the fifth crusade (1218-1221), who besieged Damiatte in Egypt for five months. It was during this crusade that Francis of Assissi (died 1226) made his celebrated visit to Egypt and had his legendary encounter with the sultan, whom he tried to convert.[79] This ruler was viewed by the Copts as the most benevolent prince they had ever had.[80] Al-Kamil attempted to rid Egypt of the crusaders. The troops of the crusaders, who had been decimated by the plague, finally retreated on their own after having won certain privileges for pilgrims and the return of a supposed splinter of the cross. Seven years later, Emperor Fredrick II (1220-1250) undertook a new expedition, the sixth crusade (1228-1229). He was able by means of his diplomatic conduct and a treaty with al-Kamil, with whom he shared intellectual and political interests, to gain possession of Jerusalem, Bethlehem and Nazareth, as well as a corridor to the harbors of Sidon and Jaffa (1229). In the treaty equal rights and complete religious freedom were guaranteed for both Moslems and Christians. It was not long, however, before the successor of al-Kamil retook Jerusalem in 1244.[81]

The Mongols

The Mongols forged a kingdom stretching from China to Eastern Europe. In the thirteenth century, Genghis (= higher) Khan (died 1228) conquered North China and Central Asia. While still alive, Genghis Khan divided his enormous realm among his favorite sons. Thus several Mongolian kingdoms came into existence at his death: one in the West, that of the 'kingdom of the golden horde' in south Russia (1240-1480), and the kingdom of Il-Khan (literally, 'Lord of the tribe') in Persia (and Iraq), which was established by the grandson of the Genghis Khan, Hulagu (ca. 1217-1265), who was the first to bear the title Il-Khan.

It is related regarding the Mongols that they surpassed even the most barbarous peoples in cruelty. The hardly knew the names of the peoples they destroyed.[82] The entire population of the Middle East, both Christians and non-Christians, suffered horribly under the so-called Mongol storm. The Mongols were known as the destroyers of Christianity in Asia. When speaking of the 'eclipse of Christianity in Asia' (Browne), one must think primarily of the disappearance of Nestorian Christianity, which had just recently so miraculously spread over Asia. Around the year 1200, there were still some 25 metropolitans under the Catholicos of Baghdad.

Although it is true that the Mongols must bear the blame for this disappearance of Nestorian Christianity—especially in later years—it must not be forgotten that it was precisely the tolerant politic of the Mongols that permitted the spread of Christianity in the first place. The spread of the *pax tartarica* to China helped prepare the way for the spread of Nestorianism to the Far East, and it was in the wake of the Mongol invasion that Christianity again began to penetrate into China in the beginning of the thirteenth century. It was, however, viewed as the religion of the foreigner, being present among Turkish and Mongol tribes. With the disappearance of the Mongols from China, Christianity was uprooted as well.[83]

Originally all Mongol rulers were characterized by their striking tolerance in religious matters.[84] The first Mongol princes favored Christianity and some of the great Khans were nearly converted. With the Mongol conquest, the reconquest of the old Christian regions appeared possible. Hulagu, the conqueror of Baghdad in 1258 and founder of the Il-Khanate in Persia was married to a Christian wife. He was said to have been an adherent of Christianity, although there is no evidence that he was ever baptized. At the destruction of Baghdad, Christians remained safe in their communities, a fact due to Hulagu's Christian wife, it is said. Christians were permitted to rebuild their churches and to practice their faith freely, without restriction or humiliation, in Baghdad and Damascus, which was taken in 1260. The Christians in Damascus, however, made use of their new-found freedom to treat the Moslems with great intolerance. According to one Moslem author from that period, they drank wine freely during the fast month of Ramadan, and urinated in the streets, on the clothing of Moslems, and on the doors of the mosques! They also wore crosses openly and preached in the streets: "The true faith of the Messiah will triumph today." A Christian historian praised the intolerance toward the Moslems and in so doing probably reflected the opinions of many Christians in his day. The Syrian Jacobite Catholicos and historian, Bar Hebraeus (died 1286), related that at the conquest of Baghdad, the Christians escaped death and martyrdom because of the "benevolence, the wisdom and the wonderfully great character of Hulagu." When this prince died, the same historian wrote: "There was sorrow through the whole world at the death of these two great luminaries and zealous combatants of the Christian religion." It may have required a stretch of the imagination to describe such a prince, known for his barbarity, as a "defender of the faith."[85]

There were continual direct contacts between the Mongols and the Western Christian leaders, including the pope. Innocent IV (pope from 1243 to 1254) established diplomatic relations with the Mongol Khans. This pope had three agenda items: 1) continuation of the crusades in Palestine, 2) the extension of papal authority over the Eastern church along more diplomatic than military lines, 3) a relation with the Mongols such that they would convert to Christianity. In order to achieve these, he sent missionaries to the Mongols. The papal delegation, which arrived at the court of Guyuk (died 1248) in Karakorum on 22 July 1246, found a group of Nestorians there who assured them that the prince was on the point of becoming a Christian. Whatever the case may have been, the fact is that the leader of the Mongol troops received the order to send a delegation to King Louis IX 'the saint' of France (reigned from 1226-1270), who was at that time serving as leader of the crusader army in Cyprus. The intention was a joint venture to free the Christians of Palestine. In 1248, several delegations were exchanged and received.

The conquest of Syria by the Mongols came about in part under the banner of the crusade. Under the Mongol ruler Kubilay Khan (1214-1294), one of the intermediaries between the Kubilay and the Vatican was the well-known Marco Polo (1254-1324) and his father. This Venitian merchant was the first European traveller to reach the Far East. Around 1260, he made a journey to China and returned in 1269 with the request of the Kubilay Khan to send missionaries. Kit-Buka was given charge of the conquest of Syria. He was a Nestorian Christian who was able to depend on the sympathy of the Orthodox Christians in the struggle with the Moslems. This campaign of Kit-Buka against Islam has been called the 'yellow crusade'. On 3 September 1260, however, a battle took place between the Egyptian Mamluk army and the Mongol army, which resulted in the absolute defeat of the Mongols. Kit-Buka was taken prisoner and condemned. This defeat signalled the end of Mongol expansion in the Near East, and at the same time the victory of Islam. This and other factors occasioned a further oppression of the Christian church in Syria and the end of the remaining crusader cities in Palestine.[86]

During the first three centuries of Mongol hegemony, the Mongol rulers took a tolerant approach toward Christianity. This same tolerance was applied equally to Buddhism and Islam as well.[87] The Mongols of the East were Buddhists. The Mongol rulers in the West, the Il-Khans of Persia, vacillated for a long time, however, over whether to accept Christianity or Islam. Ultimately, they chose Islam.[88] Their acceptance of Islam in the West could be connected with the fact that when in 1291 the last bulwark of (Western) Christians in Acco was surrendered, it was the ultimate proof to the Mongols not only of the weakness of the European *powers*, but also of the *religion* the Europeans confessed. That moment is viewed, in any case, as the turning point in Mongol history. "From this time on, their sentiments turned more and more against Christianity and toward Islam."[89]

For the arrogance that they had previously displayed, the Christians in Damascus would later pay when the Mongol occupation of that city ended. In 1301 all the churches of Egypt were ordered closed, since they were considered friends of the Mongols and the old restrictive measures were again laid down.

Especially under Timur Lenk ('the cripple', 1336-1405), a militant form of Islam came into being. Timur was himself a Mongol, but of Turkish descent. He became one of the most gruesome conquerors the world has ever known. He wiped out entire cities in a way that was even more cruel than that of his Mongol predecessors. In Persia, he left Isfahan in ruins with a pyramid of some 70,000 skulls, and Baghdad, with one of some 90,000. Beginning in 1394, Timur conducted attacks against Mesopotamia (Iraq) and northern Syria, over which he swept like a cyclone in 1400, and where he dealt a deadly blow to the West and East Syrian churches. The old cultural centers were plundered and left in ruins. Cities such as Baghdad, Takrit, Mosul (in Iraq) and Tur 'Abdin and Mardin (now in south east Turkey), were obliterated. Many Christians were swept away in the last mentioned region, and those that took refuge in underground caves were smoked out.[90]

The Mamluks (1250-1517)

As the name indicates, the Mamluk dynasty was a dynasty of slaves. Beginning in 1250, the Mamluks ruled in Egypt and Syria, until the Ottoman Sultan Selim (Sultan from 1512 to 1520) conquered Cairo in 1517, and even then their authority continued in Egypt. There were in fact various Mamluk dynasties, which are referred to as generations of military aristocracies. Their great historic role is seen in the fact that they succeeded at keeping the Mongols at bay, and were able to definitively defeat the crusaders. They resisted the attack of the Mongols under Hulagu, 'the destroyer of the caliph of Baghdad', and were able to halt the hordes of Turks under Timur Lenk, thus protecting Egypt from plunder. They brought the crusader principalities in Syria and Palestine to an end. Acco (then called Jean d'Acre), which had fallen to the crusaders in 1104, was subdued by Saladin in 1187 but was retaken by the crusaders under Richard the Lionhearted in 1191. The final bulwark of the crusades, Acco fell in 1291, when it was taken by the Mamluk Sultan of Egypt. The last crusader was literally driven into the sea. The preacher in the mosque at Damascus spoke in 1291 of "all those who had wanted to fight for the faith."[91] At that point in history, the fall of Acco was comparable to the fall of Jerusalem to Saladin in 1187.[92]

During the rule of the Mamluks, who were not of Arab descent, Christians in Egypt were persecuted and the last possessions of the Franks in the Middle East were surrendered. The thirteenth century witnessed the complete disappearance of Latin domination of West Asia. After that the Moslems were able to bring the Christian principalities completely under their own control. The zenith of this offensive was reached in the ascent to power of the Ottomans in the seventeenth century. This resulted in harassment, persecution and murder for local Christians. During the reign of these 'slaves', entire areas were converted to Islam or their population was pillaged. Thus, for example, the city of Antioch was plundered by Baybar in 1268. They definitively rid Syria and Egypt of any remaining crusader presence. From that time on, Damascus took the place of Antioch, whose population had been banished or enslaved. In 1366, the Orthodox Synod would choose Damascus as its see.

The Ottomans (1517-1914)

Already at the end of the thirteenth century there is reference to the rise of the Ottoman Turks. Osman (died 1323/24) gradually extended his rule at the expense of the Byzantines. In 1453, Constantinople was conquered by Mehmed II (1451-1481), which was followed by the conquest of the rest of the Byzantine empire. Most spectacular, however, was the fall of Constantinople, the most important city of Eastern Christendom. This city received the name of Istanbul (reduced to Tsambul). Outside the Ottoman empire, the name Constantinople remained in use until 1923. The fall of this city, like that of Jerusalem in 1187 and Acco in 1291, was received with great bitterness in the West.[93] As a result of the conquest of the city, the Turkish sultan was referred to as the "predecessor of the anti-Christ and a second Senna-cherib," after the Assyrian king who had besieged Jerusalem in the time of King Hezekiah of Judah (2 Kings 18: 13-37, 19).[94] A preacher, con-nected with the British embassy in Constantinople, Edward Brown, was able to write in 1677: "It is repugnant to see the half-moon raised everywhere where the cross had for so long triumphantly stood."[95] Mehmed II appointed a Greek monk, George Scholarios, as Patriarch Gennadius II in January 1454, and later nominated an Armenian bishop as Patriarch of all Armenians. The patriarchs had civil *and* religious authority. Each church became a separate entity called a nation (*millet*). Other communities besides the Greek Orthodox, received similar privileges in the nineteenth century due to the reforms (*Tanzimat*). The only exception was the Roman Catholic Church. The unofficial reason for that was that the head of this church—namely the pope—resided outside the country. Since March 1960 there has been a nuncio in Ankara but in the eyes of the Turkish authorities he represents rather the papal state than the Roman Catholic Church.[96]

In 1516 the Turks conquered Jerusalem and proved to be more hostile toward the West than the sultans of Egypt had ever been.[97]

The direct result of the fall of Constantinople for Eastern Christianity was that all Christians initially were subsumed under the Greek Orthodox Patriarch of Constantinople. The Turks viewed all Christians as a single nation, or *millet*. While the Nestorian Christians had enjoyed the place of preference under Moslem rule until then, under the Ottomans the Greek Orthodox Church assumed that role. Only later was a separate Armenian *millet* recognized, and the Ecumenical Patri-arch, as he was called, continued to claim authority over all other Christian communities, as had the Byzantine emperor before him. The Orthodox Church was called the *Rum millet*, or the Byzantine nation. The patriarch was not only the spiritual head of the Greek Orthodox Church but also the civil head of the Greek nation.

The Patriarch of the West Syrian Jacobite Church, who was re-presented in Constantinople by a *wakil*, or deputy, resided in the monastery of Dayr al-Za'faran, near Mardin in eastern Turkey. The Patriarch of the East Syrian Church—the so-called 'Mountain Nestorians'

—resided in the Kurdish mountains. He neither requested nor received recognition from the sultan.[98]

Capitulations

It is important to look more closely at the relation between Western Christians and Christians under the Ottoman empire. Immediately after the conquest of Constantinople on 2 June 1453, an agreement was made with the Turkish Sultan Mehmed II (1451-1481), in which Christians were assured of life, property and the unhindered practice of commerce and religion. In 1454, a similar accord was signed with Venice. In the reign of King Francis I of France (1515-1547), during the battle of Pavia (24 February 1525), in which Francis was defeated by Emperor Charles V (1519-1556), secret contact was made with Sultan Sulayman I (1494-1566) by the forces of Francis for the purpose of enlisting his help. In 1535, Francis I and Sulayman I made a pact. This pact is seen as the beginning of French supremacy in the Levant.[99] It was considered at the time, however, as a 'religious crime', since it ruptured the Christian unity of the West that had existed in Europe.

This pact then functioned as a model for the treaties drawn up by other Western states with the Ottoman empire. 'Capitulations' became the common term for these treaties. These 'treaties' were not viewed by the Turks as international accords, but rather as 'decisions', since the Christians with whom they were made were considered 'infidels'. Through these capitulations, the Western Christians living in Turkey were granted certain extra territorial rights: they were allowed to conduct business, enjoyed protection of their person and property, stood under the jurisdiction of the Western powers in Turkey, could to a certain extent freely exercise their religion, could safely visit sites in Palestine, and could not be forced to convert to Islam. In this, no distinction was made between Roman Catholics and Protestants. Turkey made such treaties with various Western nations, such as England, France and the Netherlands.

The treaty with the last mentioned nation was made in 1860, in which it was determined that the Dutch would not be hindered from visiting holy places in Jerusalem, and that the monks could not prevent adherents of the Lutheran faith from visiting the Holy Sepulchre.

How such capitulations functioned in reality appeared, for example, when some American missionaries were arrested by Turkish police when they visited Jerusalem in 1824, and their release had to be arranged by the British consul. British protection was of great benefit to the American missionaries. When after the battle of Navarino (20 October 1827), in which a large part of the Turkish-Egyptian navy was destroyed by the navies of the English, French and Russians, the British consulates in Turkey were closed, the American missionaries fled to Malta. As soon as the British consul returned, so did the American missionaries, who stood under their protection.

Yet it was not the American missionaries alone who profited from the protection of England. A Maronite convert to Protestantism, As'ad al-Shidyaq, also received consular protection. Sir Stratford Canning, the English emissary, protected all American citizens when there was no American consul. It was not until 7 May 1830 that a capitulation was signed with the United States. The well-known American missionary, Eli Smith, even went so far as to maintain that American citizenship was as profitable in his time as Roman citizenship was in the time of the apostle Paul (cf. Acts 22:28). "The missionary nowhere has to be concerned," he said, "about losing his life or liberty, since the power of the Christian nations was able to keep the Turks in check." When an American fleet once paid a visit to Beirut, this was interpreted as an implicit sign of respect for the mission, showing what powerful friends the missionaries had![100]

The concerns of the European powers with the Ottoman empire were expressed in the nineteenth century by the euphemistic phrase the 'Eastern Question'. The European powers, however, had their own, often conflicting, interests. Actually, the liquidation of the "sick man on the Bosporus" (the expression appears first to have been used by Russian tsar) did not take place in the nineteenth century because the European powers could not agree on the division of the spoils. Both England and France were involved in the Greek rebellion of 1821. The Turks then arrested the Ecumenical Patriarch, Gregory V (died 1821), as he celebrated the Easter service, dragged him from the church, and subsequently hanged him by his ecclesiastical vestments.[101]

The Crimean War

The European powers did not fail to make use of these concessions in the form of capitulations on behalf of various Christian, or even non-Christian, minority groups, where, of course, it coincided with their own interests. The Turkish sultan also managed to exploit the internal disputes of the European powers to his own advantage.

36

The Crimean War was fought from October 1853 until February 1856 between the Russians and the British, French and Ottoman Turks. The direct cause of the war was the Russian claim to exercise protection over the Orthodox subjects of the Ottoman sultan, and a dispute between Russia and France over Russian Orthodox and Roman Catholic monks at the holy places in Palestine.

During the Crimean War, and the Russian-Turkish War, from 1876-1878, the Turks had European allies who fought with them against Russia. In a manner similar to that in which the treaty between the sultan and the French king had been earlier condemned, so also now there was talk of the (Christian Europe's) betrayal of Russia. While the Germans (Prussians) sided with Russia—as a natural member of the European community of nations—France assumed a completely different position. The Roman Catholic Bishop of France, representing the position of the Vatican, expressly sanctioned France's part in the war. The Crimean War was then sanctified as a 'crusade' against the heresy of Photius (died ca. 895), the Byzantine patriarch who in 863 had been condemned by the pope. It bore many similarities to the crusades, especially the fourth, when the European Christians turned against the Byzantines. It is then understandable that the Russians saw in the Crimean War a breach of Christian European solidarity—in particular on the part of France and England.[102]

As soon as France was recognized by the sultan as the protector of his Roman Catholic subjects, the tsar sent an emissary to Constantinople in February 1853 in order to demand guardianship over all Turkish Orthodox Christians. When Turkey did not accede to the Russian request, Tsar Nicholas I (1796-1855) occupied the Danube principalities of Walachia and Moldavia, ruled by Turkey, in reprisal in June 1853. When diplomatic consultations produced no result, Turkey declared war on Russia on 23 October 1853. On 27 March 1854, France and England in turn declared war on Russia. In September 1856 the invasion of the Crimea took place. Only after the fall of Sevastopel (10 September 1855) did peace negotiations begin. Provisional terms for surrender were accepted by Russia on 1 February 1856. On 30 March 1856, the so-called Treaty of Paris was signed, in which the integrity of the Ottoman empire was guaranteed.[103]

The Crimean War and the gathering in Paris which followed signalled, according to Joseph Hajjar, "a decisive turning point for Christianity in the East." The defeat of the Russian Army in the Crimean War meant the dominance of the (Western) French-English alliance throughout the Ottoman empire.[104] In an appendix to the Treaty of Paris the equality of all subjects, Moslems and Christians, was confirmed by decree of the sultan.[105] It was viewed by George Khodr, the current Metropolitan of Mount Lebanon, as the first step toward the secularization of the Ottoman empire. Before that time, a Moslem who converted to Christianity was guilty of apostasy from the Islamic faith (*ridda 'an al-Islam*). In Turkey, in accordance with Islamic law, this crime was punished with death until 1844. As a result, a mission to the Moslems was out of the question. A subject of the sultan could not join the church of the 'Franks'. Those who became Protestants, in fact, stepped outside the security of the Ottoman empire.[106] On the basis of the cooperation with the French and English during the Crimean War, this traditional death penalty for apostasy from Islam and conversion to Christianity was abolished by the sultan. It was now legally permissible for a Moslem to receive baptism.[107] The sultan agreed from then on to assure all his subjects, regardless of race or religion, all the advantages of communal rights that the citizens of free (liberal) Europe enjoyed. The publication of the *Hatt-i Humayun* (Imperial Rescript) and its endorsement by the international community was the source, according to Joseph Hajjar, "of the regeneration of contemporary Eastern Christianity."[108]

The Berlin Congress

'Christian Europe' would not neglect in the following decades to demand 'reforms' from the sultan, regardless of what political, economic or military problems he would face as a result. In 1860, due to the unrest in Lebanon, an allied 'intervention' took place. Rumors concerning the massacre of Christians in Syria finally led to the removal of Sultan Abdul Aziz (1861-1876) on 30 May 1876.

When France occupied Tunisia in May/June of 1881, a great protest ensued in the Islamic East. The sultan turned to the Germany of Otto von Bismarck (1815-1898), who sent a military mission to Istanbul on 2 November 1880, which became a precursor of German influence in Turkey. This influence was apparently intended to prolong the existence of the Ottoman empire.[109] With the demise of the Ottoman empire the cultural influence of Western Europe increased.

At the 'Berlin Congress', which took place in Germany from 13 June to 13 July 1878 under the leadership of Bismarck, a great deal of time was devoted to the division of the Ottoman empire into spheres of influence: the Austrian emperor had already immediately occupied Bosnia-Herzegovina (25-29 July 1878); France sanctioned its 'rights' in

Syria, Palestine and the status quo in the holy places, while England was encouraged by Bismarck to occupy Egypt at some point. This was a "turning point in the history of Russia and the Turkish empire," according to Joseph Hajjar. "It set European expansion in motion."[110] The revolt of Ahmad 'Urabi was crushed in the English victory at Tell el-Kebir on 13 September 1882. 'Arabi Pasha was subsequently banished.

In the English bombing of Alexandria (11-12 June, 1882) and the battle of Tell el-Kebir, the hopes for independence of the peoples who had lived under Ottoman rule, especially the Arabs, were dashed for several decades. The way was opened for massive and uncontrolled penetration by the economic, cultural, social and religious power of the West.[111]

Mandate Territories

After the First World War (1914-1918) the Ottoman empire was divided up into various parts. Several areas were handed to France and England as 'mandate territories': England 'received' Palestine, Iraq and Egypt; France received Syria and Lebanon. The hope for religious freedom arose among Christians in the areas. The chairman of the *International Missionary Council* at the time, John R. Mott (1865-1955), summarized his findings as follows: "Whereas formerly indirect methods of approach were necessary on account of government restrictions and Moslem opposition and fanaticism, yet in many Moslem lands to-day the way is open to widespread and direct evangelization."[112]

Among Arab nationalists, were found both Moslems and Christians. Not only Moslem Arabs, but also Christian Arabs saw the Western Christian mission efforts to be flowing from imperialistic arrogance. Many Moslem nationalists were convinced that the missionaries were using local Christians with whom they worked as tools for the foreign powers in a divide-and-conquer politics that was intended to weaken national movements. 'Umar Farrukh and Mustafa Khalidi went so far in their book, the title of which translates as *Mission and Colonialism in Arab Lands*, a book well-known in the Middle East, as to contend that the mission movement was more harmful for Arab lands than imperialism, "since imperialism only came to our land behind the missionary veil." According to these two authors, the mission schools not only had a divisive effect, but also actually delayed the development of Arab nationalism. They refer to certain books and missionaries and draw attention to the fact that the first church in the Ottoman empire was called 'The Church of Zion'.[113]

In the Arab national awakening there was clear reference to a cooperation between Moslems and Christians. In the struggle for independence, both from Turkey and later from the colonial yoke, Moslems and Christians frequently fought side by side. Copts and Moslems together resisted British rule in 1919/1920 and the cross and the crescent appeared for the first time on the same flag. Coptic priests and Moslem 'ulama (religious scholars) walked arm in arm through the streets of Cairo.[114] At the site of Martyrs' Square in Beirut, both Christians and Moslems fell at the hand of the Turks.

In the twentieth century the Christian communities in the Middle East have suffered much as a result of the wartime conditions before and during the First World War. The definitive disintegration of the Ottoman empire had grave consequences for the Christian minorities. The massacre of the Armenians around 1915 was the most dramatic but not the only disaster that Christians, along with other inhabitants of the Middle East, suffered. Many died of hunger. The European powers, who wanted to grab as many of the crumbs that fell from the Ottoman table as possible, both encouraged (Lawrence of Arabia in 1916 and the 'Arab revolt' with Sherief·Husayn in the Hejaz) and frustrated Arab struggle for independence. They were able through these conflicting interests to make intelligent use of the trauma of the various communities. But their own European interests always had priority.[115] In the decades following the First World War Assyrian or Nestorian Christians suffered much at the hands of the Turks and Kurds. They were punished for their support for England in particular, which was viewed as 'collaboration'. There were still Greek, Armenian, Assyrian and Syrian Orthodox Christians in what remained of the Ottoman empire, the Turkey of Mustafa Kemal Ataturk (1881-1938), but many also departed for Syria and Iraq. In the defeat of Greece and Asia Minor, a new defeat for Orthodox Christianity was seen: "The illusion of a restoration of Hellenic-Byzantine Christianity in the Aya Sophia in Constantinople was nurtured but for a brief moment."[116]

On 24 July 1923 the Turks signed the Treaty of Lausanne, later ratified by the new Assembly, whereby the capitulations were abolished, the *millet* system disappeared, but minorities were given the right to organize themselves in accordance with their own laws. The exchange of population was envisaged. Between 1923 and 1930 about a million and a quarter Greeks were sent from Turkey to Greece, and a rather smaller number of Turks from Greece to Turkey.[117]

Since the Second World War the international situation had drastically changed. The actions of the European powers and the United States would have its effects of the further developments in the Middle East. The creation of the state of Israel in 1948 marks an a important new stage in the relationship of the Jews in and towards the Arab world.

Some of the problems and challenges the churches faced *vis à vis* the Moslem environment in past and present will also be discussed in the chapters on the separate churches. In the final chapter we will try to deal with the contemporary and future perspectives for both the Jews and the Christians in the Arab world of today.

NOTES

1. 1947, 124.

2. Cf. Wensinck, ch. III: "De joodse invloed op het ontstaan van de moslimse eredienst" (Jewish Influence on the Origins of Moslem Worship).

3. 44:32 (31); 45:16 (15); 2:47 (44); 2:122 (116); cf. Amos 3:2.

4. 5:12 (15); 5:70 (74).

5. 45:16 (15); 40:53 (56).

6. 7:137. Speyer, 348, says that this expression is taken either from Genesis 13:14 or Psalm 113:3. The psalm has become especially familiar through the liturgy.

7. 68:37.

8. According to Hitti, 1966, 30f.

9. Wensinck, 7, 68, 74-81.

10. Wensinck, 59, 68.

11. Bijlefeld, 160f.

12. Wensinck, 24.

13. Wessels, 1972, 184f.; cf. Barakat Ahmad, ch.4, in which he delves more deeply into the complex reporting of this history.

14. Koran 19:37 (38); 43:65; cf. also 2:253 (254); 21:93; 23:53 (55); 13:36.

15. Corbon, 1977, 15f.

16. Cf. Wilms, 1966.

17. Andrae, 282; cf. Browne, 22; Bell.

18. Gardet, 106, who unfortunately gives no reference to a source.

19. *E.I. s.v. Kuds* and *Kubbat al-Sakhra*; cf. Borrmans.

20. Fattal, 85.

21. Fattal, 72-74.

22. Fattal, 82.

23. Tritton, 115.

24. Goitein, 74.

25. Tritton, 94.

26. Arberry, 1969, 193.

27. Meinardus, 1970, 359f.

28. Every, 76.

29. Hitti, 1951, 484.

30. Quoted by Tareq Mitri, 1985, 55.

31. Every, 76; al-Baladhuri, 172, 187f.; Hitti, 1964, 1650.

32. Sahas.

33. Smith, 1976, 120.

34. Juynbol, 1910, 345, 350; Corbon, 1977, 48.

35. Meinardus, 1970, 360.

36. Arberry, 1969, 245; Betts, 10.

37. Thubron, 78-85.

38. Atiya, 269.

39. Corbon, 27; Atiya, 226, 228.

40. Meinardus, 1961, 172f.

41. Corbon, 54.

42. Spuler, 1958, 328, 331; Ronart, s.v.; Hitti, 1964, 360.

43. Meinardus, 1961, 346.

44. Arberry, 1969, 248; Atiya, 269; Müller, 162.

45. Browne, 49; Stewart, 1928, 218; *E.I.* *s.v.*, Harun al-Rashid.

46. Browne, 57.

47. *E.I.* *s.v.* al-Mutawakkil.

48. Meinardus, 1961, 346.

49. Watt, 1972, 13.

50. Hitti, 1964, 312f.

51. Hitti, 1964, 313.

52. Atiya, 1969, 195, 270f.; O'Leary, 163, 169; *E.I.* *s.v.* Hunayn ibn Ishak.

53. Hitti, 1964, 633.

54. Atiya, 199.

55. *Lexikon s.v.* Seldschuken; cf. Hitti, 1964, 473-76.

56. Atiya, 200f.; cf. Stewart, 223f.

57. Tritton, 95.

58. Rosenthal, 58; Goitein, 65.

59. Tritton, 95; Fattal, 24, 108.

60. *Lexikon s.v.* Fatimiden.

61. Meinardus, 1961, 175; Atiya, 87 n.4.

62. Meinardus, 347; Müller, 148.

63. Cf. ch.5.

64. Watt, 1972, 52f.; cf. Runciman, 1969, 27.

65. Van Erp, 75.

66. Van Erp, 76.

67. Runciman I, 1965, 287.

68. Runciman I, 1965, 286f.

69. Arberry, 1969, 258f.; Fiey, 1975, 103.

70. Every, 91; Hitti, 1967, 285; Hitti, 1964, 638f.

71. Fiey, 1975, 103; Every, 93.

72. Sivan, 1968, 180.

73. Hitti, 1972, 215; Arberry, 1969, 252; Betts, 13.

74. Arberry, 1969, 252.

75. Hitti, 1972, 211.

76. Runciman II, 1965, 466.

77. Runciman II, 467.

78. Fiey, 1975, 104.

79. See Giulio Basetti-Sani, ch. VII: "Saint Francois devant le sultan."

80. Hitti, 1964, 654.

81. Aziz Ahmad, 1975, 85; Meinardus, 1961, 180.

82. Stewart, 156f., 258, 261, 265.

83. Atiya, 273f.; Browne, 172f.; Stewart, 262; Heussi, 214.

84. *Lexikon s.v.* Mongolen.

85. Browne, 151; Atiya, 209; Stewart, 159; Neill, 123.

86. Benz, 113f., 148; Browne, 154; Stewart, 267.

87. Benz, 112.

88. Browne 172f.; cf. Spuler.

89. Thus Browne, 154, 161, 174f.

90. Browne, 172; Every, 30; Atiya, 276; Stewart, 275-84; Neill, 123; Hitti, 1964, 699.

91. Sivan, 1968, 183.

92. Atiya, 1975, 3; Ronart, 341-43; *Lexikon s.v.* Mamluks; Hitti, 1964, 671.

93. Atiya, 1975, 660.

94. Ware, 1975, 97; Corbon, 1977, 43.

95. Ware, 96; Runciman, 1969, 71; Lewis, 1968, 315.

96. Xavier Jacob, IV (1994), 2.

97. Every, 99.

98. Kawerau, 450f.; Every, 99; Ware, 98; Betts, 15; Runciman, 1968.

99. Atiya, 1975, 661.

100. Kawerau, 433-35, 440-42, 444, translated from the German text; *E.I. s.v.* Imtiyaz. Cf. page 140.

101. Arberry I, 302.

102. Every, 102; Benz, 157f.

103. Cf. *E.I. s.v.* Kirim.

104. Hajjar, 1971, 103.

105. Arberry, 1969, 302.

106. Kawerau, 442f., 452.

107. Latourette, 1947, 48.

108. Hajjar, 1971, 105f.

109. Hajjar, 1971, 110.

110. Hajjar, 1971, 109f.

111. Hajjar, 1974, 111.

112. Mott, 1926, 361, 379; Joseph, 1961, 223.

113. Farrukh and Khalidi, 1964.

114. Meinardus, 1970, 40f.

115. Corbon, 1977, 54.

116. Hajjar, 1971, 189; 1974, 418.

117. Lewis, 1968, 254, 260, 354. Arberry, 1969, 474.

II. ORTHODOXY IN THE ARAB EAST: CELEBRATED DOGMA

Every Church is a manifestation of the Holy Spirit.
John Chrysostom

Introduction

The Eclipse of Christianity in Asia (Browne) is the title of a book which offers an intriguing account of how Christianity was gradually extinguished in Asia, 'eclipsed' behind the dark clouds which have gathered over Asiatic history. Many Christians in the West are amply aware of the fact that Christianity in Asia was not originally of European or Western origin. Rather, it was "where Christianity began" (Horner), at least as far as Western Asia and the Middle East are concerned. In fact, the so-called 'major' world religions all originated in Asia. Christianity too, or rather the Christian faith, was born in the East, in Galilee and Jerusalem, and already in the first century of the (for that reason) Christian calendar spread from there all the way to Spain. The apostle Paul himself had plans to visit Spain (Romans 15:24, 28), and according to the first letter to the Corinthians of Saint Clement, an acquaintance of Paul, he did. Yet for the first thousand years of the Christian era, the nucleus of Christianity lay in the (Middle) East.

The church spread throughout the (*koine*) Greek-speaking world. *Koine* Greek was the language spoken in the East at that time, especially in the cities, although in rural areas indigenous languages, such as Syriac and Aramaic (the language spoken by Jesus), were maintained. *Koine* Greek is also the language in which the New Testament was written. It remained the predominate language until the fourth century, when the Roman emperor Constantine (306-337) moved his court to the city named in his honor, Constantinople (modern Istanbul). In the West too, the Greek language continued to be used for a long time.[1] Greek was still spoken in Gaul and in Carthage, as well as in Rome in the second century. The 'Greek' Church Father Irenaeus, for example, who came from Asia Minor and became Bishop of Lyon in the year 177 still wrote and spoke Greek.

In order to understand properly the differences that quickly arose between the various regional churches it is important to realize that the hinterlands of Syria were never completely Hellenized. The bishops from Mesopotamia who attended the major synods and councils, which were then conducted in Greek, had to make use of interpreters on these occasions. The clergy from Edessa, for example, sent to the Ecumenical Council of Chalcedon in 451 a petition in which more than one-third of the affixed signatures were written in Syriac.[2]

In order to spread the gospel to the rural areas, it was necessary to make use of the local language, which is precisely what occurred. Through the process of Christianization, these indigenous languages were 'upgraded' to literary languages. That was especially the case with Syriac and Aramaic, as well as with Coptic and Ethiopic.[3] This process could be compared to the role that Luther's translation of the Bible played in the development of the German language, or the writings of John Calvin in that of French, or the impact that the King James version of the Bible had on the development of the English language.

Several of the Orthodox churches see themselves as connected with 'Antioch'. Most of the differences among the various Orthodox churches as well as amongst themselves were viewed in the West as mainly dogmatic in nature. Therefore it is of importance to describe the christological struggle which led to certain divisions not only amongst the churches in the East but also to a certain extent with the Western church, aside from the 'national' (and political) differences. Although the national differences should perhaps be given the greater emphasis, the dogmatic differences also deserve mention. But the real character of Orthodox spirituality should be sought not so much in the theology but in the liturgy, whatever the differences amongst the various Orthodox churches may be. We will therefore discuss them in this chapter. Icons are treated here as well because they illustrate Orthodox spirituality and explain what the Orthodox want to say when they speak about the process of *theosis* or divinization: God becoming human so that humans can become divine (Irenaeus).

The Churches of Antioch

The first center of non-Jewish Christianity was the city of Antioch, situated on the Orontes river. There the new religion was first preached to the 'Gentile Greeks'. Antioch is now called Antakya, and has, since the end of the French mandate over Syria in 1939, belonged to Turkey. Although currently of little importance, it was once the third most important city (after Rome and Alexandria) in the entire Roman empire, as well as home to the first metropolitan of Eastern Christianity.

In 64 B.C., Antioch became the residence of the Roman governor of the province of Syria. With its beautiful temples (e.g., that of Apollo), colonnades (e.g., that of Herod), forums, theaters, baths, palaces and aqueducts, it was an important artistic and commercial center. Ten percent of the population was Jewish who built various synagogues there (Acts 6:5).

Early in the Christian era, Antioch played a prominent role in the beginning of the Greek mission, that is, the mission to non-Jews (Acts 11:20; Galatians 2:11ff.). Here primitive Christianity encountered Hellenistic Judaism. Antioch was chosen by Paul and Barnabas as the base from which the mission to the Gentiles would be launched, the so-called first and second missionary journeys (Acts 11:25; 13:1-3; 14:26; 18:22). It was in Antioch that the disciples of Jesus were called Christians for the first time (Acts 11:26), indicating that the name was first applied to the group by others—perhaps as a term of derision (1 Peter 4:16). According to the 'father of church history', Eusebius (ca. 260/5-339/ 340), the church in Antioch was established by Peter. In any case, he was viewed as the first Bishop of Antioch, even before he departed for Rome.[4]

Already before the dawn of the post-apostolic period, Ignatius, who died a martyr's death in Rome shortly after 110, was one of the most important bishops of this city. Many years later, bishops of Antioch continue to bear his name.

Antioch was also the third most important city in the Christian world, again after Rome and Alexandria. In the fourth century, however, the rise of Constantinople would force Antioch from this position. Constantine was the first Christian emperor to permit the building of an official church in the city. The city was struck several times by earthquakes. In 636 Antioch was conquered by the Moslems, was regained by the Byzantines in the tenth century, but fell once again into the hands of Moslem rulers (the Seljuks), only to become in 1098, on the occasion of the first crusade, the center of one of the feudal centers of the crusaders. Many of the Eastern churches claim to stem from this church. Although the heads of various churches call themselves the Patriarch of Antioch, none of them resides in the city today.

In the first centuries there was a palpable tension between the Greek (Hellenistic) and the Semitic world. These two worlds coexisted in Antioch in some form of symbiotic relationship until the fourth century, when the "Antiochian, Semitic world came of age, and slowly distanced itself from its Greek twin."[5]

The Understanding of Jesus

In the early centuries of church history the church wrestled with its understanding of the person and message of Jesus of Nazareth. What is his significance for eternal salvation, and how is he related to God? The christological struggle resulted ultimately in the birth of various 'national' churches in the East, as well as the rupture between the Western church and the Eastern church(es).

Nicea: Arius 325

Arius (died 335) lived in Alexandria, Egypt, and taught that the Son (of God) had not existed from eternity. Rather, there had been a time when the Son did not exist. According to Arius, the Son did not derive from the *essence* of the Father, but from His *will*. He is not true God. The Son was, in his view, the first creation of the Father.

When Arius published his views in 318, his bishop, Alexander, charged him with heterodoxy and he was condemned by the Council of Alexandria in 321 and subsequently removed from office. The dispute reached such high levels that in 325 the First Ecumenical Council was called in Nicea, near Constantinople, by the emperor himself. This gathering then spoke out against Arius as follows:

We believe ... in one Lord Jesus Christ, the only begotten Son of God, who is of the essence of the Father. God of God, light of light, begotten not made, being of one essence (*homoousios*) with the Father.

But this declaration did not in any way end the christological controversy. While by means of this decision the Church was able to secure the true divinity of Christ, it posed a threat to the true humanity of Christ, as was soon to become apparent.

Constantinople: Apollinaris 381

Apollinaris, who became Bishop of Laodicea in 361 (today called Latakiya and located in Syria), was among those who fully acknowledged the decision of Nicea on the divinity of the Son. But he held a unique view of the humanity of Jesus. Beginning with the conception that man must be divided into body, soul and spirit, Apollinaris thought that Jesus did indeed have a true human body and soul, but lacked a human spirit. In its place was the divine word (*Logos*). According to him, the humanity and divinity had combined to form a new being in Jesus. Viewed thus, Jesus has one nature, which was formed by the mingling of two natures.

49

Because of his views, Apollinaris is considered the predecessor of Monophysitism: the belief in the one divine-human nature of Christ. The resulting conclusion would then have to be that the human nature of Jesus was not of one essence with our own. According to Apollinaris, the divine Logos did everything to ensure that redemption did not fail.

At the Second Ecumenical Council of Constantinople in 381 the teaching of Apollinaris was condemned. The confession was made that those who desired to believe in the true redemption of the sinner by Jesus Christ also had to cling to the truth of His true and perfect humanity.[6]

While the Council of Nicea confessed the true divinity (the *vere Deus*) of Jesus, Constantinople emphasized his true humanity (*vere homo*). The question that consequently arose was: How are the two natures then related to one another? It appears that the issue engendered various opinions and schools, which are sometimes connected with Alexandria (Egypt) and the already mentioned Antioch. The direction of 'Alexandria', where greater stress was placed on religious feeling, is sometimes considered more speculative, while that of 'Antioch' was supposedly more empirical and intellectual in nature. Cyril (died 444), the Patriarch of Alexandria and representative of the Alexandrian school, placed emphasis on the unity of Christ without paying much attention to his historical reality. In his view, the divinity and humanity of Christ were combined in a single nature with the result that the divinity in Christ predominated.[7]

Ephesus: Nestorius 431

Opposed to the position of Cyril was that of Nestorius. The rhetorical gifts of this Syrian monk from Antioch helped him to the Patriarchate of Constantinople. He followed the direction of the Antiochians which emphasized more Christ's *humanity* than his *divinity*. He taught that the unity of the divine man was some form of conjunction, not unlike that of a marriage.[8] For that reason Nestorius contested the reference to Mary as 'mother of God' (*Theotokos*), a title which had been in circulation since the time of Origin (died 253/4). According to Nestorius, Mary was not the mother of the divine, but only of the human nature of Christ. In the expression 'mother of God' Nestorius heard a denial of the full humanity of Jesus. The child that Mary brought into the world could not have been God, he contended. Therefore he preferred to speak of Mary as '*Christo*tokos'. He was supposed to have said "I acknowledge no God of two or three months of age," a statement that was later used in Moslem polemic against the doctrine of the Trinity. He placed the emphasis on the division of the natures in Christ in contrast to the teaching of Apollinaris.

At the Third Ecumenical Council of Ephesus in 431 Nestorius' teaching was condemned and he was relieved of his position as Patriarch. Cyril, who became Patriarch of Egypt in 412, was primarily responsible for the condemnation. Nevertheless, many Eastern bishops, led by John, the Patriarch of Antioch, did not participate in this condemnation.[9]

Eutyches (ca. 378-454), the 'archimandrate' or abbot of one of the monasteries in Constantinople, was a follower of the Alexandrian school and was active in the struggle against Nestorius. He taught that Christ had two natures before his incarnation, but only one after his incarnation. Just as the sea absorbs a drop of honey, so also the divinity had absorbed completely the humanity of Christ. In other words, he taught an exaggerated Monophysite position, namely, that the body of Christ was unlike that of most humans. The nature of the body was transformed by the divinity.[10]

Chalcedon: 451

In a doctrinal letter Pope Leo I (440-461), the Bishop or Pope of Rome, stated in opposition to Eutyches that before the incarnation there was but one nature, which was divine; the human nature came into being only in the incarnation, so that after the incarnation both natures were present.

At the Fourth Ecumenical Council, which was subsequently held in Chalcedon in 451, the full humanity and the full divinity of Christ were confirmed:

of one substance with the Father according to his divinity, of one substance with us according to his humanity; like us in all things except sin; begotten from eternity of the Father according to his divinity, but in the last days, for us and for our salvation, born of the Virgin Mary, the mother of God, according to his humanity; one and the same Christ, Son, Lord, Only-begotten in two natures without confusion, without change, without division, without separation.

The *without confusion* and *without change* were included against Eutyches, who thought that the two natures were merged in a single divine man. The *without division* and *without separation* were included against Nestorius, who viewed the two natures as two different persons, which were only one in will. Through its four negative predications Chalcedon sought to preserve the mystery of Christ.[11]

One other important decision of the Council of Chalcedon was to accept the twenty-eighth canon in which the see Constantinople received second position in the list of patriarchates. The council assigned to the Metropolitan of Constantinople, 'the new Rome', a large area of authority and decided that the city where the emperor and the senate resided, and which possessed as much authority in the ecclesiastical sphere as Rome, should take the first position after Rome. Rome, however, never accepted this decision.

National Churches

Even more important than these dogmatic differences, however, were the more or less 'national' lines along which the churches divided. There were clergy who were imperially or melchitically (*melchos* is the Syriac word for 'prince') oriented. It was their intention to enforce the decisions of the Council of Chalcedon (located next to Constantinople, the second Rome, and the residence of the emperor) among the other metropolitans, such as those of Alexandria, Jerusalem and Antioch. This led to confrontations, some of them bloody. An identification of sorts arose between emerging *nationalistic* sentiments and *Monophysite* inclinations. Constantinople recognized only the Greek Orthodox (Melchite) Patriarch of Antioch and those clergy of Greek Orthodox bent. The 'Nestorians' moved beyond the border of Persia. Where the Jacobites remained in Byzantine territory, they were forced underground and had to endure persecution.

After the death of Patriarch Severus of Antioch (ca. 456-538), who was considered the greatest exponent of Monophysite teaching, both a Greek Orthodox and a Monophysite patriarch were appointed. The term 'Monophysitism' was often wielded by its opponents as a label, while it was viewed as a term of derision by those who bore it. Ascriptions such as 'Nestorian' and 'Monophysite' were usually applied by others, but their intended recipients typically rejected them. The Copts, for example, do not wish to be known as Monophysites. It was for them more a question of the "sense of unity between the human and the divine than the misleading unity of nature, which never occurs among the orthodox fathers of the so-called 'Monophysite' churches.[12]

In 431, after the Council of Ephesus, a break occurred when the East Syrian Church or Church of the East (also known as the Nestorian Church) came into being. After the Council of Chalcedon a West Syrian Church developed, which would later be called the Jacobite Church. These churches then broke with the Chalcedonian (those who continued to adhere to the decisions of Chalcedon) or the Melchite (imperial) Church.

The designations used above focused primarily on the 'dogmatic' or doctrinal differences which led to the break-up of the church. In fact, however, as was often the case in the history of the church, non-theological factors played just as fundamental a role in the break. There were and indeed still are dogmatic or doctrinal differences, but the actual conflicts and schisms were just as much, if not more, motivated by 'national', political, social and economic factors. Both Chalcedon and Nicea, which was the first residence of the emperor, were situated near Constantinople, the seat of power. The emperor played an important role in calling the above mentioned ecumenical councils. He had a political interest in the unity of the Church. The resistance of some of the churches to the decisions of the councils also was directly related to 'national' resistance against the central authority. Political factors played an important role in the acceptance or rejection of the decisions of the councils. Thus, for example, the Copts in Egypt perceived the deposition of their pope at Chalcedon in 451 as a national insult; likewise, the Armenians were unable to attend the Council of Chalcedon due to the wars in which they were embroiled, and later distanced themselves from its decisions; the Jacobites too were alienated from Byzantium due no less to 'national', cultural and economic considerations.

'Byzantine imperialism' came to its fullest expression under the reign of emperor Justinian (sole ruler from 527 until 565). He defeated the Vandals in North Africa, the Ostrogoths in Sicily, Italy and Dalmatia, and the Visigoths in Spain. Emperor Justinian was an important lawgiver, codifying Roman law, and was not without merit as a theologian. He was also the greatest builder of churches known to antiquity since Constantine. It was to him that Egypt owed Saint Catherine's monastery at the feet of Mount Sinai. He also had constructed the largest church known at that time, the Aya Sophia. At its completion in 537 he was supposed to have said: "The glory belongs to God, who has considered me worthy to complete this work. Solomon, I have surpassed you."

At the Fifth Ecumenical Council at Constantinople in 553 Cyril's interpretation of Chalcedon was confirmed, under the Justinian's influence. The 'national' churches of the Jacobites, Armenians, Copts and Ethiopians continued, however. It is said concerning the wife of Justinian, empress Theodora (died 548), that she was secretly a Monophysite and supported adherents of Monophysitism. Her influence in the political formation of the empire was probably considerable. The Melchites were supported by imperial weapons, while the Monophysites had their own armies of monks. In the ensuing struggle, the Syrian Orthodox or Jacobites were raided. They lived in conflict with Byzantium and had to suffer under discrimination.[13]

National resistance against Rome and Constantinople played a prominent role in the resistance of the Jacobite, Nestorian, Armenian and Coptic churches. They considered the Patriarchates of Alexandria and Antioch as their own, while they saw pope Leo I primarily as Roman.[14] That was one of the reasons why (the Egyptians and) Syrians initially welcomed the Persian and later Arab Moslems as liberators from the Byzantine yoke.

The Liturgies

The decisions of the church councils quoted above were not purely speculative, merely theoretical concerns of theologians and clergy, but rather arose from the very liturgies of the Church. Every 'Orthodox' doctrine has its roots in the *liturgy*. These were the themes of the liturgy and of the liturgical songs developed by the theologians. Before a doctrine was confessed by the Church Fathers or taught by theologians it was lived and celebrated in the liturgy and devotion of the people.[15]

Doctrine cannot be understood unless it is *prayed*; likewise, the doctrine that is prayed must be *lived*. Thus in the Byzantine liturgy, the confession of faith is introduced with the words: "*Let us love one another*, that with one mind we may confess Father, Son and Holy Spirit, Trinity one in essence and undivided.*" If one really seeks to understand Eastern spirituality, one must consider not so much the doctrine, as the liturgical life of the Orthodox churches. In fact there is no good way in which to become acquainted with these churches except through the liturgy, whether it be the quiet awe-inspiring liturgy of the Jacobites ("let all within us be silent" words taken from the liturgy of James), or the folk liturgy of the Coptic churches and its use of cymbals since the Middle Ages, or the Armenian liturgy which is among the most moving liturgies in existence, or the stately liturgy of the Byzantines. Actually it is difficult to express *in words* the uniqueness of Orthodox spirituality. It is something that must be experienced. Someone once characterized the difference between Eastern and Western spirituality with the words: *ex oriente lux; ex occidente lex* (from the East light, from the West law) (J.C. Hoekendijk). Whoever seeks to understand Orthodoxy must witness the liturgy. There is the ancient Antiochian liturgy of James, which was revised by one of the most important and versatile Jacobite writers Jacob of Edessa. The holy liturgy of the Jacobite or West Syrian Church, the oldest and richest of Christianity, is primarily that of James. It is said that James celebrated this liturgy in Jerusalem in conformity with the order he received from the Lord himself. More probably, however, this liturgy came into existence shortly after the Council of Nicea in 325 and before that of Chalcedon.[16] A Greek liturgy was also composed by Saint Basil (died 379). It then became the standard liturgy of the Greek Orthodox church. The other Greek liturgy bears the name of John Chrysostom (died 407) and is a simpler and shorter form of Basil's. The liturgy of Chrysostom is known by heart by the faithful. The genius of Chrysostom dominates the spirituality of the Orthodox churches.[17] The Copts use three liturgies: that of Basil the Great, of Gregory Nazianzus (died ca. 390) and Mark, the last of which was established and completed by Cyril the Great.[18]

The differences in the faith experiences of the various Christian traditions was once described as follows. While for Catholics the presence of Christ is experienced in the *sacrament*, and for reformation Christians primarily (and as far as the confessions are concerned in the first place) in the *preaching of the word*—during the sermon, the 'altar bell', so to speak (to use the words of K.H. Miskotte), rings: "God is present, God is in our midst"—for still other Christians, such as adherents of the Salvation Army that presence of Christ is experienced primarily in *song* (H. Berkhof). Obviously this characterization cannot pretend rigid distinctions; the boundaries are fluid. But if one were to ask what the Eastern Orthodox liturgy was all about, one could reply that it addresses *all* the senses. Not only hearing (faith is from hearing, Romans 10:17), but also sight, taste and smell. Whoever truly seeks to understand the Orthodox churches must experience the liturgy: "Taste and see that the Lord is good" (Psalm 34:9), or as Philip says to Nathanael: "Come and *see!*" (John 1:47). In Orthodoxy, sight plays a very important role. It is said that the eyes come first. Reference is then made to the words of Jesus in Matthew 13:17: "Truly I say to you, many prophets and righteous men longed *to see* what you see, and did not see it, and to hear what you hear, and did not hear it." Each of the senses is sanctified by God's saving acts. "Sight, as the primary sense, is hallowed through the visible appearance of God in Christ, just as hearing was sanctified through the word of God."[19]

Believers attend the liturgies in the church, especially that of Sunday and generally those of the high holy days, as though a 'theater' production, so to speak, where each person discovers his or her own truth in the drama played out there.[20]

The liturgy is the heartbeat of Orthodoxy. That is sometimes difficult for those from the West to imagine. Whereas in the Western approach to faith and religion the intellectual search is often the precondition for all else, Orthodoxy revolves around the liturgical and mystical life: "The Westerner, whether Catholic, Protestant, agnostic or atheist, will always try to confirm positive and negative assertions by means of a logical thought structure. In contrast, Orthodox believers, who perhaps are more conscious of the limitations of the human mind, willingly accept the fact that searching leads to silence, to not-knowing, to fascinated and joyful astonishment before the face of the Ineffable, who creates, loves, inspires, guides, and humanizes humanity."[21]

Liturgy is celebrated dogma. In Orthodoxy no distinction exists between mysticism, praise and prayer. Theology and mysticism are not, as they so often are in the West, placed in hostile opposition, but rather reciprocally complement each other. All true Orthodox theology is mysticism. In the words of Vladimir Lossky: "The Orthodox church has never made a fine distinction between the realm of theology and that of mysticism," between personal experience of the divine mysteries and the dogma taught by the church.[22] Doctrines are therefore not understood unless they are prayed: *lex credendi = lex orandi*. It is not so much the (intellectual) knowledge of faith that stands central as a lived and experienced knowledge. In the words of the Church Father, Gregory of Nyssa (died ca. 394): "It is not a question of knowing something about God, but bearing God within. It is therefore not a question of arguing about God, but of a direct and living encounter with a concrete and personal God."[23]

Icons

In order to explain further that which is understood by Orthodox spirituality, it is fitting to make reference to the icons. Icon means 'image'. It is a painted representation. The human word is not the only vehicle for conveying the presence of God—icons convey his presence as well: "Icons are not idols, but God's glorified creation, which makes God live for us."[24]

Painting icons is considered a holy art. It was and is primarily done in monasteries, and the artist must prepare himself for his work with prayer and fasting. The result can be truly aesthetic, but it is more important that whatever aesthetic gifts he/she might have be subject to the

56

'mind of the Lord' which reflects the Spirit that lives in the Church.[25] In the Orthodox faith the incarnation, the Word becoming flesh, the Son of God stands central. Thus the icons of Christ and Mary can be a reflection or glimmer of the capabilities given to a human person in order to attain to its true destination. The statement of Mary: "Behold, I am the handmaiden of the Lord, let it be to me according to your word" is the image of humanity in conformity with the will of God.[26]

Icons are the symbols of Orthodoxy. The Council of Nicea (787) determined that icons may be kissed, and may be the objects of reverence and homage, but not of actual worship. The icons were to be *held in honor*, not *worshipped*.[27]

Icons do not occupy the same position of importance in the various Orthodox churches. The Syrian Orthodox are not so attached to them, and the Nestorians do not recognize them at all, even though their use can be demonstrated back to the time of Mongolian domination. It is presumed that they rejected the use of icons, not entirely voluntarily, but in part due to the influence of the Islamic environment.[28] Whatever the case may have been, the lack of images led American missionaries in the nineteenth century to the belief that they had discovered in the Nestorians the 'Protestants of the East'. The Armenians do have icons in their churches but do not have the Iconostasis, the screen with painted icons behind which the mystery of the eucharist takes place, dividing the laity from the one officiating. It has been in existence since the twelfth century. Soon after its development, a certain traditional pattern emerged: the face of Christ, Mary portrayed from the front, the archangel Michael, Saint George and the 'Mother of Mercy' with her cheek pressed against that of the child.[29] In Armenian Orthodox churches, the icons are usually found against the apse, behind the altar.

Icons arose in the fourth century in conjunction with the desire to own an object of devotion that could give deliverance from sickness and other needs. Stories also were circulated regarding the existence of icons that had not been made by human hands. One of these, depicting Jesus, supposedly protected Edessa (modern Urfa, in Turkey). In one of the Byzantine hymns, Mary is called the 'unconquerable general' who was supposed to have liberated Constantinople once from invaders through her miraculous intervention. Innumerable miracle are attributed to the icon of the *Theotokos*.[30]

The Coptic Christians in Egypt, but also others, even ascribe human qualities to the icons, such as weeping, sweating and bleeding.[31] A similar miracle has also been reported in our time. On 5 April 1964 Maria

Malouf, the abbess of the Greek Orthodox convent of Our Lady of Sadnaya, near Damascus, had a dream. The Holy Virgin appeared to tell her that the oil from the oil lamp in front of the Chahoura, the miraculous icon of Our Lady of Sadnaya, was overflowing. She went to the shrine and collected the overflowing oil in bottles which when distributed appeared to have healing powers.[32]

It is good, however, to lend consideration to the 'usual' place and significance of the icons in Orthodox piety. The icons of Christ and Mary are in the view of Orthodoxy a reflection or glimmer of the capabilities given to humans so that they may attain their true destiny. Saints are people who are 'divinized', who have become divine. The term 'divinization' (*theosis*) is unique to the Orthodox vocabulary. The Orthodox assume that man is created in the image of God. The recovery of this likeness, which is often lost, is called 'divinization'. In support of this, appeal is made to the Psalms: "I say, 'You are gods, sons of the Most High, all of you'" (Psalm 82:6) and to the epistle of Peter who writes that through God's glory and power we are endowed with "precious and very great promises, that through these you may ... become partakers of the divine *nature*" (2 Peter 1:4). It is the saints who have attained to the true human destiny. Indeed, all Christians, not only monks, must become participants in the divine nature. The saints are able, by their lives and words, to bring to expression the reality of the Kingdom of God. That is also celebrated in the liturgy, in which heaven comes to earth. Icons depict that event. Icons are intended to demonstrate how to participate in the divine nature. Since man is the image of God, man can find God in his own heart: "The Kingdom of God is within you," as they interpret the saying of Jesus (Luke 17:21). The icon is the mirror in which the glory of the Lord is reflected. To use the words of Pachomius (died 346), one of the first hermits in Egypt: "In the purity of my heart, he sees the invisible God as in a mirror."[33]

'Divinization' means a progressively stronger participation in the presence of God. And where is God more fully present than in Christ? There is a deep understanding that the Word became flesh and that the divine fullness dwells bodily in Christ. In the story of the transfiguration on the mountain the humanity of Christ was transparent to his divinity. It was, so to speak, 'red-hot' with the divine presence. On Tabor, "the uncreated light of His Godhead shone visibly through the garments of His flesh."[34] In the resurrection of Christ, the grave broke open under the weight of divine life. For that reason, Easter and the Feast of the Transfiguration are among the two most important holy days of the year for the Orthodox. They clearly express that which is central to their belief. Christ demonstrates that for which humans are destined and what 'divinization' means. That is not to say that humans become God, but truly human. 'Divinization' is not an identification with God. The unity with God that is sought is, to turn a theological phrase, unity with the divine *energy*, not with the divine *essence*. The mystery of unity is the mystery of unity in diversity.[35] To express it in the 'theological' language that is better understood in the West, 'divinization' could best be translated as 'sanctification'.

The purpose of the icons is to demonstrate how to participate in the divine nature. The salient feature of an icon is that the perspectival point of ascent is not located in the illusory depths of the image, but within the viewer![36] The best icon of God is the human being. This is brought to expression in the Orthodox worship service when the priest applies incense not only to the icons, but also to the members of the congregation, thus "saluting the image of God in every person."[37]

The comparison of the soul of a human being with a mirror is frequently found in this connection. The mirror referred to is that of the ancient East, which was made not from glass, but from silver or copper. That means that it can become tarnished and must be polished in order to serve the purpose for which it was made. The apostle Paul must have had such a mirror in mind when he said "for now we see in a mirror dimly" (1 Corinthians 13:12) or "And we all, with unveiled face, reflecting the glory of the Lord, are being changed into his likeness from one degree of glory to another; for this comes from the Lord who is the Spirit" (2 Corinthians 3:18).

The following story can perhaps further clarify the nature of the image. Once, at the court of a prince, there was a group of Chinese and Greek painters. The Chinese said: "We are the best artists." "No," said the Greeks, "We are much better than you are." "Indeed," said the prince, "I will put you to the test and see which of you is right." The Chinese were placed in one room and the Greeks in an adjoining room, separated by a curtain. The Chinese requested many painting supplies and paint, while the Greeks requested cleaning supplies and began to wash the walls. When the Chinese were finished with their painting, they beat the drum in celebration. The prince entered and saw the painting. Its beauty overwhelmed him. He then turned to the Greeks, who pulled back the curtain separating the two rooms. The reflection of the Chinese painting shone on the walls, which had been cleansed of even the slightest stain. All that the prince had just seen in the room of the Chinese appeared even more beautiful here. The moral of the story is this: The actions of the Greeks—and here one can substitute any nation—is symbolic of the human person who cleanses and purifies his or her heart from sin. In the same way the image of the invisible God is reflected in the heart of the believer.[38]

This comparing of the soul to a mirror appears in all the mystical literature. Just as the mirror can become rusty, so the soul can be tarnished, clouded over by sin, and contact with the material world. The Church Fathers Ephraim the Syrian (died 373) and Palladius (died 431), as well as Isaac of Nineveh (second half of the seventh century) spoke of the need to polish the mirror, to cleanse or clean it so that it can once again reflect the divine image without spot or wrinkle. When the believer (or the mystic) persistently prays in purity, he or she will be worthy to see in his or her heart the light of the revelation of God that shines on it, as on a polished mirror.[39]

NOTES

1. De Lacy O'Leary, 1964, 36.

2. De Lacy O'Leary, 1964, 118.

3. *Lexikon s.v.* Christian.

4. Atiya, 1968, 169-71.

5. Corbon, 1977, 59.

6. *C.E. s.v.* Apollinaris.

7. Kleyn, 1, 2.

8. Kleyn, 2.

9. *C.E. s.v.* Nestorius, Theotokos, Ephesus; Kleyn, 3; *R.G.G. s.v.* Cyrill; Browne, 7; Atiya, 1968, 177, 240, 248.

10. Kleyn, 3.

11. Berkouwer, 85, 88, 101-10.

12. Atiya, 1968, 178f.

13. Atiya, 69,73-75; *R.G.G., s.v.* Justinian, Byzantische Kunst.

14. Kleyn, 6-8.

15. Pelikan, 138f., 141.

16. Atiya, 1968, 196, 222f.

17. Malik, 310f.

18. Atiya, 1968, 127.

19. Pelikan, 122.

20. Sartorius, 84.

21. Sartorius, 327.

22. Lossky, 1957, 49f.

23. Ware, 205.

24. Mönnnich, 268.

25. Sartorius, 24, 35; Ware, 214; Evdokimov, 153, 161.

26. Sartorius, 115.

27. Pelikan, 145; Lossky, 167; Holl, 423.

28. Atiya, 1968, 232, 224; Browne, 79, 80.

29. Patlagean.

30. Pelikan, 132, 149; Patlagean; Ouspensky, 59.

31. Meinardus, 1970, 178.

32. Meinardus, 1970, 214; Leroy, 126.

33. Pelikan, 256; Ware, 224-26; Evdokimov, 160.

34. Ware, 321.

35. Pelikan, 267; Ware, 231.

36. Sartorius, 115, 116.

37. Ware, 226.

38. Arberry, 1968, 77, 78.

39. Smith, 1976, 254.

III. THE BYZANTINE ORTHODOX:
THE MOST ARAB OF THE CHRISTIANS

Their relations to islam over the centuries may be characterized, in one word, as existentially chequered, morally subservient, and spiritually tragic, although, in the Arab world at least, they worked more closely with their Muslim compatriots on civic, social, cultural and national problems than any other Christian group.

Charles Malik[1]

Introduction

Eighty-five percent of all Orthodox Christians in the world live in (former) communist nations, primarily those of eastern Europe and Russia. Of the seven Orthodox churches located outside that area four (Constantinople, Greece, Cyprus, and Sinai) are predominantly or exclusively Greek in terms of nationality. One (Alexandria) is part Greek and part Arab and African, and the remaining two (Antioch and Jerusalem) are primarily Arab, although in Jerusalem and among the higher clergy there are still many Greeks.

In this chapter we will discuss the (Greek) Orthodox Church and its current numbers in and outside the Middle East. In order to understand its specific Arabic identity the relationship to the see of Constantinople and the Greeks must be discussed. In the search for independence by the 'Arab Orthodox' from the Greeks the Russian Orthodox church played an important role on the former's behalf. Attention will be given to the important contribution the 'Arab Orthodox' made to the so-called 'Arab Awakening' and the ideology of 'Arabism'. We will also turn to the renewal that has taken place since the 1940's in this church. Some of their political positions, in particular with respect to Lebanon, will also be discussed in chapter V. Finally, in this chapter we will look at the Greek Catholics and the relationship between the Greek Orthodox and the Protestants.

The Greek Orthodox in the Middle East

The Ecumenical (Greek Orthodox) Patriarch has his seat in Istanbul, formerly Constantinople or Byzantium, to this very day. For years this position was held by the famous Patriarch Athenagoras I (1886-1972). In

January 1964 Pope Paul VI and Patriarch Athenagoras I met in Jerusalem. The mutual anathemas that had been issued at the great schism of 1054 were repealed by him and Pope Paul VI. In their joint declaration on 7 December 1965, they nullified the mutual excommunication. In July 1967 Pope Paul VI visited Patriarch Athenagoras in Istanbul, after he had exchanged the kiss of peace with him on 26 December 1965 in Rome.

The other Greek Orthodox patriarchs, however, such as the Patriarchs of Alexandria, Antioch and Jerusalem, are not subject to this patriarch (as is the case with the Roman Catholic churches in their relation with Rome), but are autocephalous, i.e. they have their 'own heads' of their churches. 'Constantinople' assumes a position of honor among the several autocephalous churches, but as the first among equals, it exercises no central authority. Each patriarch has his own metropolitans and bishops, and convenes his own synod. Thus the unity of the Greek Orthodox Church(es) is not expressed in monarchial control, but in the common acceptance of the tradition of the Church fathers, especially, of course, the Greek Fathers. As Theodorus Abu Qurra (died ca. 820), the Melchite Bishop of Harran and the first important Christian writer to produce works in Arabic, once stated: "We are more dependent on the teaching of the (Church) Fathers than we are on our own breath."

The Orthodox churches accept the statements of the first seven ecumenical councils, a few of the most important of which were discussed in the previous chapter. These churches all follow as was mentioned above the same liturgies which are ascribed to Basil the Great and John Chrysostom. The Greek Orthodox view themselves as the keepers and propagators of the holy liturgy of Byzantium in the Middle East.[2]

The mutual anathemas of the Roman Catholic church of the West (Rome) and the Byzantine church of the East (Byzantium) in 1054 brought little change to the relationship between Rome and Constantinople at the time. This can be illustrated by the events surrounding the first Crusade. Although the first Crusade took place in part at the instigation of the Byzantine emperor, who asked the Pope for help in the struggle against the Moslems for the purpose of liberating the Holy Land, the crusades soon dealt violent blows to the Byzantines themselves. Even up to the thirteenth century the break was not yet considered irreparable. But Byzantium soon suffered more at the hands of the European Christians. The Western Christians of that time, like their Protestant descendants in the nineteenth century, viewed the churches of the East with contempt. They considered them as dilapidated and saw themselves

63

as the liberators of the holy places. "They made more of the errors of the Byzantines than of the sins of the Moslems."[3] The definite break between East and West actually began with the Fourth Crusade in 1204. This Crusade was directed against Byzantium itself! The city was occupied and plundered and many church treasures found their way to the West at that time, for example, to the famous San Marco church in Venice. A Latin empire was declared in Byzantium. The split between the Eastern and Western church became so severe that ultimately the East chose the yoke of the Asians above that of the West. On 29 May 1453 the saying "better Turkish than Popish" found fulfillment when Constantinople was overrun by the Turks.

To what degree the relation between East and West had soured became evident when on the evening before the fall of Byzantium in 1453 an important court functionary, Grand Duke Lucas Notaras, openly declared: "Better the Turkish turban ruling in our city then the Latin mitre."[4] It was therefore not so much the rupture of 1054, but the Latin actions during the Fourth Crusade that ultimately lead to the break between Rome and the Greek Orthodox church, so that the "turban of the sheik" was preferred to the "cap of the cardinal."

Subsequently the Turkish sultan had the famous Church of the Holy Wisdom changed into a mosque. One of the Moslem clergy mounted the pulpit and recited the Islamic confession of faith: "There is no God but God." He then climbed onto the altar and praised the "victorious God."[5]

Later, in 1934, the first president of the Turkish republic, Mustafa Kemal Ataturk would turn this mosque into a museum and would forbid the practice of any religion there. The whitewash was removed from the mosaics revealing such images as the enthroned Madonna with child, the emperors Constantine the Great (ca.280-337) and Justinian I (482-565), and the enthroned Christ.[6]

During the visit of Pope Paul VI in 1975, however, an incident occurred in this 'church' when the Pope suddenly kneeled down and prayed. Moslems, in turn, later performed there the *salat* (the Moslem ritual prayer) in protest against the fatal attack of certain Armenians during the seventies against Turkish consuls.

As soon as Constantinople had been incorporated into the Ottoman empire, the Greek Orthodox Patriarch was made the civil leader of all the Orthodox (thus also non-Greek Orthodox) congregations. Thus the Greek Orthodox in the Middle East increasingly learned to live under Islamic Ottoman rule. The already existing class of *dhimmi*s, i.e. the class of "protected citizens," which was in force among Christians, was expanded into a *millet* system in which the separate Christian communities, including the Greek Orthodox, became autonomous and were allowed to rule themselves, albeit within certain limits.

Gradually the Greeks extended their authority over the entire church. From the seventeenth century on, large Greek families from the Phanar quarter, i.e. the quarter of Constantinople inhabited by Greeks, had great influence with the Ottoman government and dominated the Greek Orthodox church.

While the Patriarch of Antioch was, generally speaking, a Greek, those of Jerusalem and Alexandria were and still are today only of Greek nationality. This fact has lead to some tension within this church in the current state of Israel.

But beginning in the eighteenth century there was a growing dissatisfaction with these ethnic and linguistic distinctions between Greeks and Arabs. The tension was between the hierarchy, which was almost exclusively Greek, and the "lower" parochial clergy and lay people, who were almost exclusively Arab. The tensions increased when in 1821 the Greeks broke with the Ottoman empire. The Arabic speaking Christians became even more conscious of their Arab identity. A growing breach between the hierarchy and the community was evident when the *Khatt-i Humayun*, (an official decision of the Ottoman sultan) was announced in February 1856, in which it was decreed that each community must be given a constitution in order to give sufficient support to the lay people.[7]

For the various Orthodox churches, the demise of the Ottoman empire in the First World War and the events that ensued immediately thereafter were of great importance. The war between the Turks and Greeks in the twenties occasioned a large scale relocation of the population. Many Greeks left what had become the new Turkish nation under Mustafa Kemal Ataturk (1881-1938), and many Turks, in turn, left Greece and took up residence in the new Turkish republic. One of the stipulations which were added by the new Turkish state to the Treaty of Lausanne in 1923 was that all the subjects of the Greek Orthodox religion would leave the country. Only the Greek Orthodox Patriarch was allowed to remain in Istanbul (Phanar). But the Greek Orthodox population of Anatolia, about two million people, left. While the Greek Orthodox population of Istanbul in 1927 where they were allowed to remain numbered 156,000, the present number of Greek Orthodox members in the city is less than 3,000.[8] The Israel-Arab war of 1947-48 brought in its wake the exodus of tens of thousands of Orthodox from the newly created state of Israel to Lebanon, Syria and Jordan, or elsewhere outside

65

the Middle East. In the fifties (during the regime of the Egyptian president Gamal Abdel Nasser (died (1970)) the Greek Orthodox community in Egypt all but disappeared, leaving only a few ten thousands behind. Tens of thousands of Orthodox of Lebanese and Syrian origin have emigrated since 1955. In the sixties, approximately one hundred thousand Orthodox moved from Syria to Lebanon. The number of Greek Orthodox in Egypt currently numbers about 5,000, of whom approximately one-third are Greek. The others are Egyptian citizens of Syrian, Lebanese or Palestinian origin.

In March 1983 five bishops of Greek nationality were asked to leave the country. Only the Patriarch, Nicholas VI was left undisturbed. He has been part of the general emigration out of Turkey, Egypt, Syria, and Israel.

Lebanon often functioned as a stopover of Christian on the way to somewhere else in the world. The gradual disappearance of the Greek Orthodox from Turkey and Egypt is more cultural and political than religious, as is evident from the primarily Greek composition of the movement.[9]

In Israel, including the occupied territories, there were, according to the estimates of 1972, 39,000 Greek Orthodox and 26,500 Greek Catholics or Melchites.[10] The statistics given in a 1989 publication are as follows: the largest group of Christians, numerically speaking, within the borders are the Greek Catholics, with 40,000 members, followed by Greek Orthodox, with 30,000 members.[11]

In all, approximately 700,000 to 750,000 Greek Orthodox Christians are to be found in the Middle East under the leadership of the Greek Orthodox Patriarch of Antioch (200,000 to 250,000 in Lebanon and 400,000 in Syria). In all countries they are minorities among the Christians except for Syria.

Since 1977 the position of the patriarch has been occupied by Ignatius IV Hazim, head of the second largest Arab speaking Christian community (after the Copts). The patriarchy consists of ten dioceses: five in Syria (Aleppo, Latakiya, Hamah, Homs and 'Akkar). Numerically they form the largest Christian group in Syria: 450,000 or 4.94% of the population. Four other dioceses are located in Lebanon (Beirut, Mount Lebanon, Tripoli and Zahlah-Baalbek). In Lebanon they form 20% of the Christian population, or 300,000 Christians, surpassed in numbers only by the Maronites. The diocese of Baghdad was overseen by a bishop who normally resided in Kuwait. At least one million Greek Orthodox (i.e. originating from the Middle East!), however, live in the diaspora outside the Middle East.[12]

Rum *Orthodox*

It may seem strange, at first, to hear someone speak of the Greek Orthodox Christians as the 'most Arab' of the Christians in the Middle East. After all, the adjective 'Greek' would seem to indicate that they, of all Christians, must be considered part of a non-Arab tradition.

Their name, however, is *Rum* Orthodox. *Rum* is the Arabic name for Byzantium. It actually stands for Roman, but was used as the designation for the (East) Roman empire. One of the chapters (*suras*) in the Koran bears this title. In this (thirtieth) chapter of the Koran, the conquest of Jerusalem by the Sassanids in 614 is alluded to (30:2-5). All of Syria and Palestine fell under Sassanid control at that time. This text of the Koran also contains a prediction of the expected reconquest of Jerusalem by the Byzantines. The future victory of the Byzantines over the Persians is predicted. The 'believers' referred to there, who would rejoice at the victory of the Byzantines over the 'heathen' Persians, are probably the followers of Mohammed. In any case, the sympathies of the prophet Mohammed for the Christians (the Byzantines) and his preference for them over the Sassanids are clearly evident in this passage.

The church of Jerusalem and especially that of Antioch have become indigenized in the Arab world. They are rooted in the Arabic language and culture. The liturgy is also celebrated in Arabic.[13] If any Christian group in the Middle East can be referred to as *Arabic*, it is the *Rum* Orthodox Church. Although the patriarch is still called the Patriarch of "Antioch and the whole East," he has resided for centuries in Damascus.

The Byzantine Orthodox church must be distinguished from both the West and the East Syrian churches (the Jacobites and the Nestorians respectively) as well as from the Coptic and Armenian churches, all of which are among the so-called non-Chalcedonian churches, since they do not subscribe to the decisions of the Council of Chalcedon. The Byzantine Orthodox Church, in contrast, is Chalcedonian, as is the Roman Catholic church, or the church of the undivided West (the churches standing in the tradition of the sixteenth-century Reformation could also be named among the Chalcedonian churches). In the end, it was the letter of Pope Leo I that prepared the way for the statements and eventual decisions of the Council of Chalcedon in 451.

As a result of the fact that from 960 until the time of the crusades Byzantium controlled large portions of Syria, the Syrian 'Melchites', as these Greek Orthodox Christians were originally called, bore the strong stamp of the Byzantine church. When shortly after the death of the prophet Mohammed in 632 the Moslem Arabs began to conquer parts of the Middle East, Byzantine Orthodox Christians were suspected, especially by the Islamic rulers, of having 'political sympathies' with 'East Rome'. It may be that their quick transition to the use of Arabic was motivated by their desire to throw off this suspicion by adapting to their new surroundings. From the ninth century on, the process of 'Arabization' continued unabated.[14] It was the Greek Father John of Damascus (died 749) who first took up a theological position as one of the newest Christian heresies: "The heresy of the Ishmaelites" (Sahas).

Relations with Russia

When one refers to the Greek Orthodox Church in the Middle East, it is important to keep in mind the special relation that came into existence in the past, and actually continues to exist today, between these Orthodox Christians and the Russian Orthodox church. It was the missionaries from Byzantium who brought the Gospel to the Slavic peoples in the ninth century. It is therefore no surprise that an intimate relation with Byzantine culture has remained. Moscow saw itself as the child and heir of Byzantium, as the 'third Rome', since the 'first Rome' had fallen away (so they said) and the 'second Rome' had fallen into the hands of 'unbelievers' in 1453. In the seventeenth century, the Patriarchs of Alexandria and Antioch maintained direct relations with Russia and sought from them both spiritual and material support. Just as the English supported the Druzes and Protestants in the Ottoman empire, and the French took it upon themselves to protect the Christians united with Rome (the Melchites and the Maronites), so too the Russians protected the Greek Orthodox. In 1774 a treaty was made between Russia and the Ottoman sultan, in which Russia was officially given the right to act as the protector of the Orthodox church in the Ottoman empire. That entailed that the sultan recognized that there was a Russian interest in the freedom and welfare of its Christian subjects. When the need arose, the tsar intervened on behalf of the Orthodox in Istanbul. It is evident that the interventions were not separate from the tsarist politics of expansion into the region of the eastern Mediterranean. This Russian protection of the Greek Orthodox continued even after the communist takeover of Russia in 1917.[15] According to the well-known Lebanese Greek Orthodox philosopher and diplomat Charles Malik, the Greek Orthodox Church would have been orphaned without the Russian Orthodox Church:

The churches of the West come to it—Orthodoxy—as to something alien: they want to change and convert it. Russian Orthodoxy comes to it as to bone of its bones and flesh of its flesh. It is not another, it is the same, at least in liturgy and in spirit.[16]

In 1858 Russia established a continual ecclesiastical mission in Jerusalem which was intended to strengthen the sentiments of rebellion among the Arab Orthodox churches against the Latinizing and Protestant zeal for conversion. The great affinity between the Arab Greek Orthodox and Russian Orthodox is deeply rooted in their common Byzantine heritage. Especially in the nineteenth and twentieth centuries, the links between the two churches were strengthened as much as possible. That was in part due to the fact that the Russians were also the ones who strongly supported the rising Arab nationalism, in which the Greek Orthodox played such an important role. In 1882 the *Société impériale orthodoxe de la Palestine* was established in order to enhance the prestige of the Orthodox Church in Syria and Palestine. That was the beginning of the development of cultural and social institutions that extend to the Patriarchate of Antioch in Syria and Lebanon. In 1898 the Russians had 64 schools, 213 teachers, and 6,739 students in Syria and Palestine, a number that would later be doubled.[17]

From 1724 until 1899 the seat of the Patriarch of Antioch was occupied by Greek prelates. They could be appointed due to the authority that the 'Greek' Greek Orthodox Patriarch of Istanbul enjoyed under the Ottoman government. For a long time the Greeks attempted to retain their supremacy over the Greek Orthodox church of Antioch. That led to conflict between the dominating Greek hierarchy and the rising indigenous Arab clergy. After 1878, Russia attempted to help the Arabs obtain the Patriarchates of Jerusalem and Antioch in order that they might wrest themselves free of the Greek domination from Istanbul. While it succeeded in the case of Antioch, in that of Jerusalem it failed.

In the Patriarchate of Antioch the hierarchy, which was predominantly Arab, did not wait for political independence before achieving ecclesiastical emancipation. On 31 January 1898, the mixed Synod selected Meletius II, the Metropolitan of Latakiya (Laodicea) as Patriarch. For the first time in centuries, the patriarchate was definitely transferred to an Arab, and has remained in Arab hands until the present. The hegemony of the Greeks that had been established by the Ottomans in the sixteenth century had come to an end. From that point on the further replacement of the Greek hierarchy took place without difficulty.

The patriarchate once again actually enjoyed its autocephalous status. In Jerusalem, however, the Greek hierarchy continued in place. To this very day, as was mentioned before, there is tension between the higher clergy and the laity.[18]

The relationship with the Russian Orthodox church remained in tact after the communist takeover in 1917. The celebration of thousandth anniversary of the Russian Orthodox Church in 1988 went hand in hand with public relations contacts with the church of Antioch. During his visit in 1991, at the invitation of the Patriarch of Antioch, the Russian Orthodox Patriarch Alexis II did remind him of the old relationships between 'Antioch' and Moscow. The current renewal of the Russian Orthodox Church gives hope for a new support to their church.[19]

In an interview held in 1990 Bishop Georges Khodr said that the Orthodox in the Holy Land include Palestinians and Jordanians, thus Orthodox Christians whose first language is Arabic, while their bishops are all Greek. According to him a real "conversion is needed to put an end to this tragic and absurd contradiction between faithful and their shepherds." The consecration of one or two educated Palestinian bishops would show the willingness of the patriarchate for renewal."[20] In 1992 in Jerusalem a committee was founded for Arabic-Orthodox initiatives. The two most urgent problems which were raised by this committee were: the bad management of the properties of the Orthodox church and the refusal by the ('Greek') hierarchy to accept Arabs in the running of the community. They want one or more Arab bishops to be nominated. The last Arab bishop, Symeon died in 1981. The last Arab Patriarch of the Greek Orthodox was Atallah and he died in 1534![21] The present Greek Orthodox 'Greek' Patriarch Diodorus rejected the allegations. The initiatives of the Arab-speaking Orthodox against the Greek hierarchy were described in the press as a fruit of growing Palestinian nationalism.[22]

Arab Awakening and Arabism

It was primarily the Greek Orthodox who at the close of the last century and the beginning of this century contributed to the so-called Arab awakening. The renaissance (*nahda*) of the Arabic language and Arab culture in general would have been unthinkable without them. It was the Greek Orthodox from Lebanon in 1875 in Alexandria who established the Egyptian daily, *al-Ahram* (The Pyramids) which continues to be published to this day.[23]

70

During the First World War, tens of thousands (some estimate hundreds of thousands) of Christians died as a result of starvation and deprivation, not to mention the victims of the pogroms against the Armenians. During that time, the Orthodox suffered less, relatively speaking, than the Maronites and the Catholics. That was in part due to the fact that the Greek Orthodox Patriarch, Gregory IV Haddad (died 1928), maintained good relations with the Arab political entities. He was among the first to recognize Faisal (1883-1933), the son of Sharif Husein of the Hejaz, with whom England began the so-called 'Arab Revolt' (against the Turks) in 1916, as king of Syria. Later, as is known, King Faisal was removed and 'compensated' by the British with the throne of Iraq (from 1920). There were many, primarily Greek Orthodox, Christians who spoke out on King Faisal's behalf.[24]

One could say that Arab nationalism originally was in part inspired by the struggle of the Greek Orthodox Arabs to throw off the Greek yoke. It was the Greek Orthodox Arabs who made such an important contribution to Arab nationalism and Arab socialism *(istirakiyya)*. A Greek Orthodox Christian, Michel Aflaq (died 1989), was an ideologue and founder of the Arab socialist Ba'th party *(Ba'th* literally means resurrection). Michel Aflaq equated Islam with Arab nationalism.

The Arab Christians should recognize that Islam forms for them a national culture in which they must immerse themselves so that they may understand it and love it, and so that they may preserve Islam as they preserve the priceless element of their Arabism.

With respect to the prophet Muhammad whom he regarded as the founder of Arab nationalism, he said: "The life of the prophet Mohammed, and that is what the Arab soul in its absolute reality represents, can not be recognized by the intellect. The way to understand it is not to recite the verses of the Koran, but to live it."[25]

The well-known Greek Orthodox bishop, Georges Khodr, has expressed himself frequently over the course of the years on the 'Arab cause'. As he said in a speech on Arabism *('uraba)*.

It is above all important that the Christians who live in Arab territory feel completely at home there. It is their destiny to become an indispensable presence in order to give witness to their belief in Arabism. The original significance of Arabism for Eastern Christianity lay in the fact that the Arab factor can form a true ecumenical ferment in the area. Only if all Christians place themselves in the service of the liberation of man, can they come closer to one another. They

71

will make a contribution by recreating a non-Greek, and a non-Latin Christianity, that is in search of its own identity and at the same time enriches the Christian world, that in its place structures itself in a creative way and dialogues with the various religions of the Arab continent, after having internally liberated itself from all foreign mortgages, I am fully convinced that no Christian renewal is possible in the East if it is linked, no matter how remotely, with a form of confessionalism of an ethnic group that is necessarily anti-Arab.[26]

With the closing sentence Bishop Khodr undoubtedly had in mind the Maronite groups, such as that of the Falangists, under the leadership of Pierre Jemayyil—and later his son Bashir Jemayyil—who defend such 'confessionalism' (*ta'ifiyya*). This would become all too clear in the subsequent Lebanese civil war (1975 and the following years). The friction existing between Greek Orthodox and Maronites is expressed by a Lebanese saying: they get along about as well as garlic and *baklawa* (an Arabic sweet).

Spiritual Renewal

The Orthodox Youth Movement, founded in 1941-1942, and which celebrated its 50th anniversary in 1992, has played a very important role in the revitalization of the Greek Orthodox church. It has still 7,000 active members.[27] Among the founders was the still very influential (in the ecclesiastical sphere) layman Albert Laham, and the already mentioned Georges Khodr, who is currently Metropolitan of the Greek Orthodox church of Mount Lebanon (Jabal Lubnan). In 1953, the latter of the two took part in the world organization of Orthodox youth, *Syndesmos*. The current Greek Orthodox Patriarch, Ignatius IV Hazim, was among those who took the initiative in the establishment of *Syndesmos*, the world-wide, pan-Orthodox youth movement. For a number of years Hazim was co-chairperson of the World Student Christian Federation. He was also Bishop of Latakiya, Syria for several years. From 1962-1970 he was superior of the Balamand monastery near Tripoli (Lebanon). He lent his leadership there to the Theological Institute of St. John of Damascus. Since its founding in 1974, he has acted as one of the presidents of the *Middle East Council of Churches*. In 1977 he was chosen as the Greek Orthodox Patriarch of Antioch. He later joined a group founded by Marcel Marqus and Gabriel Sada in Latakiya. This Orthodox Youth Movement held Bible seminars and rallies, established schools and published a magazine, *al-Nour* (light), and other religious materials for the purpose of catechization. It was also involved in social work and applied itself to the fight against poverty. Two monastic communities were also established: Dayr Mar Yaqoub (for women) near Tripoli, and another in Deir al-Harf (for men) near Beirut.[28] "Our church,", said the Patriarch in 1963, "is healthier today than it has been in the last thousand years." Three years later this same sentiment was echoed by the leading Orthodox layman, Constantin Zurayq, who in the laying of the first stone for the new Orthodox seminary in Balamand saw a testimony to the "spiritual renaissance of the Orthodox community of Antioch."[29]

The new spirituality that surfaced in the Orthodox Youth Movement and exerted no little influence in the Orthodox church was a combination of spirituality and action, which was very similar to recent models in Latin America.

The process of internal renewal of the church was accelerated since the return of peace to Lebanon in 1990. At the occasion of the Synod of 1993 Metropolitan Georges Khodr recommended a pastoral council which would be dedicated not to doctrinal matters but would be dedicated only to writing a catechism, prayer and common services.[30]

With regard to ecumenism, the *M.E.C.C.* has since its inception been under the direction of the general secretary (until 1994), the Greek Orthodox Gabriel Habib. This organization plays an important role within the ecumenical relations between the churches.

The Greek Orthodox are not, as their best representatives show, simply out to survive as a church, but to take on the challenge of what it means to be a church in the complicated context of the Middle East. Especially in this church of Antioch one finds those who are working for a church in the Arab world, in which the existing confessional, ethnic and cultural gaps between Christians could be bridged, so that one can really speak of a church by and for the Arabs.[31] Or as Patriarch Ignatius IV Hazim declared in an interview in Lebanese daily *al-Nahar*:

We can say that the contribution of the oriental Christians to contemporary Arab nationalism and to the elaboration of her master ideas is not only a search for a new political framework that guarantees the perfect equality between Moslems and Christians .... It is also an expression of their profound attachment to a Islamic-Christian co-existence and their refusal to transform themselves into a religious or ethnic community.[32]

The Orthodox did give to the Orthodox the *summa theologiae* of John of Damascus and his defence of the icons, but never knew the regime of a triumphant Christendom which established itself at the end of the first millennium in Byzantium as well as in Europe. The church of Antioch has to be a church of humility without the glory or the illusions of the first, second or third Rome.[33]

The Greek Catholics or Melchites

Since the fall of Constantinople the name (or rather label) Melchites is no longer in use for the Greek Orthodox. It has now become the designation for the church which broke away from the Greek Orthodox and linked itself with the Church of Rome. Today the designation Melchite is usually used to describe those of the Byzantine rite who have joined Rome (approximately 250,000) in the Patriarchates of Alexandria, Jerusalem and Antioch.

In the seventeenth and eighteenth centuries there were attempts at unification (i.e. with Rome) which culminated, however, in the establishment of a separate Greek Catholic church in the nineteenth century.

In his instructions to his new ambassador to the papal court in 1728, the French king, Louis XV, (reigned 1715-1774) made clear that the French government had three objectives in spreading the Roman Catholic faith: the Christianization of the Moslems, the conversion of the schismatics and the removal of the seed of heresy. Rome forbade the first, and the emphasis came to lie in the conversion of schismatics. In the first half of the nineteenth century, Maximus Mazlum (1833-1853) became the first Greek Catholic Patriarch. He was able to bring the external and internal organization of his community to a successful conclusion. Under his energetic leadership his church gained the status of a unified and, with respect to civil status, independent church. Indicative of the situation and his positions is the fact that in 1822 he became a French citizen and enjoyed French legal protection under the system of the so-called capitulations (see chapter I). Both France and the Latin clergy took part in the process of consolidating the Greek Catholic Church and its separation from Orthodoxy.

The reaction of the established parallel hierarchy came in 1838 when the Orthodox patriarchs in the Middle East published a declaration in which the Latinizing activities and separation were condemned.[34]

In the second half of the twentieth century, there was an improvement in the relations between the Vatican and the Eastern churches. Pope John XXIII (1881-1963), who worked for a time in Istanbul (1934-37), had great compassion for the Eastern churches.

The primary dogmatic differences are the doctrine of the infallibility of the pope issued by Vatican I in 1870 and the "immaculate conception of Mary" in 1950. The problem of the procession of the Holy Spirit from the Father and the Son (*filioque*) and the way in which the Eucharist is celebrated was apparently no longer viewed as such a problem.[35]

The number of Melchites in Israel, the largest groups of Palestinian Christians in the Holy Land, is 45, 000. The current Melchite Patriarch Maximos V Hakim (since 1967), who was Archbishop in Galilee became well known. He was able to regain large tracts of ecclesiastic holdings in Israel/Palestine that had been confiscated after the Arab-Israeli war of 1948.

The Greek Catholic and Maronite population of the villages of Iqrit and Kafar Bir'am in Galilee did not have such success. In 1948 these villages were occupied and the population was forcibly deported by Israeli troops. In spite of promises of resettlement of new lands, these 4,500 people received neither. They finally returned, with the support of the Melchite Archbishop of Galilee Joseph Raya, without permission to demand what remained of their houses and land. Over the course of the years, however, much of it had been given to Jewish immigrants.[36]

The Israeli premier at the time, Golda Meir (died 1978) refused to give them permission to settle in their former villages.

Another Melchite bishop Hilarion Capucci from Israel was arrested by the Israeli authorities in 1974 on the charge of smuggling arms to the Palestinians. Pope John Paul II used him in 1979 as an intermediary to the new regime of Khomeini in Iran.

From 17-24 June 1993 the eighth session of the theological dialogue between the Orthodox and the Catholic Church took place in the Greek Orthodox center, St. John of Damascus Orthodox Theological Institute in Balamand (Lebanon). In the document which was finalized there the Orthodox Churches present recognized the existence of the Catholic Churches of oriental rite and the Catholics no longer see them as a model or method for future unity. They see each other as sister churches. 'Unitatism', as a method of bringing about the union of the churches is rejected. By excluding any form of Catholic proselytism and any wish to expand at the expense of the Orthodox Church in the future the committee hoped to overcome the obstacles of some of the other autochephal churches who postponed their participation in the dialogue so far (from the Patriarchates of Jerusalem, Bulgaria, Serbia, Georgia and Greece).[37]

Maximos V. Hakim, the Greek Catholic Patriarch, delivered an interesting address at Algiers University on 13 April 1978 where an honorary doctorate was conferred upon him. In his address, titled "Christians and Arab Nationalism," he stated concerning the role of Christian Arabs:

The Umayyad caliphate was indebted to Christians for its organization, expansion and survival. ... The grandson of Sargun, our St. John of Damascus, held for several years the position of Finance minister .... The Christian poet al-Akhtal, known as the bard of the Umayyad, table companion of Yazid and of John of Damascus, immortalized in a famous poem the part his fellow tribesmen played in this struggle in support of the legitimate authority.

He states how, "for our Melkite church, as for Islam, Arabic is the language of prayer. To some extent since the 8th century and more generally from the 11th century onwards, we have been praying in Arabic in a great number of patriarchates." He continues to report that "the vicissitudes of history drove many Christians, especially Melkites, to Egypt, They there became founders of Arabic newspapers and distinguished themselves in this field: Jirji Zaydan and his journal *Al-Hilal*, Gabriel Taqla and his famous paper *al-Ahram*."

The (Arab) renaissance, therefore, at the beginning, was due to the efforts of Syro-Lebanese, Christians mainly, who were reacting against Ottoman occupation and who, for this reason, often lived as emigrants, a voluntary form of exile. ... The first cry of revolt against Ottoman occupation, raised in the name of Arab nationalism and not of liberation of the Christians, was that of Najib Azuri, the Lebanese author, in his book *Réveil de la nation arabe*. ... The reality of an Arab nation having to reconquer its independence and its historic pride progressed. The idea was taken up by nationalist in Syria and Lebanon, Christians as well as muslims. The occupying power became conscious of the revolt and resolved to drown it in blood. So it came about that in al-Marja Square, in Damascus, and in the Place des Canons, in Beirut, rightly known as *Shahat al-Shuhada* one could see the first martyrs of the Arab cause swinging at the end of a rope.

His conclusion is that

The Arab muslim world and Arab christian communities are made to complement each other. They will overcome their common enemy only through their complementarity. ... Moslem Arabs and Christian Arabs, we belong to a single race. We adore the same God. We venerate the same prophets. Our salvation lies in recognizing each other's distinctiveness in the values each incarnates, and in the capacity of each to complement the others. The christians' openness to the West does not make him a false brother. Rather it makes him a link between two civilizations, two cultures, two religions which confess belief in the same God.[38]

In this context something more might be said about the relationship of the Vatican and the churches in the East. The creation of the Latin Patriarchate of Jerusalem goes back to the First Crusade in 1099. Baldwin the brother of Geoffrey of Bouillon founded the Latin kingdom of Jerusalem. The installation of Latin clergy gave an enormous boast to pilgrimage from Europe to Jerusalem. After a long eclipse the Latin Patriarchate was reinstalled in 1847 and entrusted to the Franciscans. At present for the first time a Palestinian Arab (Michel Sabbah) hold the see.

On the 30th of December 1993 the Vatican signed an agreement with the state of Israel which means more a political recognition of two states (the Vatican and Israel) than a treaty between two religions.[39]

The Greek Orthodox and the Protestants

In the nineteenth century the work of primarily American Protestant missionaries resulted in Protestant churches which counted not a few former Greek Orthodox among their ranks. In 1837 one of these American missionaries, Eli Smith, said to the Greek Orthodox Christians of Beirut: "It is not our intent to establish a separate sect and we in no way desire to offend the Greek church. Our goal is higher than the ecclesiastical. It is the saving of souls." The intent initially was to work into the hearts and consciences of the oriental Christians, without attacking the doctrine, constitution and rites of the Eastern Church, in order "to cause the corrupt, idolatrous churches to be destroyed from the inside out."[40]

It is no wonder then that such an institution led inevitably to a split in the Church. Several former members of the Greek Orthodox Church belonged to the Protestant church established in Hasbaya, near Beirut, in 1844. An attempt by the Greek Orthodox church to suppress the Protestant church by means of an anathema failed, primarily due to the position of the Druzes, who were united with Turks against the Maronites.[41]

Such activities by the Protestant missionaries, as well as by the Roman Catholics in the Middle East, which amounted to nothing other than proselytism, gave occasion for the Orthodox see of Antioch to accompany a delegation to Russia in 1842 in order to plead for help in combatting these activities.[42]

NOTES

1. Malek, 305.

2. Arberry I, 1969, 297.

3. Mönnich, 438.

4. Meyendorff, 100; Ware, 96; Runciman, 1969, 71; Lewis, 1968, 315.

5. Runciman, 1967, 149.

6. *Encyclopedia of Islam, s.v.* Aya Sofya.

7. Hourani, 1962, 273, 296.

8. Jacob, 1, 6.

9. Arberry I, 1969, 333.

10. *Religious Life*, 51-60.

11. Horner, 1989, 107.

12. Horner, 1989, 109, 115.

13. Ware, 139; Arberry, I, 1969, 33.

14. *Lexikon s.v.* Christen.

15. Arberry I, 1969, 306, 333; Betts, 27.

16. Arberry I, 1969, 311.

17. Hajjar, 1971, 373; Latourette, 302.

18. Hajjar, 1971, 373; Arberry I, 1969, 327f.; Betts, 28; Meyendorff, 164.

19. Valognes, 314, 315.

20. Khodr, "Orthodoxie et histoire au Moyen Orient," in: *Contacts* 43 (1991) 34, 35.

21. According to *Courier Oecumenique du Moyen Orient* XVIII (III 1992), 48.

22. *Het christelijk Oosten*. (October 1993) XLV Afl. 4, 283, 284, 286.

23. It was founded by two Lebanese brothers, Salim and Bisharah Taqla. Cf. Hitti, 1967, 466.

24. Arberry I, 1969, 304. On the events surrounding the expulsion see *Le Monde*, 23 March 1983.

25. Haim, 62.

26. Khodr, 1973, 185, 199.

27. Valognes, 308

28. Horner, 1989, 12.

29. Arberry I, 1969, 333, 338, 317; Ware, 144f.; Meyendorff, 165; Betts, 145.

30. Valognes, 308.

31. Arberry I, 1969, 340; Corbon, 1977, 320f.

32. *Islamochristiana* X (1984), 217.

33. Valognes, 307.

34. Arberry I, 1969, 313, 316f.; Betts, 45; *Lexikon s.v.* Christen.

35. Betts, 152.

36. Ryan.

37. *La Documentation Catholique* 75 (1993), 15, 711-14 and *Service d'infomation* N. 83, 1993, 100-03; *MECC News Reports* July/August 1993, 2; cf. *Het Christelijk Oosten* (October 1993, XLV Afl. 4, 242-57.

38. *Islamochristiana* V (1979), 243-48.

39. Henry Laurens, "Le Vatican mise sur l'Etat d'Israël," in: *Le Monde Diplomatique*, March 1994.

40. Kawerau, 320f.

41. Kawerau, 294f.

42. Arberry I, 1969, 306.

IV. THE SYRIAN ORTHODOX AND ASSYRIAN CHURCHES

The sun of righteousness has married the daughter of darkness and he has spread his beauty upon her face and she is clothed in light.

The Syrian Liturgy

Introduction

We will first describe the emergence of two (of the three) 'branches' of the 'Syrian' Church: the Syrian Orthodox and the Assyrian Churches. The third, the Maronite Church, will be discussed in the next chapter. We will also deal with the importance of two of its original theological centers—Edessa and Nisibis.

As far the Syrian Orthodox Church is concerned, the 'founder', Jacob Baradaeus, will be discussed as well as an exponent of its early spirituality and piety: Simon the Stylite. How these churches faired under Moslem domination until recent times will be described as well as their current numbers.

We will also treat the role of the Assyrian Church in Arabia and its remarkable missionary outreach. Its relationship with the Mongols and its fate in being 'discovered' by the West in modern times and its ensuing decline will be discussed as well. The role of the Protestant missionaries and in particular the influence of the Roman Catholic Church which led to the creation of the Chaldean Church concludes this chapter.

'Syrian', 'Assyrian'

The name Syria was apparently originally a Greek adulteration of Assyria, at that time situated on the upper Tigris river in the 'land of two rivers', i.e., Mesopotamia (modern Iraq). The area lying between Assyria and the Mediterranean sea would later be called Syria.

The Syrian Orthodox are among the oldest, if not the oldest, of the Christian churches in the Middle East. In southeast Turkey there are various monasteries around Tur 'Abdin, i.e., the mountain of the worshippers of God, frequently called the Mount Athos of the Middle East, after the famous center of Greek Orthodox monasteries on Mount Athos in Greece.[1]

The language that has been spoken there since before the time of Alexander the Great (356-323 B.C.), and therefore also in the time of Jesus, is Aramaic or Syriac. It is also the language that Jesus probably spoke and it is still in use in the liturgy of the church today. There are some villages in Syria, Sadnaya and Ma'lula, situated not far from Damascus, where this language is still spoken.[2] The former was built by the Byzantine emperor Justinian I around a Greek Orthodox monastery. The latter contains the Greek Catholic monastery of Saint Sergius, one of the oldest churches in the world.

The city of Antioch, situated on the Orontes river, was the capital of the region since the time of Alexander's successors, the Seleucids (the Syrian dynasty that succeeded Alexander). Originally, the inhabitants of this region were called Arameans, but in the Christian era, when Aramean came to mean 'pagan', the Christian Arameans began to refer to themselves as Syrians. Both names, Assyrians and Syrians, are used to this day as names for the Christians belonging respectively to the East Syrian and West Syrian Churches.

The West Syrian Church is also called the Jacobite Church, after a certain Jacob Baradaeus (ca. 490-578). Currently, however, these Christians prefer to be known as the Syrian Orthodox Church, in part to avoid the heretical connotations of the Jacobite name. The East Syrian Church is sometimes referred to as the Nestorian Church, after Nestorius. But especially since the last century they prefer to be known as Assyrians, since they view themselves (whether rightly so need not be decided here) as descendants of the ancient Assyrians. Ancient Assyrian names, such as Assurbanipal the last great king of the New Assyrian empire (ruling from 669-629 B.C.), are still current among them today. In biblical times, when the name of the Assyrians was mentioned, it sent shivers of fear up and down the spine. It is tragic in a sense, that such a weak (in every sense of the word) Church bears the name of a once powerful people, known for its fierceness.

Since the work of Anglican missionaries in the nineteenth century, the designation Assyrian has become common for the East Syrian Church, partly in order to avoid the heretical implications of the name Nestorian.[3]

The Syrian Orthodox Church stems from the oldest, originally Christian church—the church of Antioch. The apostle Peter is said to have been its first Patriarch, in the year 37. The gospel made its first inroads in cities like Antioch, Damascus, and Edessa, and it became the religion of members of the gentry, the artisan class, as well as of the poor and the oppressed. The upper strata of the population was Hellenized and a gulf between the Greek or Hellenized Christians *and* the Syrian Christians appeared. For many years the language of the first

Christian documents remained Greek, such as those of Ignatius of Antioch, who would later die as a martyr (ca. 110). His martyrdom took place under the reign of the Roman emperor Trajan (98-117). Ignatius was the second Bishop of Antioch, after the apostle Peter.[4]

Edessa

In the beginning of the third century a Christian city came into existence in Edessa for a short period. According to a legend, related by Eusebius and said to have been taken from the archives of Edessa, the origin of the church there was traced back to Jesus himself! King Abgar V of Edessa is said to have carried on a personal correspondence with Jesus. In any case, the only historical certainty is that Abgar's successor, at the end of the second century, who bore the same name, was a Christian.[5·]

Edessa developed into the center of Syrian theology. When Nisibis in northern Mesopotamia was conquered by the Persians in 364 the leading minds departed to Edessa. For example, Ephraim of Syria (306-73), the most important representative of (at that time) unified Orthodoxy, left Nisibis in 363 and taught until his death in Edessa. His work gained significance in the entire Christian church. Edessa's theological school grew to become a bulwark of the Syrian Orthodox tradition, while Antioch became increasingly Hellenized. Nevertheless, the public breach did not come until the Ecumenical Council of Ephesus in 431.

In his own (Syrian Orthodox) church, Ephraim is further known as "the Great." He is, however, claimed by both the Nestorians and the Syrian Orthodox (Monophysites). Ephraim was a fruitful poet and exercised great influence through his biblical commentaries, songs, hymns, and treatises in verse form on important questions of faith, known from Ireland to China.[6] His orthodoxy did not prevent him from using in his church the Diatessaron, Tatian's famous harmony of the gospels (ca. 170), which was for a long time accepted as a canonical text. Later Rabula, the Bishop of Edessa (421-435), would introduce the 'Syrian Vulgate', the Peshitta.[7] In the wake of the christological controversies, the Byzantine emperor Zeno (474-491) decreed the closing of the school of Edessa and expelled all Nestorians from his empire. This prompted the relocation of the school of Edessa to the city of Nisibis, beyond the reaches of the Roman empire. Since then, Nisibis has been the spiritual center for Nestorians. From that time until its conquest by the Arabs in the seventh century, Edessa formed the center of the Syrian Orthodox or Monophysite Christianity. A few centuries later, during the first crusade,

Edessa was for a short time the capital of the principality of the Count of Baldwin of Flanders (died 1118).[8]

Nisibis

In 363 the ancient Mesopotamian city of Nisibis passed definitively into the control of the Persian empire. Apparently, around the year 300, a theological school was formed, which was moved in 363 to Edessa by Ephraim the Syrian. From that time on it was known as the 'mother of science', the intellectual center of Nestorianism, with as many as 800 students, most of whom lived together as monks. In addition to theology, Syrian liturgy and biblical interpretation, the school pursued the study of medicine and philosophy. The majority of Nestorian ecclesiastical leaders received their training from this school. Many Greek writings on christology, but also on philosophy were translated here from Syriac to Arabic. Thus the Nestorians who had finished their studies became the teachers of the Arabs. In 639 the city of Nisibis fell into Islamic hands, yet retained its theological significance. As a result of the plundering and destruction of the library in 1171 and the fire set by the Mongolian prince Timur Lenk in 1395, as well as the attack of the Kurds in 1403, Nisibis fell into ruin. In 1516 the city became part of the Ottoman empire.[9]

The Syrian Church expanded its mission to Persia, Armenia and Arabia. From their primary centers in Tur 'Abdin and Nisibis, preachers were sent out. In this way the foundation was laid for the later expansion of Syrian Orthodox Christianity. The fact that the whole of Asia (the entire East) was ascribed to the Patriarch of Antioch reflects this. After the Ecumenical Council of 431, the lines between East and West, Syriac and Greek, Semitic and Byzantine, Dyophysite and Monophysite, Nestorian and Orthodox were drawn ever more sharply.[10]

As was noted already in the first chapter, the differences were not purely, and perhaps not even primarily, theological in nature. In the city of Antioch the upper social class sought ties with the capital Byzantium and were referred to as 'imperials' or 'Melchites' as the derisive term indicated. The 'common' people, in contrast, who had not been Hellenized, remained Semitic. Thus a 'national' gulf grew between the Greeks and Greek-oriented population on the one side and the 'Semitic' or Syrian population on the other.

The Monophysite Church: Jacob Baradaeus

Consequently, a 'national' resistance to the imperial, 'Melchite' domination by Byzantium contributed to the establishment of a separate Syrian Orthodox Church. The exponent of this national Syrian resistance was Jacob Baradaeus (Yacoub Bourd'ono). He breathed new life into Monophysitism in the sixth century.

The survival of the Syrian Church can be ascribed to two factors. First, one must take into account the support lent by the empress Theodora, the wife of emperor Justinian I. She is reported to have been the daughter of a Syrian priest and to have secretly fostered strong sympathies for the Monophysite churches in general. Secondly, the persistent and tireless efforts of Jacob Baradaeus must be noted. Emperor Justinian wanted his unified empire to have but one universal church. Although he was not himself as much a defender of orthodoxy as has been assumed, he did follow a policy of suppression toward the Monophysites and exiled or jailed their leaders.[11] The Monophysite resistance was concentrated in the monastic centers of Scetis, or Wadi Natrun, in Egypt, and on the border of the Arabian peninsula, in the territory of the Ghassanids, as well as in various places in northern Syria and Mesopotamia.

In the middle of the fifth century, the number of bishops sympathetic to Monophysitism had been so reduced that the church was at the point of dying out. The year 543 was decisive. At the instigation of the empress Theodora, who had great influence over the emperor, and at the request of the Arab king, al-Harith ibn Jabala (529-569), the old Coptic patriarch assigned two metropolitans to the regions of Asia: thus Jacob became the Metropolitan of Edessa and Theodorus the Bishop of Bostra. His primary residence was Hira on the northeast side of the Arabian peninsula. Three interacting cultural currents, the Persian, the native 'heathen' Arab, and the Byzantine ran together in this city, the capital of the Lakhmids. As the see of the Nestorian Bishop, it became the center from which Christianity penetrated the Arabian peninsula.

The Ghassanids, a tribe from the northwest corner of the Arabian peninsula, were 'Byzantinized', although they remained Arabs and tied to Monophysitism. They lent a contingent of troops to the Byzantine army in the war against the Persians. Their most important political and military contribution was delivered during the reign of al-Harith ibn Jabala, when they defeated the Lakhmids at their capital, Hira. The Ghassanids played an important role in the history of Syrian Monophysitism. Through the efforts of king Harith, the Monophysite church was given new life, after it had been dislocated by the emperor Justinian I. The missionary activity of Harith and his son Mundhir gave an important stimulus to the propagation of Christianity in the south of Arabia. They were responsible for the construction of several churches and monasteries for the Monophysite church. Some of the Christian Arab families in the Middle East today trace their lineage back to the Ghassanids.[12]

The nickname Baradaeus ('camel saddles') refers to Jacob's attire. Such clothing was better suited to a poor monk than to a respected clergyman. It looked like a piece of patchwork, and he wore such clothing in order to be able to hide from imperial persecutors. He had no fixed place of residence, and he wandered, as the apostle Paul once had, as a sort of missionary bishop in order to encourage his fellow believers. He was so hardened by asceticism that his skin felt like stone. In accordance with the instruction of Matthew 10:9f., he took neither money nor provisions for the journey, while travelling night and day, sleeping seldom (never on a bed), and never making use of a horse or donkey. Over the course of thirty-five years he travelled great distances on foot. As a missionary bishop, he was given an audience with Arathas, king of the Ghassanids. In 550 he ventured over the border of the Byzantine empire in order to ordain priests there as well. He established churches and installed two patriarchs and around thirty bishops. By his efforts he laid the foundation for a new church, the Syrian Orthodox (Monophysite). Without him this church would never have come into existence. The church found its greatest following among the people of the Syrian hinterlands, while the 'Greek' cities were more inclined toward Greek-Byzantine Orthodoxy. Unlike such Monophysite churches such as the Coptic and the Armenian, the Jacobite church was never exclusively a national church.[13]

Simon the Stylite

Characteristic of the Syrian Orthodox church was the appearance of the 'stylites'. Such hermits distanced themselves, so to speak, not horizontally, but vertically from their surroundings. In this way it was possible to remain in the centers of the populated world and to exercise unprecedented influence over the masses. Around the year 400, after the time of persecution, enthusiasm for the monastic ideal, which in a certain sense took the place of martyrdom, increased greatly. Stylites mounted existing pillars or pillars of their own making in order to sit or stand there. The stylites were not, therefore, completely isolated from others. A hanging ladder was used by disciples and admirers to provide the barest necessities. Sometimes a small support was mounted on the pillar against which the stylite could lean when necessary, since most of the time was spent standing. In this world of the stylites the intention was to imitate the standing of the angels and their liturgical service before God. It symbolized a turning away from the world and proximity to heaven. There was a tendency to make the pillar ever higher. This practice was continued in the Byzantine empire until the tenth century.[14]

The founder, as well as an important advocate of this form of asceticism, was the legendary Simon the Stylite (390-459). He was also the most renowned of these saints. He was the son of pious parents from the city of Sis, in the border area between Syria and Cilicia (now Turkey). For thirty-seven years he practiced this form of asceticism somewhere between Antioch and modern Aleppo. The ultimate height of his pillar was 20 meters. Persian, Arab and Aramean pilgrims came from many lands in order to see him. From his pillar he exercised great authority and delivered exhortations to the crowds gathered around his pillar. In this way he is said to have converted thousands of Arabs and other nomads. He healed diseases and performed a judicial function as well. In addition to his regulation of ecclesiastical affairs and his combatting of heresies, he also had great influence in public affairs.

Today one can still see in northern Syria, near Aleppo, the remains of *Qal'at Sima'n*, as well as the ruins of the church that was constructed around the place where Simon perched on his pillar. Emperor Zeno (died 491) gave the order to have a basilica built around the famous pillar, which was destroyed in 499. It was considered during the reign of Justinian the most beautiful and detailed architectural undertaking of Christian antiquity until the construction of the Aya Sophia.[15]

It has been asserted that the Islamic minaret, from which the Moslem is called to prayer five times a day, was inspired by the pillar of Simon, as a continual call to prayer.[16]

The Syrian Orthodox Church
and its Moslem Environment until the Present

In 559 the see of the Catholicos (a high bishop) was established in the Mesopotamian city of Tikrit, the same city from which the famous Moslem prince Saladin (died 1193), as well as the current Iraqi president, Saddam Husein (purportedly), hail. This see would remain in existence until 1860.[17]

On the eve of the birth of Islam, the persecution of the Monophysite church (a similar persecution was also underway among the other national churches, such as the Coptic church) by Byzantium was so severe that the Arab Moslems were, at least at first, greeted as liberators from the Byzantine yoke. With the Arab 'occupation' of Syria in 635 and Persia in 640-644, the majority of Jacobites fell under Islamic domination and became so 'Arabized' over the next three centuries that their West Syrian dialect survived only as an ecclesiastical language, while Arabic became the language of commerce and literature. The weakening of Hellenism by Islamic conquest brought in turn a strengthening of the Jacobite position. During this time they expanded, in part at the expense of the Nestorians, also in the northern part of Mesopotamia, taking Mosul as their center. There, or in the immediate vicinity, the primate of the East, who is called the Maphrian or "fructifier," since as the head of the Eastern ecclesiastical province he could appoint bishops, has resided since the seventh century.[18]

One of the great Jacobite writers and churchmen to gain notoriety was Bar Hebraeus (Gregory Abul-Faraj 1225/6-1286), the son of a Jewish doctor. As a boy he must have endured the horrors of the invasion led by the Mongol prince Hulagu (died 1265). While fleeing from the Mongols, he found himself in Antioch. He first became a hermit and later was named Bishop of Aleppo. In 1264 he was named the high Metropolitan of the eastern portion of the Jacobite Patriarchate of Antioch. In his time there were still twenty metropolitans and hundreds of bishops in the West (one in Cyprus, among others) and eighteen bishops in the East (i.e., in East Syria and Mesopotamia). He died just before the Mamluks definitively defeated the Crusaders in 1291.[19]

Since the thirteenth century the center of the Jacobite church has been in the area around Nisibis, Edessa, and Tur 'Abdin. Although connected in name with Antioch, their patriarchs have for the most part had no fixed place of residence, living in numerous places and monasteries in the area, among them the city of Homs in Syria. Since 1292, these patriarchs have borne the name Ignatius, in memory of Ignatius of Antioch.

Although the Syrian Orthodox may have escaped the Byzantine yoke with the Arab conquest, many Jacobites subsequently converted to Islam. Especially in the thirteenth and fourteenth centuries, they lost many members to Islam as a result of bloody persecution. In the seventeenth century, a portion of the church united with Rome. Rome had on several occasions made overtures to the Jacobites, but it was not until 1760 that they succeeded in creating a Syrian Catholic church under its own

'Catholic' Patriarch. In 1783 an official line of Syrian Orthodox Patriarchs was established and officially recognized by Rome. In 1830, this new church was accepted by the Ottoman sultan as a separate nation, or *millet*.

At the end of the nineteenth century the Syrian Orthodox suffered from persecution by the Ottoman Turks and Kurds. The same occurred during the First World War in Turkey and in the regions of northern Syria and Iraq, as a result of which great numbers of Syrian Orthodox felt compelled to move to various other locations in the Arab East.

The Syrian Orthodox church of Lebanon, Syria and Iraq, which today numbers approximately 175,000 members, almost formed a majority among the rural population in the Patriarchate of Antioch until the thirteenth century. After the conquest of the crusader's principalities, the demise of the Syrian Orthodox church set in, and the number of members had dropped by the nineteenth century to approximately 200,000. They lived primarily around the Patriarchal see of Dayr Za'faran, near Mardin, which in 1920 became part of Turkey, where they never received an official legal recognition like the Armenians, Greek Orthodox and Latins.[20] Of the 200,000 Jacobites and Syrian Catholic Christians in the area surrounding Tur 'Abdin in southeast Turkey, many suffered the same fate as the Armenians during the First World War. Subsequently, many emigrated to Syria, Iraq and Lebanon. According to estimates, approximately 100,000 Jacobites and Syrian Catholics died in Urfa (Edessa) and Mardin as a result of hardship and pogroms, while it is estimated that an equal number of Chaldean (Catholic Nestorians, see below) and Nestorian Christians suffered the same fate in the mountains north of Mosul. In 1933 the Patriarchal see of Dayr Za'faran was relocated to Homs in Syria, which was at that time still under French mandate. In 1959 the patriarch was finally relocated to Damascus and currently stands under the leadership of Moran Ignatius Zakka I, the 122nd Patriarch of Antioch in the East.[21]

When he was still a priest he was invited as observer at the Second Vatican Council in Rome. On the 10th of October 1993 the Syrian Orthodox Patriarch inaugurated a new church building, Mar Ephream, al-Souriani in Ashrafiyah (Beirut) not far from the 'hot' demarcation line between East and West Beirut during the Lebanese civil war in the hope that this might contribute to the revival of his community.[22]

The Chaldean, Syrian Orthodox (Jacobite) and Syrian Catholic Churches suffered a great deal during the first World war in Turkey. But during that war the Nestorian church which numbered about 100,000 before the War virtually disappeared in Turkey. The Nestorians or Assyrians had joined forces with the Russians against the Turks with the promise of compensation in land. When Czarist Russia collapsed, they found themselves abandoned and took refuge in Iraq. Half of their number perished during their escape in the winter of 1917/1918, having been constantly harassed by hostile Kurds in the mountains. Only some isolated families or individuals are left, without clergy or church buildings. The following numbers are given for the churches currently present in Turkey: Chaldean, 2,000; Greek Orthodox, 3,000; Melchite, 7,000; Syrian Orthodox, 13,000; Syrian Catholic, 3,000; Roman Catholics 6,000; Protestants of various denominations, 1,000. Relatively speaking, the Armenians with 52,000 (plus Armenian Catholics (4,000)) are in the majority.[23]

At this time the Syrian Orthodox Church has twenty-six archdioceses throughout the world, twelve of which are in the Middle East: four in Syria (Damascus, Aleppo, Homs and al-Hasaka), three in Iraq (Baghdad, Mosul and Basra), and two in Turkey (Midyat and Mardin), two in Lebanon (Beirut and Mount Lebanon) and Dayr Mar Markos in Jerusalem (under which Amman also falls).[24] At present, their number is estimated in the Middle East at 115,000 to 150,000, of which 50,000 to 60,000 are in Syria and 20,000 in Lebanon.[25] The membership of the Syrian Orthodox Church has dwindled, especially in southeast Turkey, since the seventies. Whereas a generation ago there were still approximately 40,000 members in the cities and villages surrounding Tur 'Abdin, there are now at the most 8,000, of whom the majority are aged. Some have moved to Istanbul, while others have emigrated to the United States and Europe—especially Sweden and the Benelux countries have become the home of many Syrian Orthodox Christians.[26]

The East Syrian or Nestorian Church

In the early centuries of the Byzantine empire Persia was its arch-enemy. In part as a result of persecution, East Syrian Christians, or Nestorians, moved to Persia. With the hope of removing from themselves suspicion of sympathies with the Byzantine emperor, the Christians in Persia then organized themselves separately from Byzantium. Although it sounds odd, the Nestorian church was organized years before the Nestorian controversy took place. The influx of Nestorian leaders into Persia led to a split with the 'imperial' church and made the church definitively Nestorian when Nestorian christology was officially adopted in 484. The church was never, however, connected with the person of Nestorius, who was Patriarch of Constantinople from 428 until 431, when he was deposed by the Council of Ephesus.

Originally these Christians were ecclesiastically dependent on Antioch, but since they lived in the Persian empire, it was necessary for them to have their own head. Since the beginning of the fifth century, they have had their own Patriarch in the former capital of the Persian empire, the twin cities of Seleukia and Ctesiphon, situated a few miles to the southeast of Baghdad. It was at the time the most important Christian center outside of the Roman empire. In 499 the Persian church became autocephalous, and from that time on the title 'Patriarch of the East' has been used, indicating equality with and independence from Antioch, Alexandria and Rome.[27]

The Jacobites and Nestorians coexisted in Persia until the arrival of the Arabs. There they enjoyed the legal protection they never had under Byzantium.[28]

The Syrian Orthodox and Nestorians in Arabia

Christianity was known in the Arabian peninsula even before the arrival of the Nestorians. Around 225 there were bishoprics in Beth Katraye and in the region of Qatar. Christianity found its way into the Himyar, Ghassan, Taghlib, Tanukh, Tayy and Quda'a tribes long before Islam arrived on the scene. An Arab queen, Maria, was also a Christian. She extended an invitation to a certain bishop Moses to come and live among her people.[29] The Ghassanids, who were vassals of Byzantium, belonged to the Monophysites, while the Lakhmids of Hira, which was affiliated with Persia, were Nestorians.

In the fifth century, there were five bishoprics in Arabia of which that of Hira was subject to the Nestorian Metropolitan of Kashkar. There were Nestorian bishops in Bahrain, Qatar and Oman also. Christian churches were built in Sa'na (a cathedral was built there by Abraha al-Asnam) Aden and Zafar. The well-known mystic from the second half of the seventh century, Isaac of Nineveh, was born in Qatar. At the end of the sixth century there was a thriving Christian community in Yemen as well.

In most cases the Arab Christians of the pre-Islamic era were followers of the Eastern Church (Nestorians), although some fell under

Jacobite influence. It is said that a merchant brought Christianity to Najran via Hira. Christianity was further strengthened there by the influx of Monophysites who took refuge there during reign of Justinian. The monk Bahira, who purportedly met the prophet Mohammed while still a youth, was a Jacobite (some say a Nestorian). The preacher to whom Mohammed purportedly listened in the market at Ukaz, Quss ibn Sa'ida, was supposedly a Nestorian. In the later years of his life, Mohammed received a delegation of Christians from Najran with whom he made a treaty,[30] according to which no harm was to be done to them, and help would be lent them in the rebuilding of their churches. Priests and monks were released from the poll tax. The fact that the relationship with Nestorians was more positive than it was, for example, with the Monophysites is attributed to the fact that the christology of the Nestorians was closer to that of Islam. It was claimed by one of the Patriarchs of Seleukia (Ishoyabh 628-643) that he had first made a treaty with the prophet Mohammed and later with caliph 'Umar ibn al-Khattab in which he obtained important concessions on behalf of the Nestorians. Mohammed's successors gave Nestorians important positions in the royal court and as governors of the Persian provinces. Persia consisted at that time of the caliphates of Kerman, Balkh, Bokhara, Seistan, Khorasan and Afghanistan.[31] Nomads like the Banu Salih clung to their Christianity even when the 'Abbasid caliph al-Mahdi (775-785) sought to impose Islam upon them in 779 and when the caliph al-Ma'mun (813-833) persecuted them in 823. In the ninth century the last traces of Nestorian Christianity were swept from Arabia.[32]

The 'Abbasid era (750-1258) was a time of great literary activity both in terms of the number of authors and the volume of works produced. Nestorians who served as the doctors of the caliphs had a measure of political influence, especially under caliph Harun al-Rashid (786-809) and his two immediate successors. The caliphs granted high offices of great distinction at court to Christians. When the center of power was relocated to Baghdad, the Nestorian Catholics also made the trip. He functioned as the spokesman for all Christians at the court of the caliph, just as the Greek Orthodox Patriarch exercised that function in the Ottoman empire after the Turkish conquest of Constantinople in 1453. The Nestorians were the mediators of the Hellenistic heritage in the Middle East, not only as teachers and doctors, but also as translators of philosophical, natural scientific, and especially medical works from Greek antiquity.

Later the heritage passed down by them would be transmitted to the West by Arabs living in Sicily and Spain.[33]

The Nestorian Church as Mission Church

Although the western border was closed to the spread of the Nestorian church, the eastern border was open to missionary activity. For centuries the Nestorians were, geographically speaking, the largest church— even larger than the Roman Catholic church in the West. In the Middle Ages they had tens of millions of members. Nevertheless, like the Jacobites, they nowhere became a national church, unlike the Copts and the Armenians, and they remained a religious minority wherever they went, whether under the Persians (Sassanids), or under the Moslems.[34]

From west to east, north to south, the Nestorians travelled through almost all of Asia as messengers of the gospel, following the trade routes along the coast and inland. And so they became the representatives of the most zealous mission church that the world has ever known, although there are those who contest this title due to the (supposedly) superficial way in which they went about gaining converts, e.g., the Keraites.[35] Wherever they established a diocese, they also founded a school with a library, and a hospital with medical facilities. They were renowned not only for their medical skills, but also for their technical experience and scholarship. They lived from their manual labor and were supported by those among whom they worked.[36]

It is said that their ethical and practical theology as well as their medical knowledge accounts for the success they enjoyed in China.[37] In the thirteenth century, the Nestorian church in Asia numbered two hundred diocese and twenty-seven metropolitans.

Due to the efforts of the Nestorians, the gospel was also brought to the Turkish and Tartar tribes of Central and East Asia. In 781, an unknown king of the Turks wrote a letter to Timotheus I (780-823), whose term of office more or less coincided with the reign of Harun al-Rashid (783-809), the most capable patriarch ever to serve among the Nestorians, in which he asked the metropolitan to give guidance to his people, who had become Christians with him. Timotheus selected eighty monks and assigned bishops who were then sent to the East to preach the gospel. He appointed a metropolitan for Turkestan, to be stationed in Samarkand, and two bishops in Bukhara and Tashkent. Marco Polo (1265-1323) saw a church in the Keraite capital. Around the year 1143 the people of Europe began to hear for the first time of the existence of an extensive Christian kingdom under Prester John in Central Asia. Prester John also held the titles of either Unc Khan or Owang Khan. Some identify Prester John as Owang or even Genghis Khan (died 1228), who was less hostile toward Christians than Timur Lenk (died 1403). The Pope was convinced that somewhere in the East there existed a large Nestorian kingdom.

In the thirteenth century Christianity was wide-spread throughout Turkestan. In the Middle Ages the Turkish and Mongol Christians in Central Asia, Persia and Mesopotamia were so numerous that Nestorians translated hymns into Mongol.[38]

The missionary activity of the Nestorian church reached as far as China! The Nestorians must have arrived in China in the early Middle Ages. The first mission took place in 625, under the Patriarch Yeshuyab II (625-643), by a Syrian whose name was pronounced as A-lopen in Chinese. This was attested by a great stone monument in Singanfu in the province of Shensi in Central China that was discovered by the Jesuits in 1625. The monument was erected in 781 (779) during the days of the Catholicos Hanan Shua and indicates a substantial Christian presence. In the inscription not a single word was mentioned about the miracles of Jesus, nor was any reference made to his crucifixion, death or resurrection, making its content somewhat less than evangelical. This is one of the reasons that the mission work has been spoken of as 'superficial'. In the seventh and eighth centuries the Nestorians apparently met no opposition to their preaching of Christianity. In the ninth century, on the contrary, they did indeed encounter resistance. Many priests and monks reverted to secular life. Yet Christianity in China was not completely uprooted until the late Middle Ages.

With the arrival of Roman Catholic missionaries, the position not only of the Nestorians, but also of Latin Christians was considerably weakened by disputes in the face of the advancing Moslems. When the Nestorians first entered China again under the Mongols in the thirteenth century, a persecution of 'foreign' religions began under the Ming dynasty. The total elimination of Christianity in China took place around 1400, when the pogroms of Timur Lenk wrecked havoc in the rest of Central Asia as well. Traces of Nestorianism are still in existence in Lamaism in Tibet. Frequently listed among the reasons for this first failure of Christianity in China is the fact that the church had remained primarily 'foreign'. The seventy-five names mentioned on the Nestorian monument described above were almost without exception Syrian.[39]

Another important factor in the demise and ultimate dissipation of the Nestorian church in Central and North Asia, including Turkestan and Mongolia, was the ascent to power of Genghis Khan and the expansion of Mongol domination in the first half of the thirteenth century. The demise came primarily in the wake of the second Mongol invasion. Timur is referred to as 'the undertaker' of the Nestorian church. He stands as one of the most merciless conquerors known to human kind. He governed Transoxania, Central and West Asia with terror, and with the exception of Syria and Iraq, wiped the Nestorian church off the Asian map. Since that time, Nestorians survive in Asia almost exclusively around Lake Urmia and in Kurdistan in modern Iraq.[40]

'The Protestants of the East'

In the nineteenth century the Nestorians were 'discovered', so to speak, by the West. In a certain sense this discovery would be as disastrous for the Nestorians as the discovery of America in 1492 was for native Americans. The story of discovery begins with a certain Claude James Rich, at the time resident of the British East Indies Company in Baghdad. In 1820 he visited the ancient biblical site of Nineveh. His report caused excitement in scientific circles and among missionaries in England and the United States. He related to the English public the facts concerning, what he called, the Assyrians, who still spoke a language similar to the language of Jesus.

Reverend Justin Perkins (1805-1869) of the *International American Board of Commissioners for Foreign Mission*, who was sent in 1833 to work among the Nestorians, emphasized the aversion that the Nestorians had to the ecclesiastical use of images. He found them to be much simpler and more scriptural in their practice of faith and religion than the other Eastern Christians: oral confession, the doctrine of purgatory, and many other dogmas and practices of the papal, Greek and Armenian churches, which he considered corrupt, were unknown among the Nestorians. The Scriptures were at least held by them in higher regard than human traditions. Since they used no images or crucifixes, but only a simple and symbolic cross, and their view of the virgin Mary was very similar to that of the Protestants, it was thought that they constituted the 'Protestants of the East', crypto-Protestants of sorts.

The simplicity of their church interiors may reflect a concession to the Islamic objection to religious pictures in places of worship, or it may merely attest to the poverty of an isolated Christian people. The former

94

explanation is suggested by their long and uneasy coexistence with the Moslem majority, the latter by the lack of any pronouncements against icons in their decrees.[41]

According to Perkins the great fault of the Nestorian church was that they lacked true personal piety. This attitude of the Western missionaries —which will be further addressed in the eighth chapter—led ultimately to a negative disposition toward the Nestorians.

The renowned American mission secretary, Rufus Anderson, later contended that the experience of thirty-six years had shown that the old, dead Nestorian church could not be reformed and awakened to new spiritual life. He saw no other alternative for the 'enlightened' than to leave the church and to begin again on the apostolic foundation. By this he meant a separate Protestant church.[42]

In 1833 Americans began their mission work in the mountains of Kurdistan. From 1842 until 1844 a certain Reverend George Badger also resided in Kurdistan. He was appointed representative to the Eastern Churches and especially to the Nestorians of Kurdistan by the Archbishop of Canterbury and the Bishop of London. In 1850 he visited Kurdistan again. The sending of a representative to the Eastern Churches was in agreement with the position of the Anglicans at that time. Badger was 'high church', and was a fierce opponent of non-episcopal communities. He went there with the express purpose of working against the efforts of the American 'dissenters' among the Nestorians.[43]

The Decline of a 'Nation'

Before the arrival of Western missionaries, the Nestorians lived in relative peace with their 'primitive' Kurdish neighbors. This harmony was disturbed by the sympathies shown by the Western missionaries for the Nestorians. The disposition of the Westerners seemed to promise more than just instruction and social welfare. It seemed to offer the prospect of political independence as well. The presence of missionaries heightened the Kurdish suspicion of the 'mountain Nestorians', who maintained a precarious independence under the patriarch. The Turks, for their part, feared losing their minimum of control and exploited the anxiety of the Kurds and their desire for booty in order to carry out a program of liquidation and subjection.[44] This promise, whether accurately understood or not, undermined the relationship between the Nestorians and their environment, namely the Kurds. The conflicts which erupted between the Kurds and Nestorians beginning in 1843 were the result.

Reverend Badger gave asylum to the patriarch. What ensued were the greatest mass murders to take place, as is said, since the time of Timur Lenk. Thousands of Assyrians died and many others fled to Russia. The Nestorian patriarch appealed to the world powers for help.[45]

The First World War only intensified the tragedy of the Assyrians. Having been battered by the Kurds, the Nestorians decided to descend from their mountain refuge to the lower areas around Mosul and to join the allies—the British—against Turkey in the hope that they would thereby gain independence. Nestorian conscripts served the British and the Russians. The death rate among the women was very high. In 1917 their great leader, Patriarch Shim'un Benyamin XX, was murdered on the Iranian border by a Kurd.

When the conscripts were released after the signing of the Treaty of Versailles in 1918, the Assyrian refugees were a people without a home, huddled on the banks of the Euphrates and Tigris rivers in Iraq, which fell under British mandate. A series of incidents led to the worsening of the relations between the Assyrians and their Moslem neighbors. The fact that the British assisted them in the League of Nations did the relations no good. The Assyrians from the *wilayat* Mosul refused to allow themselves to be integrated into the general structure of the newly established Iraqi nation. Their inability to come to terms with the new situation resulted in disaster. They were pushed back and forth between the local national movements and the illusion of European protection. In 1933 thousands of armed Assyrians attempted to relocate in Syria. They were, however, turned back. Upon their return, at the instigation of the Kurds and the Bedouins a mass murder took place. Yet many refugees found their way to Syria, as had also been the case in 1914, 1921 and 1924. The Iraqi government accused Mar Shim'un of insurrection, deprived him of his Iraqi citizenship, and in 1932 deported him to Nicosia, Cyprus. He remained there for eight years. In 1940, in response to the invitation of a large number of Assyrian immigrants in the United States, he left Nicosia for Chicago, where he established his residence. Assyrians remaining in Iraq were forced to face being assimilated as citizens of Iraq, which a large number became.[46]

Patriarch Mar Eshai Shim'un, who became Patriarch already as a child, was reconciled in 1971, after more than fifty years exile in Cyprus and the United States, with the Iraqi government under Hassan al-Bakr, which returned his citizenship to him in a solemn ceremony. He was not permitted, however, to reestablish his residence in Iraq. He later caused quite a stir when at the age of 65 he decided to marry, thereby surrendering his office. He died in the United States in 1975. In 1968, encouraged by the Iraqi authorities, a minority of Nestorians chose an alternative patriarch. The current legitimate Patriarch is Mar Dekha IV, who had previously been the Patriarch of Iran. He was appointed in 1976, visited Iraq in 1978 and was received by the president, but like his predecessor was not allowed to take up residence there. He resided for a time in Chicago, and now has his residence in Tehran and holds Iranian citizenship.[47]

Currently the church is thought to have no more than 150,000 members throughout the world. Only half of these still live in the Middle East. There are six dioceses: two in Iraq (excluding the two dissidents, who at the instigation of the Iraqi authorities have followed the alternative patriarch), one in Lebanon, one in Chicago, and one in Modesto, California. Already in 1943, long before the other Orthodox churches, this church decided to join the *World Council of Churches*.[48]

The Chaldeans

Since the Crusades, the Roman Catholic Church has made attempts at rapprochement with the Nestorians. In 1551, the Assyrian community refused to accept the appointment of Shim'un VII Denka as Patriarch of the Church of the East. They sent a monk, Yuhanna Sulaqa, to Rome, where he was appointed Patriarch of Babylon and head of the first church in the Middle East to unite with Rome. While the name Assyrian refers to an ethnic identity, the name Chaldean refers to the (Catholic) 'rite'. He later died as a 'martyr' in Diyarbekr (Eastern Turkey) at the hands of the anti-Catholic community.

In 1672 more than a century after the failure of Patriarch Sulaqa to effect the 'return' of the Nestorians, a separate Chaldean rite was organized. Chaldea was originally the name for the area south of Assyria, and Chaldean has become the name for the Nestorians who have united with Rome. It was not until 1830 that a fixed hierarchy could be established for this so-called Chaldean patriarch, who was then recognized in 1845 by the Turks as the leader of a separate nation (*millet*). The Chaldean church succeeded in overshadowing, both in power and number, the original Nestorian church. Since 1834 the Chaldean church has become an effective power, especially in Baghdad.

The Chaldean church, less affected by the mass murders which took place in 1915-1917 and 1933 among the Assyrians, grew under the leadership of the long-ruling Patriarch Emmanuel II Thomas (1900-1947),

97

who, as the only Christian in the Iraqi senate held an important position, into a strong community (in 1958: 176,000 members). The Chaldean church is numerically the largest church in Iraq. They make up 70% of the Christians in Iraq.

The following figures concern the various Christian denominations in Iraq: Greek Orthodox, 2,500; Melchite, 500; Syrian Catholic, 40,000 to 50,000; Assyrians/Nestorians 50,000 to 70,000; Chaldeans 350,000 to 400,000; Armenians 17,000 and Armenian Catholics 3,000.[49] The Chaldeans are also found in Iran (11,000), Syria (6,000), Lebanon (5,000) as well as in North and South America (25,000).[50] The Iraqi minister of foreign affairs, who was much in the news during the Gulf crisis that ensued after the Iraqi invasion of Kuwait on 2 August 1990, Tariq (Hanna) Aziz (later the vice-president of Iraq) is a Chaldean Christian.

At the moment the Chaldean church has dioceses in Iraq, in Baghdad and Basra, and seven concentrated in Kurdistan. There are further three in Iran, and Turkey, Syria, Lebanon, and Egypt each have one.[51]

During the second Gulf War (1991)—the first Gulf War was the one between Iraq and Iran between 1980-1988—and its aftermath many Chaldean Christians left Iraq. Many became victims during the ordeal the Kurdish people underwent. Among the refugees who had to take refuge in the mountains in the northern Iraq near the Turkish border as well as in Syria were Christians.

From 1958 until 1989 Paul II Cheikho I was the Chaldean Patriarch. The current Patriarch is Raphael I Bidawid (since 1989), who served his church for twenty-three years in Lebanon. He is viewed as loyal to the Iraqi regime, since the Chaldean Church shows loyalty to the Ba'athist government.[52] He has been opposed to the economic sanctions that have been enforced against Iraq since the Gulf crisis and Gulf War and has spoken out against the sending of allied troops to Saudi Arabia because it "hurts the feelings of the whole Arab world who considers this country as forbidden for non-Muslims" (sic!).[53]

The Patriarch warned at the time that a reunion of Pope John Paul II with, among others, the seven patriarchs of the Catholic Churches of the Orient in Rome at the end of the Gulf War in March 1991 would entail risk for the Christian minorities if the government in Baghdad changed hands. Could the Christian minorities in general, in contrast to the Kurds, for instance, he asked, survive in dignity in Iraq?[54] In his message to the Patriarch of Babylon of the Chaldeans, his Beatitude Raphaël Bidawid, and the Catholic bishops of Iraq on 28 April 1993 Pope John Paul II declared among other things:

I share with you the desire that they (the Christian minorities) might remain in this land of yours to perpetuate the inheritance of their forefathers, nourished by their traditions and supported by their priests. Together let us entrust this intention to God's goodness, hoping that improved conditions, of benefit in the first place to Iraq, will enable them to stay and to continue to be recognized as hardworking and honest citizens, as well as sons and daughters of the glorious Church of Saint Ephrem. In this way they would be spared the trauma of being uprooted and the threat of losing their identity.[55]

NOTES

1. Atiya, 1968, 231; Strothmann, 28; Gülkan, 288-97.

2. Leroy, 33.

3. Atiya, 239; Joseph, 3-21.

4. *R.G.G.* *s.v.* Syrien; Atiya, 173.

5. *R.G.G.* *s.v.* Syrier; Atiya, 248.

6. *R.G.G.* *s.v.* Efraïm and Alt Christliche Dichtung; Atiya, 249.

7. *R.G.G.* *s.v.* Rabula.

8. *R.G.G.* *s.v.* Edessa.

9. *R.G.G.* *s.v.* Nisibis.

10. Atiya, 247; Browne, 10.

11. Kleyn, 24.

12. Atiya, 180-82; *E.I.* *s.v.* al-Hira and Ghassan.

13. Kleyn, 53f., 56, 62, 72; Müller, 134.

14. *R.G.G.* *s.v.*; Mönchtum II, 3b; Atiya, 185, 189; Leroy, 127-30.

15. *R.G.G.* *s.v.* Symeon; Leroy, 127-30; Smith, 1976, 21; Atiya, 226, 228.

16. Moubarac, 165.

17. Horner, 1989, 34.

18. *R.G.G.* *s.v.* Jacobiten; Every, 62; Browne, 10f.

19. Atiya, 204; Arberry I, 254f.

20. Valognes, 355.

21. Meno; *R.G.G. s.v.* Union; Betts, 45f., 110f.; Horner, 1989, 34.

22. *Courier Oecumenique du Moyen Orient.* XXII (III 1993), 23.

23. Jacob, 5, 7.

24. Horner, 1989, 35.

25. Valognes, 838.

26. Rolandus; Horner, 1989, 35.

27. Benz, 107; *R.G.G. s.v.* Nestorius; Atiya, 253; Horner, 1989, 20f.

28. Atiya, 184.

29. Trimingham, 1978, 3-10; Atiya, 258.

30. Ibn Hisham, 401.

31. Stewart, 214-16.

32. Atiya, 258f.; *E.I. s.v.* Nestorians and Najran.

33. Benz, 108f.; Stewart, 221; cf. O'Leary.

34. Reed, 4; Benz, 108; *R.G.G. s.v.* Assyrische Kirche.

35. Browne, 107; Trimingham, 1979, 280.

36. *R.G.G. s.v.* Nestorianen; Atiya, 257.

37. Stewart, 187.

38. Atiya, 261; Stewart, 138f, 145, 153, 161, 267f.; Arberry I, 1969, 291.

39. Atiya, 254, 262f.; Browne, 93, 95, 99; Stewart, 170ff.

40. Stewart, 256.

41. Horner, 1989, 23.

42. Atiya, 280f.; Kawerau, 313f.

43. Shaw, 95f.; Van der Werff, 117f.

44. Van der Werff, 117.

45. Atiya, 282f.; Van der Werff, 117.

46. Atiya, 284-86; Strothmann, 68, 72.

47. Horner, 1989, 22; Valognes, 431.

48. Horner, 1989, 23f., 118.

49. Valognes, 838.

50. Betts, 16f., 53f.; Stewart, 308; Horner, 1979, 278. The *Courier Oecu-menique du Moyen Orient* XX (II 1993), 17, cites the figure 600,000—80% of the Christians in Iraq.

51. Valognes, 437.

52. Valognes, 437, 441.

53. Valognes, 441.

54. *Le Monde*, 7/3 1991. But the same newspaper reported that a group of 153 Christians were arrested in August 1984, three of whom were hanged in February, and 85 were accused of separatism. Cf. *Le Monde* 16 March 1985.

55. *Islamochristiana* XIX (1993), 246.

V. THE MARONITES: THE CEDARS OF LEBANON

The Maronite community's history is a continuous struggle to maintain national and religious identity in a dominant Moslem environment.

(Istifan Duwayhi, 1625-1705)[1]

Introduction

The cedar is the national symbol of Lebanon and is prominently displayed on the national flag. At the start of the Lebanese civil war, which erupted on 13 April 1975, one of the paramilitary groups tellingly called itself 'Defenders of the Cedar'. They were referring, of course, not to the protection of this now endangered tree, of which there are increasingly fewer in Lebanon, but rather to the threat, or at least the perceived threat, to the (numerically speaking) most important Christian community in Lebanon, the Maronites. Their numbers is estimated at 700,000 to 750,000.[2]

On 19 April 1986, the Maronite synod of bishops chose a new patriarch. The previous patriarch, Petrus Antoine Khoreishi (born 1907) had held office since 1975, and was elevated to cardinal in 1983. The new patriarch, who is the seventy-sixth, and like the patriarchs of so many other churches in the East bears the title 'Patriarch of Antioch and the entire East', is named Nasrallah Sfeir (born 1920). His seat is in the city of Bkirki, some twenty kilometers from Beirut, The see was brought to this city in 1790 from Qannubin, which is in the mountains.

The Lebanese members of the Maronite church in Lebanon are distributed over eight dioceses: Beirut, Tripoli, Saida, Byblos-Batroun, Tyre, Zahle-Baalbek, Serba and Jounié. Theological training is provided by the pontifical theological faculty of the university of the Holy Spirit, in Kaslik situated between Tripoli and Beirut. This faculty claims to be the only indigenous theological faculty in the Middle East. There are, in addition, smaller groups of Maronites in Syria, with two dioceses: one in Aleppo and one in Latakiya. There are also dioceses in Cairo and Cyprus. More than one million Maronites, far more therefore than in Lebanon itself, live in the diaspora.[3]

The story of the Maronites begins with the founder St. Maron and their 'heresy'. The Maronites were related to the Arab conquerors and to both the 'Franks' and the French at the time of the crusades as well as in the nineteenth century during the eighteenth-century civil war and ever since. Since the fate of Lebanon is closely interrelated to that of the Maronites we are dealing with the whole predicament of the country: how do Maronites relating to the Druzes, Turks, and Moslems? In order to understand the position of the Maronites in the recent Lebanese civil war, which broke out in 1975, it will be enlightening to discuss the respective attitudes of the Maronites as well as the Greek Orthodox towards similar conflicts in the nineteenth century. It seems as if history is repeating itself today. After describing the Maronite attitude towards the Arab Awakening (cf. also the Greek Orthodox in this respect, chapter III) and the creation of Greater Lebanon (1920), we will deal with the Lebanese civil war and the attitude of the Maronites towards the Moslems, the Palestinians and the state of Israel. Finally we deal with the future prospects for their role and position.

Saint Maron

The Maronites derive their name from a Christian hermit named Maron, who died in 410. After his death, his followers relocated to Apamea, near the Orontes river in Syria. In the second half of the seventh century, a group of Maronites settled in North Lebanon, which would become their permanent home.[4] The real founder of the Maronite 'nation', however, was Yuhanna Maron (died 707), the first Maronite patriarch. The language of the Maronite community is also Aramaic, which is still used in the canon of the liturgy. Like the other Syrian Christians, the Maronites came into conflict with Byzantium (the Byzantine church), which destroyed their monastery on the Orontes river in 694. In order to escape the violence of the Byzantines, they moved south of Antioch, between Homs and Hama. The Arab-Islamic invasion was in part the reason for their move into the mountains of Lebanon, where they intermingled with the Greek-Phoenician and Mardaitic population, which had already been Christianized. In this way the Maronites became gradually more isolated "and developed the individual traits characteristic of mountaineers."[5] This type of existence could lead to a minority complex, or as A. Hourani has put it, "The price they paid was character deformation. The majority was inclined to follow the arbitrary ways of uninhibited power, while the minority developed the vices of servitude."[6]

Heretics?

One of the reasons given by the Byzantines for their persecution of the Maronites was their purportedly heretical doctrine. At least, that is what was stated, although the Maronites themselves usually deny that they were ever heretics.[7] Yet, the renowned historian of the crusades, William of Tyre, who witnessed the unification of the Maronites with the Roman Catholic church, wrote: "The heresy of Maron and his followers is and was that in our Lord Jesus Christ there exists, and did exist from the beginning, one will and one energy only."[8]

The last great exponent of the theory of the 'eternal orthodoxy' of the Maronites was Yusuf al-Dibs (died 1970).[9] Pierre Dib attempted once again, like al-Duwayhi, to refute the statement of William of Tyre.[10] One of the most important counter-arguments used by these men was that the Council of Constantinople (680/81), which rejected Monotheletism as a heresy, did not specifically mention the Maronites:[11]

Monothelitism: i.e., the belief in the one divine/human will of Christ, a variation on Monophysitism, the belief in the one divine nature in Christ.

Regardless of what one may conclude from this, the fact remains that the Maronites maintained contact with the West for many centuries, not only with respect to economic and political concerns, but also with respect to religious concerns. Under the influence of the crusaders, in 1182 the Maronite church began gradually to ally itself with Rome. The Maronites were (re-)confirmed (depending on one's viewpoint) in their orthodoxy in 1439 by the Council of Florence. The complete union with Rome was achieved at the Synod of Luwayzeh in 1736 when the *filioque* (i.e., the statement that the Holy Spirit proceeds from the Father *and the Son (filioque)*), the shibboleth of the Roman church, was accepted by the Maronites. The unification was the climax of a process that took centuries.[12]

Maronites and Arabs

Because of the anti-Byzantine attitude of some Christians in Syria and Egypt, it is assumed that Arab Christians were pro-Arab during the Arab conquest. That was indeed the case, as has already been described, with the Jacobites and, as we shall see, with the Copts.[13] This was not so, however, with respect to the Maronites. It is important to keep that fact in mind in order to understand their current attitude toward their Moslem environment properly. In spite of the fact that over the centuries they have been 'Arabized', and now use Arabic in business and literature, they frequently saw and see themselves not as Arabs, but as descendants of the original inhabitants of the area they now inhabit, the Phoenicians. Accordingly, the Maronites resisted the Arab 'invasion' in the seventh century. Their monasteries in the mountains served as refugee centers at the time of persecution. They viewed the mountains as an island in the surrounding and increasingly threatening 'sea of Islam'. Christians from other parts of the Arab world also found temporary refuge among them, or went there to escape taxes or other discriminatory measures imposed upon them by the Umayyad caliph 'Umar II.[14] Thus, for example, the Maronite monastery was established on Cyprus after the general persecution under al-Ma'mun.[15] In spite of the emigrations out of Lebanon, the population of the mountains of Lebanon has remained Christian for centuries and has maintained Syriac as its language.[16] Today the use of Syriac is limited to a small portion of the liturgy. For the rest they use Arabic.

Maronites and their Relationship to the Franks/French

At the time of the crusades the Maronites maintained friendly ties with the crusaders and offered the Franks military assistance. This occurred for the first time in 1099 when the Franks stopped to celebrate Easter near 'Arqa on their way from Antioch to Jerusalem. On that occasion, Christians descended from the mountains of Lebanon and welcomed them, helped them with their provisions, and offered them guides for the journey to Jerusalem. Maronites continued to assist the crusaders in Syria for the duration of their stay.[17] The relations of the Maronites, especially with the Franks, can be illustrated by what Louis IX (1214-1270), 'the Saint', is reported to have said on 21 May 1250: "We are convinced that this nation, which we have established under the name of Saint Maron, is part of the French nation."[18] The crusaders left behind traces of their presence not only in the form of castles, the ruins of which can still be seen in Syria, Jordan, Lebanon and Israel, but also in the form of names which betray a European and especially a French connection, such as Salibi (which means 'crusader'!) and Franjiy (which means 'Frank', 'French', or 'European'). These names are usually borne by Maronites. Thus, for example, the Lebanese president (and therefore a Maronite) from 1970-1976 was Solayman Franjiy. The fact that the Maronites threw in their lot with the crusaders meant that as soon as the tide turned against the crusaders, the Maronites felt the consequences directly. Immediately after the conquest of Jerusalem in 1192, for example, many Maronites fled with King Guy de Lusignan to Cyprus. Guy was king of Jerusalem in 1186 and of Cyprus from 1194 until 1205. They settled in the mountains north of Nicosia, "which reminded them of their Lebanon."[19] During the reign of the Franks the Maronites were the most privileged of the groups in Syria. Under the Mamluks, however, the Maronites lost this privileged position. The Mamluks feared that the Maronites would assist the Franks in an attempted return to Syria. Already in 1283, before the defeat of Tripoli, Qalamun (1279-1290) had organized an expedition to the heart of Maronite Lebanon, an expedition that resulted in the complete defeat of the Maronites, the imprisonment of their patriarch and the destruction of several of their forts. The persecution of Maronite clergy by the Mamluks in 1366 was justified as revenge for various naval attacks on Beirut by the Cypriots and Genoese, and for the two large fires in Damascus (1339 and 1353), for which Christians were held responsible. The direct cause of the persecution was the naval attack against Alexandria by Franks from Cyprus. The Mamluk regime began then to persecute the Christians who lived within their empire. Until 1510, in the last throes of the tyrannical rule of the Mamluks, many Maronites continued to leave the region. It was not considered unusual for the Maronites who remained after the departure of the Franks, who had provided constant contact with Rome, to return to their 'heterodoxy'.[20]

During the reign of the Mamluks, anti-*dhimmi* measures were imposed, i.e., discriminating regulations directed against 'protected citizens' (*dhimmi*s), especially Jews and Christians, who were forced to wear special clothing and they were not permitted to ride a horse. It is worth noting in this connection that the Mamluks—and this is also true of other Islamic princes in other times and places—were not only out to suppress Christians, but also equally, if not more so, Islamic minorities, especially the Shi'ites. The Mamluks restored after a type of Shi'ite interregnum in Lebanon during the Fatimids' (909-1171) Sunni hegemony there.[21] This also helps to explain the 'friendship' that existed at times between the Druzes (an Islamic sect in the Shi'ite tradition) and Maronites, a friendship that continues in spite of conflicts. This also could explain the good relations experienced sometimes during the Lebanese civil war between the Shi'ite (or more precisely Alawite) dominated government in Syria, under the leadership of president Hafez al-Assad, and the Maronites in Lebanon (especially those surrounding the former Maronite president al-Franjiy).

After the crusades, the Maronites further developed their friendly ties with France and Rome. When the Turks occupied Arab lands in the sixteenth century, however, it became more difficult to maintain relations with Europe. Since such relations were still important for them, Pope Gregory XIII established a theological seminary called the Collegium Maroniticum, in order to provide the Maronite church with better trained priests.

Among the recognized Maronite scholars is the philologist Yusuf Sim-'an al-Sim'ani (Assemani; 1687-1768), who received his training at the seminary. Jibra'il al-Sahyuni (1577-1648), whose name literally means 'the Zionist'!) taught Syriac and Arabic at Sapientia College in Rome and later held the chair of Semitic languages at the Sorbonne in Paris. He was a prolific translator. He took part in the compilation of the polyglot Bible, which contained a Syriac and an Aramaic version. He was librarian of the Vatican library and represented the Pope at the Maronite Synod of Luwayzeh (Lebanon) in 1736. In this capacity he helped bring to completion the reunification of the Maronite church with the Vatican. Patriarch Istifan al-Duwayhi was, a well-known historian who has wrote a history of the Maronite Church, using the work of William of Tyre as well as that of the Islamic historian al-Mas'udi (died 957).[22]

The friendship between the Maronites and the French has remained unshaken since the time of the crusades. In 1860, in the wake of a massacre (see the next section for more details) the French, under the emperor Napoleon III (1808-1873), imposed an agreement upon the Turks, primarily for the sake of the Maronites. And in the 1920's the French obtained the mandate over Lebanon again, which was executed under the French general Henri-Joseph-Eughéne Gouraud (1867-1946), the creator of the so-called 'Greater Lebanon' (*Grand Liban*), i.e., Lebanon as we know it today. To the (Maronite) Christian enclave of Mount Lebanon were added the Beqa'a valley and such cities as Beirut, Tripoli and Saida (Sidon). Although the Christian majority did not disappear, the number of Islamic residents in the new Lebanon increased to about fifty percent of the population. In 1978 when the first troops were sent to southern Lebanon under the auspices of the United Nations, it was again the French who initially made up the majority and are still there today. They also were part of the international troops stationed in the area around the capital city of Beirut in 1982, after the Israeli invasion of Lebanon, and supervised the withdrawal of the Palestinian resistance fighters at the time.

In order to understand the current position of the Maronites, it is important to consider the events and developments that took place in the nineteenth century. Studying the history of Lebanon is sometimes like viewing a repetitive drama. W.B. Stevenson once wrote:

Syria [i.e., both Syria and Lebanon] is a stage which waits from century to century for a repetition of the same drama. Its destiny is to be invaded and to be conquered—Egyptian, Assyrian, Babylonian, Persian, Greek, Roman, Arab, Turk, a long succession of aliens have been the makers of Syrian history.[23]

At present one could add the English, French, Palestinians and finally the Israelis (in 1978, 1982 and 1993). What events of the nineteenth century are being repeated today? Conflicts and struggles that in reality are socio-economic in nature are projected into and experienced as religious conflicts. It is also striking that, generally speaking, there is a clear difference between the disposition of the Maronite Christians on the one hand and the Greek Orthodox Christians on the other towards their Islamic environment. The Maronite clergy played a major role in the events that took place from 1840 to 1860, in both the conflicts between peasantry and 'nobility', and between Maronites and Druzes. There were also tensions between the clergy and the laity, as well as between the higher and lower clergy.[24] In the previous century the differences between the Druzes and Maronites led to open conflict several times. In 1859 Karl Marx analyzed the Maronite resistance to the Druzes as a social and agrarian revolution.[25] In 1860, a bloodbath took place in which thousands of Maronites were slaughtered at the hands of the Druzes, assisted by the Turks. This and similar events continue to live in the memory of the Maronites and were in their eyes re-enacted at the onset of the civil war in Lebanon in 1975.

In the previous century a certain colonel Churchill spent ten years in Lebanon and witnessed the civil war of that century first hand. It is striking that in the description of the conflicts in the 1840's and in that of 1860 the same warring factions lined up in exactly the same formation as they did in the seventies and eighties of the twentieth century, so that one could indeed speak of a repetition of history. The difference in the positions assumed by the Greek Orthodox and the Maronites in the previous century is also similar to the difference between their contemporary positions. The Greek Orthodox regarded the war as a social, economic and political conflict while the Maronites viewed it as a religious conflict. Thus during the disturbances in the 1840's Churchill stated

The Greek Orthodox ... declared their preference for Druze rule over them; thus belying the constantly repeated assertion of the Maronites, that the Christians could never be happy under the Druzes and that death would be preferable to submitting to their intolerable tyranny. .... This preference on the part of the Greek Christians is a most important and instructive fact. It proves that Druze resistance and even violence, was not so much directed against Christendom as against Maronite ambition and presumption, and the domineering views of an intolerant priesthood.[26]

In evaluating Churchill's assessment, one must of course keep in mind that he was English, and that England at that time supported the Druzes - politically, while France supported the Maronites. Churchill reports further how weeks and months went by without progress in the attempts to reconcile the two parties: "The Maronites, exited by their clergy, talked loudly of the intolerable yoke of Druze oppression, and declared their determination never to submit to it again."[27] He went on to report that, "Assassinations and their necessary reprisals soon gave tokens of the coming storm," and added that

The Turks ... delighted at the prospect of renewed miseries ...ever busy in the work of underhand intrigue ... they warned the Druzes against yielding one iota to the contemptuous demands of Christian insolence; while at the same time, so far from preventing hostilities, they absolutely encouraged the Maronites to attack the Druzes, openly telling them they had their leave to do so.[28]

The Maronites in the mixed Maronite and Druze areas declare:

We cannot exist with the Druzes, either they or we must be destroyed or leave the country .... The self-constituted municipal body of Maronites at Deir-el-Kamar gave the strictest orders to all their co-religionists, on pain of death, not to enter into friendly or indeed into any intercourse whatever with the rival sect. To speak to a Druze became a misdemeanor, to associate with him was punished as a treason. ... Knowing that the great body of the Maronites would not engage in a war, simply to destroy the political rights of the Druzes, the justice of which indeed, the more dispassionate amongst them were ever ready to admit, he made a war of party into a war of religion. The Druzes the "enemies of the cross" the infidels, were to be exterminated or driven out of the land. ... The Maronites ... encouraged the Christians to be ready for the hour of trial. The Maronite clergy preached the holy war in their churches and led on their flocks in person to their various places of rendezvous.[29]

In 1845 in the Shuf, an area where Maronites and Druzes co-existed and where in the first months of 1983 conflicts between Druzes and

109

Maronites (Falangists) would break out, with the Israeli army (performing a similar role until 1985 as the Turks in the previous century) supplying weapons to both sides, the Maronites were led into battle by bishops with crucifixes in hand:

The Turks backed the Druzes, and then it was the same old story: and then came the old story of villages in flames, property was destroyed, and Christian fugitives pursued by Druzes and Turkish irregulars slain. Hopes of Maronite ascendancy scattered to the winds, Christianity itself, betrayed, insulted and abased.[30]

Churchill described the oppression of the Christians who lived under the Druzes: "A Christian could hardly call his life his own."[31]
Concerning the events of 1850 he stated:

The Moslems hourly vowed death to the Christians .... From the very commencement of the hostilities the mob leaders of the Maronites in the Kesrouan, and even bishops, had despatched letters couched in the most inflated and bombastic terms .... The men of Zahle, Deir al-Kamar, of Jezeen, Hasbeya and Rashe were told to be of good cheer; *this was a war of religion.* ... The standard of the Cross blessed by their priests, had been elevated amidst enthusiastic rejoicings. The Maronites had embroidered the Cross on the sleeves of their right arms ... One of these letters was intercepted by the Druzes. This then is a war of religion, said they, "so let it be".[32]

As Churchill further pointed out:

Even from the mosques and minarets the shout for blood arose, and, mingled with the muezzin's call to prayer might be heard a cry informing the faithful that by an imperial *firman* the Christians were devoted to destruction and their lives and properties had become a lawful prey.[33]

The massacres took place not only in Lebanon, but also in Damascus. There is a well-known story concerning legendary 'Abdal-Qadir (1808-1883), who saved a large number of Christians from death. This North African leader, who had been exiled by the French, calmly gave the order to saddle his horse, put the harness on it and put on his helmet. As he mounted, he drew his sword. As soon as the fanatics came into view, he rode completely alone into their midst and said:

Scoundrels. Is that the way to honor your prophet? You should be ashamed! You will yet live to regret this. You think that you can do to the Christians what you will, but the day of retribution will come. The French will turn your mosques into churches, I will deliver no Christian. They are my brothers. Keep your hands off, or I will give my men the order to shoot.[34]

110

With respect to this last incident Hitti states: "The chivalrous conduct of 'Abd al-Qadir al-Maghribi, a refugee from French rule in Algeria, who was instrumental in saving over a thousand lives, stands out as a luminous spot against a dark background. Lebanon had no 'Abd al-Qadir."[35]

Maronites and the 'Arab Awakening'

It would be unfair and incorrect to say that all Maronites displayed the attitude Churchill ascribed to the Maronites in the previous century. One cannot speak of a definitive position of either the Greek Orthodox or the Maronites. This can be illustrated through the example of the Maronite attitude toward the 'Arab awakening' (Antonius) at the end of the previous century and the beginning of this one. In 1905 a Maronite, Najib Azuri, wrote a book with the programmatic title *Réveil de la nation arabe (dans l'Asie turque en présence des interêts et des rivalites des puissances étrangères, de la curie romaine en du patriarchat oecumenique).*[36] In this book he contends that there is one Arab nation to which both Christians and Moslems belong. He regards the religious problems which were manifest among them as actually being political in nature and as being provoked by foreign powers.[37]

It is true that Christian and Islamic Lebanese fought the Turks together. Between the two World Wars, the Lebanese writer, Tawfiq Yusuf 'Awwad wrote a novel entitled *Al-Raghif* (the name of a round bread eaten by the Arabs). It is the story of the events that took place during the First World War. Many died of hunger. Moslems and Christians rebelled against Turkey. One of the characters in this novel says:

There are no Moslems who fight against Moslems or non-Moslems, only Arabs who fight Turks to win their freedom, and Turks who fight Arabs to keep them under their control. Today the true Arab nation is born. It is born of this rebellion, in which I, an Arab Christian, am taking part along side of you, Arab Moslems, to struggle against our common enemy, the Turk, be he a follower of Mohammed, Christ or the devil. ... The Turks have persecuted us whether we were Moslems who believed in the Koran, or Christians, who believed in the Gospel. ... You, Kamal [who spoke of a holy war between Arabs and Turks] have spoken in this way because you are inspired by the past and the fact that the major part of it is based on Islam. I am not reproaching you. It could not have been any other way. In the past religion was for all nations the unifying factor that secured for them their national character. In our time it would be a scandal if we were to build our new state on religion. The Arab nation that was born today is as little concerned about the caliphate as the Italians are about the papacy.[38]

111

The Middle East was part of the battle field during the First World War. The Allied Forces were fighting at the side of the Arabs against the Turks. It is estimated that nearly 100,000 Lebanese, nearly all of them Christians (especially Maronites), fell victim to disease, hunger and execution. The Maronite Patriarch, Ilyas Butrus al-Huwayyik (1843-1932) told the American King-Crane commission that Lebanon desired complete independence, and if support was necessary, then it should come from the French. In October 1918, Feisal (the son of Sherief Husayn of the Hedjaz and a friend of 'Lawrence of Arabia' 1888-1935), who was for a time king of Syria (Damascus), incorporated Lebanon in spite of almost unanimous Christian opposition. Lebanese nationalists, such as the Maronite Emille Edde, the father of Raymond Edde, who since the Lebanese civil war (1975/1976) has remained in 'voluntary exile' in France, wanted French rule. The patriarch went to Paris in 1919 with the request for Lebanese independence. General Henri Gouraud was sent, occupied Damascus, and ended the rule of King Feisal in Syria. In September 1920, 'Greater Lebanon' was created.[39]

Greater Lebanon

In the First World War, the Ottoman empire came to a definitive end. The Turks allied themselves with Germany and a German Orientalist attempted at the time to convince the Turks that the war against the Allies was a 'holy war'. The Dutch Orientalist, Snouck Hurgronje once denounced this position in an article with the biting title: "Holy War Made in Germany." Germany's defeat dealt the death blow to the Ottoman Empire as well. The British, who in 1916 helped to incite the Arabs to revolt against the Turks (the Arab revolt with which Lawrence of Arabia was connected), soon made it apparent that they had colonial objectives. The same was true of France. In the place of the promised independence, many countries were placed under French and British mandates, and others became colonies. Just as Palestine became a British mandate, so also Lebanon became a French mandate. General Gouraud, a convicted Catholic, created 'Greater Lebanon'. In other words, to Mount Lebanon (*Jabal Lubnan* or 'Lesser Lebanon'), which was populated by a Christian majority, areas were added that were inhabited primarily by Moslems—Sunnis and Shi'ites. These Moslems had been part of the province of Syria in the Ottoman empire, where they had been a majority. In the newly created Greater Lebanon, however, overnight they became one of the many minorities of which Greater Lebanon was composed. It was primarily the Maronites who were advocates of this creation. They thought they would be able with the help of the French to extend and maintain their control over the Moslem areas. It goes without saying that the Moslems, especially the Sunnis and to a lesser degree the Shi'ites, were not about to submit to this new situation. They remained extremely negative in their attitude toward Greater Lebanon and continued to long for their original unity with Syria. In 1936, in the so-called 'confrontation on the coast', there was still a group of Sunnis who pleaded for the re-unification of the Moslem coastal cities and the Beqa'a Valley with Syria. It was said in jest at the time that the greatest political activity of the Sunnis was making trips to Syria.

The Unwritten Constitution

Gradually, however, a change in the attitude of certain Sunni families came about. One must remember that Lebanon was still feudal in structure and the influence of certain families was very great. A certain Sheik Mohammed al-Jisr, a Sunni lawyer from Tripoli, cooperated with the Lebanese government and the French high commissioner. Although the general Sunni population could not appreciate his views, the success of his efforts led to a degree of change in the attitude of some Sunnis. The most well-known and important example was Ri'adh al-Solh. He was from Sidon, but lived in Beirut, at the time still a predominantly Sunni city.

After the outbreak of the civil war in 1975 and the continual ravaging of the Shi'ite south of Lebanon, the number of Shi'ites—primarily refugees—sharply increased in the Lebanese capital.

In 1936 a change began to take place in Ri'adh al-Solhs originally negative disposition. He then became a proponent of cooperation between the various confessional groups in Lebanon. He began to speak not only of an Arab state, but also of an independent Lebanese republic, free from Syria. He considered the Lebanese people an integral part of the Arab nation, but also with a unique character, that called for an independent existence. A positive response came to this Sunni disposition from the party of the leading Maronite politician Bishara al-Khoury. It was thought that there was sufficient ground for cooperation between Moslems and Christians. On 22 November this rapprochement resulted in the closing of a 'gentleman's agreement' between the two men on a national pact (*mithaq al-watani*), which since that time has become the unwritten constitution of Lebanon. Bishara al-Khoury, representing the Christians, declared the recognition of Lebanon as an Arab state and promised never

113

to ask assistance from any European power at the expense of a brother Arab state. Riadh al-Solh, in turn, pledge Moslem loyalty to the Lebanese state and promised that it would never be absorbed into a larger Arab political unification. The Maronite Bishara al-Khoury and the Sunni Ri'adh al- Solh could be considered the 'founding fathers' of the independent Lebanese republic. But this agreement also contained the dynamite that could rupture these cooperative ties. It explains the tension under which Lebanon continued to live even after it gained its independence from France in 1943. This agreement also contained an implicit double denial, since it made Lebanon neither completely Arab nor completely Western. At the time the well-known Lebanese journalist and diplomat, Georges Naccache (1902-1972), wrote what has become a renowned article: "Two Denials Do Not Make a Nation." He pointed out that Christianity and Islam had forged their ties in a double denial. He said that Lebanon was a combination of "two-fifth columns." For writing this he was given six months in prison.

Lebanization

The Lebanese political system became utterly segregated. To each of the various religious groups a specific area was designated. As a temporary measure, for the sake of justice and harmony, or so it was formulated, the communities were evenly represented at public functions and in the cooperative cabinet, so that no damage would be inflicted on the general welfare of the state. Since 1943 it has been established—falling back on the regulations of 1860—that the president of Lebanon would always be a Maronite Christian, the premier would always be a Sunni Moslem, and the chairman of Lebanese parliament would always be a Shi'ite Moslem.

Thus the resigned Maronite president Amin Jemayyil (1982-1988) transgressed this unwritten rule when he appointed in september 1982 a Maronite, general Michel Aoun, as premier pro tem.

The parliamentary seats were divided in accordance with a fixed quota. The census held in 1932 (the last!) showed a slight majority of Christians. The key to the division of the seats was 6 to 5 in favor of the Christians. Thus the number of parliamentary seats has always been a multiple of 11 (6 + 5). For many years it was officially 99, although the official number of parliamentary members was, for more than ten years, smaller due to the deaths of several of them. The accord of Ta'if, signed in 1989, determined that there would from henceforth be a division of 5 to 5, even though in the meantime the Moslems have clearly become the majority.

The Role of the Shi'ites.

In August/September 1992 the first elections since 1972 were held, although they were boycotted by most of the Maronites. In contrast to the Sunnis, the Shi'ites did not play a dominant role in the establishment of the political system. The Shi'ites belonged to (and still do) the weakest social group in Lebanon. They were primarily poor farmers and tobacco growers. Socially and politically, they were significantly behind, not only with respect to the Maronites but also with respect to the Sunnis. This was the case especially with the traditional leaders (*zu'ama*). The Shi'ites were continually under-represented in bureaucratic appointments and the officers corps of the army, as well as in business and commerce. In 1962, for example, only two of the seventy more important civil positions were in the hands of Shi'ites. It is now generally recognized that the Shi'ite community is numerically the largest separate group in Lebanon. Thirty-five percent of the Lebanese living in Lebanon are Shi'ite, or about one million. Sunnis, in contrast, make up only twenty percent of the population.

The Maronites during the Civil War (1975-1990)

At the beginning of the Lebanese civil war, the Maronites, at the behest of the Catholic University of the Holy Spirit in Kaslik, published a number of pamphlets. They dealt with the relations between Christians and Moslems and gave a definite 'Maronite' perspective of some kind on the beginning of the civil war. Leading to the (negative) reaction were, among other things, certain statements made by prominent Lebanese Moslem leaders on 24 November 1975, which comparing the Christians of Lebanon with the whites in Rhodesia (now Zimbabwe).[40]

According to the authors of one of the pamphlets, the Moslems were seeking to reinstate the *umma*, i.e. the dominance of the Islamic community.[41] Since the Lebanese presidency of Charles Helou (1964-1970), it was believed that references to an *Arab* Lebanon entailed a *Moslem* Lebanon. Christians, however, view Lebanon as one of the few places, if not the only place, in the Arab world where Christians enjoy complete political freedom. How the authors understand and explain the most recent civil war is evident when they say:

115

A religious war has arisen from a political social crisis. Certain political and religious leaders have not hidden this aspect of a holy war from the eyes of their people. On the Christian side, the fighters bore the insignia of the cross. A childish display? Perhaps, but full of significance. They are defending the last bastion of Christianity in the Arab world against Islam. Elsewhere in this Islamic world that surrounds us Christians are not full citizens.[42]

One could call it a holy war on both sides. But with two essential differences. The Christians among us have nothing but this mountain or the sea, that is to say, either put down roots ... or emigrate, while the Moslems of Beirut, 'Akkar or the Beqa'a valley are supported by the Arab world, in spite of its lack of unity, and what is more, by the whole Islamic world.[43]

Or as another pamphlet states:

Christians, especially Maronites, would rather sacrifice all than capitulate and resign themselves to living as *dhimmi*s in the Islamic empire. Christians—and especially Maronite Christians—have, from the Islamic conquest in the seventh century until the fall of the Ottoman empire, refused to live as *dhimmi*s.[44]

This same theme was repeatedly broached in other pamphlets as well: "Christians, and especially Maronites, would rather sacrifice themselves to the extreme than live as *dhimmi*s in the Islamic *umma*."[45]

In contrast, illustrating the opposing perspectives on the conflict held by Maronites and Greek Orthodox (reflecting again those described by Churchill in the previous century), is the message published by the holy (Greek) Orthodox synod on 23 August 1975, during the civil war, for (Greek) Orthodox Christians living in Lebanon:

You have lived here in the Middle East for 2000 years in continuous strength and with a spirit of deep-rooted ancestry; you are neither vagabonds nor of abject origin. You have received from him who stood up for knowledge and prestige the conviction that you should loathe every 'Christian' ghetto and every 'Christian' existence for Lebanon, for any closing of the ranks must be nationwide, motivated by our common destiny. In your awareness of that you have borne, together with other citizens, the torch of national (*qawmi*) liberation since the last century. Since the dawn of Arab history you have had your share in the transmission of the ancient heritage to Arab civilization. Throughout all aspects of Arab life you have disseminated graciousness, human understanding, and sympathy.[46]

The Role of the Palestinians

In the past, Lebanon more or less managed to avoid getting directly involved in the Palestinian conflict and the Arab-Israeli wars. Even before the declaration of the state of Israel in 1948, many (especially the wealthier)

116

Palestinians sought out Lebanon. The well-to-do neighborhood of Hamra in West Beirut was primarily Palestinian. The Lebanese always hoped to stay out of range of the battle, both literally and figuratively. The disposition of the Lebanese, especially that of the Maronites, toward the Arab-Israeli conflict was once depicted in a political cartoon as follows. A rabbi prays, "O, Blessed One, give us the victory." And an *imam* prays, "O, Allah, give us the victory." But a Maronite priest prays, "Lord, hear their prayers." Such sentiments typified the Maronite/Lebanese attitude of non-interference and neutrality.

After the Six Day War of 1967, this situation drastically changed. When bloody confrontations broke out between the Palestinian resistance and King Hussein of Jordan in 1970—especially in the month of September, from which the 'Black September' (*aylul al-aswad*) movement derives its name—the resistance and its leadership moved to Lebanon. In 1983 a Palestinian spokesman said:

When we left Jordan [in 1970], we went to Lebanon, not at the invitation of the authorities, but because it was not a walled garden. Lebanon was, during the twelve years we spent there, very generous. Beirut is the capital that loved and hated us most. We who ruled Lebanon, and were a state, are today without shelter and without desks.

His comments referred to the forced removal of Yasser 'Arafat and his followers from Lebanon after the Israeli invasion in the fall of 1982.

Israel and the Maronites

During the Lebanese civil war the contact between the Maronite leaders and Israel increased. Under the government of Israeli Prime Minister Begin (1977-1982) the contact became increasingly more open. Israeli leaders had earlier toyed with the idea that Lebanon, as a Christian enclave, would be a good ally of the Jewish state. This notion apparently enjoyed a long life in Jewish Zionist circles. In 1937 David Ben Gurion said at the Zionist congress in Zurich: "Lebanon is the natural ally of the Jews of the land of Israel. The Christians of Lebanon have a destiny similar to that of the Jewish people." A similar point of view was expressed during the civil war by Camille Chamoun, the former president of Lebanon (1952-1958) and a prominent leader until his death. In August 1978 he visited Israel, where he was viewed as the most faithful and resolute ally of Israel. When he was asked why he had visited Israel, he answered that he did not understand why he should not visit Israel when president Sadat of Egypt had done the same (in 1977). The cooperation between Israel and the Christian forces reached its high water mark during the invasion of Lebanon by Israel in 1982, even though Bashir Jemayyil declared that Israel had not invaded Lebanon "because of my beautiful eyes." "Nevertheless, complicity by the Christian right in the invasion seemed beyond dispute. The action, 'Peace for Galilee', brought the Israeli army in September 1982 to the Lebanese capital and kept a strangle hold on the Palestinian resistance for a long time. International mediation finally secured the withdrawal of the Palestinian resistance fighters from Lebanon. The Israelis ensured that 'their' man, Bashir Jemayyil, was appointed the new president of Lebanon by the parliament. In this they succeeded, but before he could assume office he was killed. A few days later, when West Beirut was also under Israeli control, the massacres at the camps of Sabra and Chatilla were carried out by the 'Lebanese Forces' under Israeli 'supervision'. It would be another two years before the Israelis withdrew from Lebanon, the Shuf hills and Sidon to the south of Lebanon, leaving the border area until today under the control of a collaborating Lebanese military group.

The Lebanese government dissolved the 'Lebanese Forces' in March 1994 after they were held responsible for a bomb attack on a Maronite church in Beirut (27 February 1994). It was seen as a plot with Israel to destabilize Lebanon.

Deconfessionalization?

The Maronites have had more political and economic power and have controlled the key positions in the government and economic life of Lebanese republic composed of sixteen different minorities. The Lebanese author cited above, Tawfiq Yusuf 'Awwad, shortly before the outbreak of the last civil war, wrote a book with the prophetic title *Death in Beirut*. At one point in the book, students protest the exploitive Lebanese feudal system, where religious loyalties make it impossible to build a functional social-political system: "Shout in their faces, 'We don't want your broken-down crutches! We don't want your system! And reject your counterfeit religions!'" At the beginning of the civil war in 1975-1976, there appeared on walls all over Beirut the slogan "No to confessionalism, yes to secularization" (*lal lil-ta'ifiyya na'am li'l 'almaniyya*). It expressed a rejection of the confessionalist system on which the Lebanese republic was built. The cause of the dissatisfaction of many was in part the fact that certain groups, especially the Maronites, had predominance over other confessions—like that of the Sunnis over the Shi'ites. The question was (and continues to be) whether true non-confessionalism or actual secularization can be achieved; whether there actually is room for true religion or only for its exploitation in order to achieve other ends. Another character in 'Awwad's novel says:

God is one of our great problems. Not the God that Moslems and Christians divide among themselves, that we divide up between us, into little pieces, with every group wanting the biggest share for itself. Not the God that stands between us to prevent mixed marriages between the different religions, or raises his hand in protest at civil marriage. That kind of God can be dealt with and done with.[47]

Has an actual deconfessionalization ever been possible in Lebanon? The following was written a few years ago about the *Kata'ib*, the name of the Falangist party that consists predominantly, if not entirely, of Maronites: "In the 1960's ... the Kata'ib emerged as a modernizing party dedicated to national integration and social reform. But by the 1970's it had reverted its primordial origins and remembered its deep anti-Muslim prejudices ...."[48] The question is whether Christians are or can be put into a position by the Moslem majority, to be and feel part of the Arab world and not fall prey to the temptation to emigrate, physically or mentally. The later has already occurred for many, and has occurred out of disappointment and doubt after, and in spite of, the great contribution they—not least of all the Maronites—have made to Arab culture, language and (political) affairs. They feel betrayed, trapped, and see behind this "uncivil war"[49] a conspiracy not only to remove Christian privileges, but to annihilate the Christian presence itself. Rene Habachi predicted the hasty end of Christianity in the Middle East. Then he added: "Perhaps with the exception of Lebanon."[50] One could ask whether Lebanon will remain the exception in the future. The Maronites have decided that they will not permit themselves to be driven out. They have used every means to defend themselves and intend to do the same in the future. The question then becomes whether they will manage to avoid the ghetto existence spoken of by the Greek Orthodox Synod of 1975.

The Dilemma of the Christians in Lebanon

The dilemma faced by Christians in Lebanon is whether they should opt for a ghetto existence or should continue to work for and believe in a society with Moslems. The former option has been advocated by Mgr. Haddad, a Maronite Bishop of Zahle, who was obsessed with the thought of protecting the Christian presence. He thinks that if the Christians in Lebanon are weakened, all Christians, throughout the world will deeply feel the loss. "Lebanon must remain a place of refuge for all Christians. Even though we are in a minority, this land must remain Christian. We have a right to a Christian land in the Arab world." A similar mentality dominates the so-called Lebanese armed forces and the Falangists, who advocate what has been called a sort of Marounistan.

But there are also proponents of the other option. Adherents of this position can be found among the Maronites, although the majority are Greek Orthodox. Thus, for example, a Greek Orthodox spokesman said in response to the statement quoted above: "They [the Maronites] have the catastrophic feeling that they are a nation and from there come their errors and our unhappiness." The well-known Lebanese scholar, Georges Corm, has pointed out how the Christian leaders vacillate between a conservative, *militant* Lebanism, which is concerned with survival, and a *liberal* Lebanism, that is concerned with integrating into the difficult Arab environment.[51] He himself clearly chooses the later option. Ghassan Tweini, the well-known Greek Orthodox publisher of the most important Lebanese newspaper, *al-Nahar*, and several years representative of Lebanon at the United Nations, was of the same mind. He criticized militant Maronitism severely as some sort of twisted crusade, with an ideology that in his opinion was a type of social fascism. At the same time he condemned radical Islam. He wanted to destroy the myth that Lebanon was undergoing a war of religions. This simplification only served the purposes of the 'crusaders' on both sides. The security and the status of the Christians would not be won through confrontations, but through a permanent dialogue with Moslem comrades, according to Tweini. Whether Christians will be won to the position of openness held not only by the Greek Orthodox, but also by Maronites in the past and present, such as Youakim Moubarac, a scholar of Maronite background, will depend to a large extent on the position of the Moslems. In that regard, Péroncel Hugoz posed the rhetorical question to the Moslems: "Do you view the Christian as a believer, as a brother, or do you view him as an unbeliever and a traitor?" If the first is the case, a symbiosis will be possible; if the second is the case, it will mean the end of the presence of Christian Arabs in an Arab land. Mgr. Neophytus Edelby, the Melchite Metropolitan of Aleppo in Syria, said in an interview that the entire Arab world was threatened by Moslem extremism. "It has been temporarily suppressed in Syria [referring to the bloody actions of the Syrian authorities against the 'Moslem Brothers' in February 1982 in Hama), but could break out again at any moment. Christians can live with Islam, but not with Moslem extremism."

In September 1990 the Lebanese civil war was more or less brought to an end. Syria, which has always had such a important say in Lebanon (though never having an ambassador there) was allowed by the U.S.A., because of its support of the Allied forces in the Gulf War against Iraq, to 'take care' of (Christian Maronite) general Michel Aoun, who had held the position of prime minister since the end of President Amin Jemayyil's term (1988). In Lebanon the agreement that had been reached earlier by the Lebanese members of parliament in Ta'if (Saudi Arabia) in 1989 (the Ta'if document was adopted as a basis for reconciliation and reform in Lebanon) was approved by the patriarch but rejected by General Aoun.[52] The agreement was implemented whereby the parliamentary division of the seats between Christians and Muslims have become adjusted more realistically to the actual figures of the population (fifty/fifty).

Patriarch Antonius Khreish, who took over from Patriarch Ma'ushi in 1975 and was made cardinal in 1983, tried to stay out of politics, in contrast to his predecessor. He saw secularization as the only solution to Lebanon's confessionalism. That meant a separation of church and state.[53]

On 26 November 1990, at the opening of the yearly session of the assembly of the bishops of the Patriarchate and Catholic bishops, the present Maronite Patriarch Nasarallah Sfeir declared in his speech on "Examination of Conscience after Sixteen Years of Trial:" "If solidarity was established among us, our people would not have been exposed to the contempt to which it was subjected. Is we would have had unanimity about the common good, the agents of disunity would have not been able to infiltrate us and disband our ranks."[54]

Sfeir wishes the Maronite Church to accept her Arab cultural heritage, without giving up its ties to Rome and Europe, so that it will not give the impression of an alien entity. Its members speak the Arabic language and its future is in the East.[55]

NOTES

1. As quoted in Khalaf, 43.

2. Horner, 1974, 89; *idem*, 1989, 109; Valognes, 838.

3. Horner, 1989, 38f.

4. Hitti, 1967, 247f.

5. Hitti, 1967, 249.

6. Hourani, 1961, 76.

7. Hitti, 1967, 251; cf. Crawford.

8. Hitti, 1967, 251.

9. Atiya, 394, 416; Salibi, 1959, 33.

10. Salibi, 1958, 92-104.

11. Hitti, 1967, 251.

12. Hitti, 1967, 406; Salibi, 1959, 16, 20f., 33; Betts, 48.

13. Dib, 11, 51.

14. Hitti, 1967, 255; Fattal, Tritton.

15. Dib, 83.

16. Hitti, 1967, 447.

17. Salibi, 1959, 131, 133; Hitti, 1967, 247; cf. Moosa, 280.

18. Hitti, 1967, 321: "We are persuaded that this nation, which we found established under the name St. Maron, is a part of the French nation."

19. Hitti, 1967, 321; see also Dib, 65.

20. Salibi, 143-45, 151, 153; Hitti, 1967, 321.

21. Hitti, 1967, 327.

22. Hourani, 1961, 57; *R.G.G.* I, 529; Faris, 345; Hitti, 1967, 404, 464; *R.G.G. s.v.* Sionita and Polyglotten.

23. Stevenson, 1.

24. Hitti, 1967, 96.

25. *Le Monde*, 25 August 1983; Churchill, 81.

26. Churchill, 81-82.

27. Churchill, 82-83.

28. Churchill, 83-84.

29. Churchill, 85f., 89f.

30. Churchill, 92.

31. Churchill, 135.

32. Churchill, 158f.

33. Churchill, 177.

34. Churchill, 217.

35. Hitti, 1967, 439.

36. Paris, 1905.

37. Hourani, 1962, 278; cf. Rabbath.

38. Makarius, 88f.

39. Betts, 31f.

40. *Report*, 12.

41. *Report*, 2.

42. *Liban 1975*, 10f.

43. *Liban*, 11.

44. *La crise*, 1.

45. *Lumiéres*, 15.

46. *Cemam*, 1976, 60; 'Awwad, 1976, 114.

47. 'Awwad, 1976, 128.

48. Hudson, 1967, 117.

49. Hudson, 1976, 104.

50. Habachi, 126.

51. Corm, 1983.

52. Valognes, 399.

53. Moosa, 296, 301.

54. *Courier Oecumenique* XIII (I-1991), 50, 51.

55. Valognes, 405.

VI. BLESSED BE MY PEOPLE EGYPT: THE COPTS

The Copts are the noblest of the foreigners, the friendliest in action, the highest in quality and the most closely related to the Arabs in general and to the Quraysh [the tribe to which Mohammed belonged] in particular.

Tradition of the Prophet Mohammed[1]

Introduction: Paradise or House of Bondage?

In the Bible, Egypt plays a double role. On the one hand, Egypt is called the 'house of bondage', where the Hebrew 'laborers' were exploited and oppressed until God liberated them. On the other hand, however, Egypt is a place of asylum, a place of refuge in times of hunger. Egypt is even compared with paradise, with the court of Eden (Genesis 13:10). The prophet Isaiah addresses unusual words to Egypt: "In that day Israel will be the third with Egypt and Assyria, a blessing in the midst of the earth, whom the Lord of hosts has blessed, saying, 'Blessed be Egypt my people, and Assyria the work of my hands, and Israel my heritage'" (Isaiah 19:24, 25).

Egypt has, as it were, retained that dual character up to the present day. In the second half of this century Egypt has been the arch-enemy of the state of Israel. In the years 1948, 1956, 1967 and 1973 the state of Israel was enmeshed in bloody wars with various Arab neighbors, and in each of them, Egypt played a vital role. Although other Arab states joined the fray, Egypt was the nation that always paid the heaviest price. That was the case until after the Yom Kippur or the October War in 1973, and the breakthrough of 1977, when the late president Sadat (died 1981) made his historic visit to Jerusalem. In spite of the protests of practically the entire Arab world at that time and over the next ten years, this surprising initiative on the part of the Egyptian president has set in motion a process of increasing rapprochement with the state of Israel. It reached its high point in the Camp David accord, as a result of which Israel withdrew from the occupied Sinai peninsula, a withdrawal that was completed in April 1982. The Muslim fundamentalists are still opposed to this process.

In this chapter some characteristic features of the history of the Coptic church of Egypt will be described from the story of the visit of the 'Holy family', the great church fathers like Athanasius (ca. 299-373) and Cyril (died 444), and the role of the desert fathers, since one finds references to the 'desert fathers of the twentieth century' (Meinardus). The relation of the Christians to the Moslems has been depicted since the Arab conquest of Egypt, the time of the crusades and of Napoleon, the nineteenth century and during the national awakening. What was the way in which the Christians related to the colonial authorities and their native Moslem compatriots in their search for national identity? The current situation between Christian and Moslems (in particular fundamentalist) in Egypt is discussed. Finally there is a brief mentioning of the Ethiopian Church, the Coptic Catholic Church and role of the Protestants.

The Flight to Egypt

"Egypt will always be blessed, since this land gave asylum to Christ." Such was the opinion of someone who had long worked in Egypt and had come to love its people. Many are familiar with the story of Mary and Joseph's flight to Egypt in order to escape King Herod's troops (Matthew 2:13-15). The Egyptian Christians, the Copts (literally 'Egyptian', from the Greek word *aigyptos*), point out several places where the holy family supposedly lived. In Matariyah, near Cairo, there is even a tree under which they are said to have rested. The founding of the monastery of the 'Blessed Virgin Mary' in Dayr al-Muharraq[2], not far from Assiut in Upper Egypt, has been associated by the Copts with the journey of the holy family to Egypt.

There is a legend circulated among the pious which explains that after leaving Palestine with the nursemaid Salome, the holy family travelled in a south-westerly direction until they reached the fertile Nile river valley. In Arab Coptic writings, Salome is referred to as Mary's niece, and is said frequently to have accompanied Jesus and his mother. She was with them at the burial of Elizabeth the mother of St. John the Baptist. She brought Mary the sad news of the crucifixion of Jesus, went with her to Golgotha, and followed her to the grave. They travelled into Egypt through Tell al-Bastah, Bilbais, Samalut, al-Matariyah and Babylon, on the site where Ma'adi, a suburb of Cairo, is now found. There they travelled by boat to Upper Egypt until they arrived at Qusqam, where Joseph built a small house of stone covered with palm branches. The Koran speaks of the birth of Jesus ('Isa' in the Koran) as having taken place under a date palm (Koran 19:23, 25). The holy family remained there for three years, six months, and ten days. The place was Dayr al-Muharraq. According to one tradition, the first church in Egypt was built there shortly after the arrival of Mark (ca. 60). Pachomius (or Anba Bakhum, died 349), or one of his immediate successors established a monastery there. When Joseph received the command to return, Mary asked Christ to attend to the house that had given them protection during their

125

exile, so Christ blessed the house and said: "May the blessing of my good Father remain on this house forever."[3]

The Largest Christian Church in the Middle East

The Coptic church is said to have been founded by the evangelist Mark, who is considered the first Coptic patriarch. The church in Egypt has endured much persecution, especially during the brief reign of the Roman emperor Decius (249-251). The Copts, however, view the persecution during the reign of emperor Diocletian (284-305), which was carried to the East in subsequent years, as the worst of the persecutions. It is said that a multitude of martyrs died in the wave of violence. The Copts begin their calendar with the year of the martyrs, which corresponds to 20 August 284 A.D., the year in which emperor Diocletian began to reign. During the last years of his government, beginning in 303, the last major persecutions of Christians took place. One famous martyr is Catherine of Alexandria, who died in 305.[4] Her remains, in particular her head, are preserved in the St. Catherine's Monastery in the Sinai desert at the foot of the mount of Moses (Jubal Musa).[5] At the end of the sixties, Pope Paul VI caused quite a commotion in Egypt when he declared Catherine one of the saints whose historicity was doubtful.

The Christian Church in Egypt did not start with the move to separate from the main Catholic Church. A "formal separation from Catholicism was accomplished with reluctance, indicating that the expression of religious nationalism followed Chalcedon, for the most part, rather than preceded it".[6]

For centuries, the Coptic church played a leading role in the worldwide church, sending out missionaries possibly as far as Ireland. Irish Christianity, which played such an important role in the Christianization of the European continent, is sometimes called the 'child of the Coptic church'. The Irish Stowe missal, the oldest missal of the Irish church, makes reference to Egyptian hermits of the fourth century (Paul of Thebes and Antony (died 356). The church of Egypt and Ireland have fairly intimate connections. It is said that seven Coptic monks lie buried in Ulster.[7]

Athanasius and Cyril

Athanasius and Cyril were central figures in the church of the first centuries. Athanasius (295-373) was originally from Alexandria and is sometimes called 'the father of Orthodoxy'. He lead the fight against Arius, a presbyter in the church at Alexandria, who viewed Jesus as a

126

creation and not as 'of one essence with the Father', as the Council of Nicea (325) would later declare (Cf. Chapter II). He spent years with the so-called 'desert fathers' and won recognition for Coptic monasticism in Rome. Though at the time he was only a deacon, Athanasius' eloquence at the Council of Nicea, although at that time only a deacon, brought him triumph.

Cyril, Patriarch of Alexandria in 412, was the principal opponent of Nestorius, Patriarch of Constantinople. It was feared at the time that Constantinople would begin to dominate Alexandria. At about the time of his death, the church of Alexandria still occupied a leading position in the church. This was decisively and definitively changed, however, at the Council of Chalcedon (451). In addition to the dogmatic statements on the understanding of Christ, it was decided (in the 28th canon of Chalcedon), that from then on Constantinople would be made equal to the dioceses of Rome, Antioch and Alexandria. Most damaging to the Copts, however, was the fact that the Coptic Patriarch from 444-451, Dioscurus of Alexandria (died 454), was deposed by the same council and exiled. The deposition and exile caused Chalcedon to be seen not only as a condemnation of Coptic christology, but as a *national* humiliation. The Copts would continue to view Dioscurus as a saint, however, and the pro-Byzantine hierarchy could only be installed and maintained with the assistance of the army. It should not be considered a complete surprise then that the Copts welcomed the Arabs as liberators from the Byzantine yoke.[8] The break has not been repaired, even though there have been attempts at reconciliation between the Coptic and the Roman church, as evidenced by the visit of the Coptic Patriarch Shenuda to Pope Paul VI in Rome in the seventies.

The Desert Fathers

When speaking of the church in Egypt, one thinks immediately of the desert fathers. Deserts have always attracted men and women who sought to walk the path to God through strict asceticism. Antony is the most renowned example. This 'father of monasticism' has had countless followers to this very day, such as the hermit Abu Matta al-Miskin (Matthew the Poor) having the same name as a hermit from the eight century.[9]

Soon after the death of Antony, Athanasius related his life in *Vita S. Antonii*. The example of Antony was also related in *The Paradise of the Fathers* written by Palladius (ca. 290-346) with stories from the life of Macarius (Abu Maqar), among others. Macarius (ca.300-390) was one of the greatest desert fathers of the Coptic church. He was a 'disciple' of Antony. With him began the actual history of monastic life in the Scete desert or, as it is now called, Wadi Natrun, in the Egyptian desert between Cairo and Alexandria. Wadi Natrun has a Christian history that supposedly dates back to the visit of the holy family to Egypt. This place was said to have been blessed by the virgin Mary. Some Christians took refuge here during the persecutions in the East under Emperor Diocletian. Macarius, who lived in the desert as a hermit for sixty years, made this place the center of monasticism in lower Egypt. The monasteries of the Scete desert, especially that of Macarius, were called 'the paradise of God'. The monastery of Saint Macarius produced more patriarchs than any other desert monastery.[10] The monks view monastic life as similar to that of the angels. The desert fathers were quick to quote as justification for their ascetic lifestyle the words of the epistle to the Hebrews regarding the former saints, described as "wandering over deserts and mountains, and in dens and caves of the earth" (Hebrews 11:38).[11]

The bishops and patriarchs were and are chosen from among the desert monks. The thermometer of the spirituality of the church is monastic life. The monastic reform that took place after the Second World War is a case in point. It brought in its wake a spiritual renewal in the Coptic church, and its effects are still being felt. Many of the new bishops including the present patriarch are 'products' of this renewal.

The motivation for becoming a monk and entering the desert was and is frequently a specific religious experience. For example, Macarius received a vision of a valley that would become a dwelling place for his followers. He distributed his possessions and began to live according to the ascetic lifestyle. The conversion of Pachomius, whose name means 'eagle' or 'falcon', to Christianity was influenced by the courageous testimony of the martyrs during the persecution under Diocletian mentioned above. Moses the 'robber' was driven to the desert by feelings of guilt. And the teaching of the gospel itself, such as Matthew 19:11 ("If you would be perfect, go, sell what you possess and give to the poor"), drove Antony into the desert.[12]

'God's Athletes'

The desert fathers were sometimes called 'God's athletes'. Human passions, both anger and desire, were thought to strangle the life of the spirit. Thus passions had to be uprooted and removed. The *Verba Seniorum* (Words of the Elders) forms the core of the desert tradition. The compilers of the *Verba Seniorum* were less concerned with asceticism than they were with the virtues it produced: generosity, humility and kindness. It is well to ask what this desert experience has contributed to human thought. According to Helen Waddell, it is useless to try to express the mystery of the desert in words. It was the humility, kindness and the moving nobility of the desert fathers that formed the seal of the holiness of the desert fathers for their contemporaries.[13] The following example illustrates what she meant by this:

The abbot Arsenius once approached one of the desert fathers to seek counsel from him. Some one who saw him go, asked him, "Abbot Arsenius, why is it that you, who are such a scholar of Latin and Greek, come to ask advice from a man 'from the outside?'" Arsenius answered: "I have indeed grasped the wisdom of the Greeks and the Latins, but I am not yet capable of learning the alphabet of this man 'from the outside.'"[14]

The quintessence of the desert teaching is to love mercy and walk humbly with God.[15] It has been said of the desert fathers that "although dwelling on earth, they lived as citizens of heaven."[16] This may appear to imply only abandonment of or flight from the world, but when properly understood it does not entail a lack of concern for the people of this world. On the contrary, as an ancient scribe noted, there was not a city or village in Egypt that was not surrounded as by a wall with the dwellings of hermits.

The monks were seen, also because of their prayers, as defenders and protectors of peace in the world, since they continually stood watch at the borders for the sake of humanity. "It is clear to all who dwell there that through them the world is kept in being, and that through them too human life is preserved and honored by God."[17] This is reminiscent of the Jewish tradition according to which the world continues in existence as long as one righteous person is still living.[18] The practice of forsaking the world is sometimes taken to extremes, for example when the use of food is reduced to a minimum. The desert fathers were aware, however, that such ascetic practices were in and of themselves no guarantee. The following story attests to the fact that they found and followed the most excellent path.

Two fathers once asked God to reveal to them how far they had advanced along the way. At that moment a voice said: "In such and such village in Egypt there is a man called Eucharistus and his wife Mary. You have not achieved their level of virtue." The two clerics set out toward the village. When they arrived, they asked concerning the man and were directed to his house, where they found Mary. "Where is your husband?" they asked. "He is a shepherd," she answered, "and he is watching the sheep," and she invited them in. As evening fell,

Eucharistus returned with his sheep. As soon as he saw the aged gentlemen, he prepared the table and brought water to wash their feet. The men said to him, "We will eat nothing until you relate to us the way in which you live." Eucharistus answered them with all humility, "I am a shepherd and this is my wife." The old men continued to press but he provided them with nothing more. Finally they said, "God has sent us." At these words Eucharistus became afraid and said, "Here are the sheep. We received them from our parents. If we with the help of God make a small profit, we divide it into three parts: one for the poor, one for hospitality, and one for personal needs. Ever since my wife and I have been married, we have never lived together, for she is a virgin. We live separately. At night we wear sackcloth but by day we wear our regular clothing. No one has known anything about this until now." At these words the fathers were filled with awe, and went out praising God.[19]

The stories regarding harlots can also be mentioned in this connection. They deal both with extreme sinfulness and extreme holiness and were especially important for the monks, whose lives were dominated by questions of sin and repentance: "Each of the harlots was involved in commercial transactions about sex, from which each was set free to live on the heights of ascetic love and prayer. Such accounts provided a stimulus and an encouragement for all Christians, but especially for monks."[20]

Such desert monasteries and hermitages appeared not only in the first centuries but continue to exist today. There are several monasteries in Wadi Natrun and in the desert near the Red Sea, of which those of Antony and Paul of Thebes are perhaps the most well known. Bishops and patriarchs of the Coptic church, also in our time, have usually spent years in the desert monasteries, or have gone through solitary hermitage, before being called to such high office, often against their own wishes.

The Arab Conquest of Egypt

The old Arab Islamic writers referred to Egypt as 'the house of the Copts' (dar al-Qibt). It is known from Arab sources that the prophet Mohammed received from a governor of Egypt, whom the Moslems call al-Muqawqis, a Coptic maiden as a gift. He took her as his concubine and she bore him his only son, Ibrahim, who died very young. Mohammed is reported to have said to his second successor, caliph 'Umar ibn al-Khattab, "Allah will open Egypt to you after my death. So take good care of the Copts in that country, for they are your kinsmen and under your protection."[21] 'Amr ibn al-'As (died 661), the renowned Arab conquerer of Egypt, is said to have referred to this saying in his first sermon after the conquest of that land (640-642). The Copts, at the time of the

Arab conquest, were still under Byzantine control. Emperor Heraclius (610-641) named Cyrus as prefect, commander of the army, and patriarch of all Egypt in 631. He was not an Egyptian, and was probably the one referred to in the Arab tradition as Muqawqis. The emperor hoped through this appointment to promote religious uniformity in that part of the empire. Cyrus pressured the Copts to renounce Monophysitism (the belief in the one divine/human nature in Christ) in favor of the Byzantine-Chalcedonian confession (see chapter II). The indigenous Patriarch Benjamin (623-665), chosen by the Copts themselves, fled to a desert monastery and remained in hiding until the 'imperial' Greeks were expelled from Egypt.

It was during this time that the Arab conquest of Egypt took place. Cyrus saw that he was fighting a losing battle. The Copts, however, were positively disposed toward this change of masters. The difference between the old and the new master was that the new master was interested in the civil and financial, but not religious affairs of the Copts. The Moslems also paid little attention to the differences between the Melchites (those who followed the 'emperor' or king: the Byzantine Christians) and the Monophysites. All Christians fell under the same rules of protection (*dhimma*) and had to pay a head tax (*jizya*) and a property tax (*kharaj*). Initially, this was less oppressive for the Copts than the Byzantine taxes. The regulations regarding clothing, on the other hand, were new. Copts were not permitted to wear white or colored turbans, to possess a weapon, or to ride on a horse. These regulations were followed more carefully in the cities, however, than they were in the villages.[22]

When Alexandria was finally conquered by the Arabs in 641, the Greek Melchite population was given safe passage to Cyprus. The indigenous Patriarch Benjamin, with whom the Moslems dealt very sympathetically, was able to reappear from hiding. He returned in triumph from Upper Egypt and was greeted everywhere by the people. 'Amr ibn al-'As was very impressed by him and paid his respects to him in Alexandria. Benjamin functioned both as a representative of the church and of the people. The church buildings that had belonged to the Melchites, were turned over to the Copts.[23]

The Relation between Copts and Moslems

In order to understand the subservient position to which the Copts were relegated by the new rulers it is important to examine the significance of the collection of taxes. The tax collectors were not only out to raise as much income as possible for the central government, but also to gain their share. Consequently, in times of economic recession, there was often an increase in the tax burden on the Copts. Many Copts, therefore, sought to enter the desert monasteries in order to escape the head tax! Originally, the elderly, women, children, the poor, blind, sick, and priests and monks were exempted from the tax. Becoming a monk was seen as a means of avoiding the tax. For similar reasons, many Copts converted to Islam. Under certain caliphs, mass conversions were even sometimes discouraged for fear of a loss of revenue![24] In 868, one of the caliphs doubled the property tax (*kharaj*) and the head tax (*jizya*) and even the clergy lost their tax-exempt status. In times of stability, under some of the ruling dynasties, the Copts were reasonably well treated and enjoyed a certain prosperity. In 726 and 773, a few, unsuccessful Coptic uprisings took place. Meinardus concludes that an uncoerced cooperation between church and state was rare in these centuries.[25]

The first independent Islamic dynasty was that of the Tulunids (868-905). Ahmad ibn Tulun (835-884) had a Coptic architect build the now famous mosque bearing his name, which still stands in Cairo. Perhaps typical of the relations of that day is the fact that Ibn Tulun had the custom of retreating from time to time to a monastery.

During the Shi'ite dynasty of the Fatimids (969-1171), with the exception of the regime of al-Hakim bi 'Amr Allah (996-1021), the Copts actually received official favor. Copts held high positions during the reign of al-Mu'izz (969-975), who was sympathetic towards them, and of al-'Aziz (975-996), whose wife was a Christian. The latter suppressed the social differences between Moslems and *dhimmi* Christians. During the reign of his son al-Hakim, however, persecutions of the Jews, Christians, and even fellow Moslems took place. Included in some of his regulations were provisions for destroying churches or turning them into mosques. The possessions of certain churches and monasteries were confiscated and the regulations regarding dress were again enforced. Crosses had to be removed from churches, and even from wrists on which they had been tattooed (a custom that prevails even to this day among the Copts). He gave Christians a five-pound cross and the Jews a heavy bell to wear around their necks. Al-Hakim forced Christians to renounce their religion and persecuted them. He also levelled many churches, especially between the years 1012 and 1014. In 1009/10, the Church of the Holy Sepulchre in Jerusalem was set ablaze at his insistence. Toward the end of his life, al-Hakim was influenced by certain Coptic monks. The position of the Copts then improved somewhat again. In 1013, he even permitted Jews and Christians who had converted to Islam to return to their original religion or to emigrate to Byzantine territory. In turbulent times, the monastery of Abu Maqar became an important place of refuge. During the regime of al-Zahir (1020-1036) permission was given to rebuild churches and Christians who had been forced to convert were again given permission to return to their original faith.[26]

The Relation between Copts and Moslems at the Time of the Crusades

The lot of the Copts in Egypt was undermined by the onset of the crusades. The Copts tried to retain a neutral position toward both the 'Latins' and the Saracens. The Egyptian Christians were aided by the fact that Syrian Jacobites had fled to Egypt before the approaching crusaders. As long as the city of Jerusalem was in the hands of the crusaders, no Copt was permitted to make a pilgrimage there since they were viewed by the European Christians as heretics. Thus the Moslems were fully aware that the Monophysite Copts did not fully identity with these Melchite Christians.[27]

With the rise to power of the Sunni dynasty of the Ayyubids (1169-1250), internal stability returned to Egypt and the confusion that had prevailed during the reign of the last Fatimid caliph came to an end. Saladin (1123-1193) was the great opponent of the crusaders. He defeated them at Hattin in 1187 and proceeded to conquer Jerusalem. For the Copts his rule in Egypt meant the reintroduction of certain regulations on clothing and the removal of Copts from civil service. He also ordered the cathedral of St. Mark in Alexandria to be demolished in order to prevent it from being used as a fortress by the crusaders.

But his opposition, which would come to be known as exemplary chivalry in Europe (cf. the noble role played by him in the famous piece by G.E. Lessing (died 1781), *Nathan der Weise* (1779) was not extended to the individual crusader. The period of Ayyubidic rule was not exclusively marked by intolerance and persecution. The Ayyubids did not place the position of Christians in imminent danger. They left the majority of Coptic churches intact and refrained in general from entering into religious affairs. Saladin gave the Copts a monastery next to the Church of the Holy Sepulchre (*Dayr al-Sultan*), which remains in Coptic possession to this very day. Apparently, the successes of this prince against the crusaders and his conquest of Jerusalem in 1187 pacified the fear harbored by Moslems against the Copts.[28]

During the fifth crusade to Egypt, in which Francis of Assisi (1181/1182-1226) had his famous meeting with the sultan in Damiatte in 1218, the Copts assisted in the defence of the city and suffered much at the hands of the crusaders. During the crusade led by the French King Louis 'the saint' in 1249/50, Copts were found in the camp of the sultan. In the late Middle Ages, the Copts were entangled once again in difficulties. Especially during the rule of the Mamluks (1250-1517), the number of Copts greatly declined to the numerical levels at which they are present. The Copts were forced to assume a defensive position. They were still a minority to be reckoned with, but they posed no real threat to the Islamic state, if indeed that had ever been the case. The Copts were still vulnerable to pillage. As soon as they managed to acquire wealth, they were forced to withdraw and their possessions or their churches were destroyed. From 1127 to 1447, 44 churches were destroyed in Cairo alone.[29] The local Mamluk (mis)rule continued in Egypt into the era of the Ottomans, which began in Egypt in 1517, with the result that the period in which Egypt belonged to the Ottoman empire is known as the 'neo-Mamluk' period.[30]

Moslems and Christians in the Napoleonic Era

Ever since Napoleon's expedition to Egypt (1798-1801), Egypt has been open to Western influence. Due to what apparently were very opportunistic motives, Napoleon pursued a peaceful policy with respect to Islam.[31] On 2 July 1798 Napoleon issued a proclamation, the first of a series published by the French in Arabic. It began with the words: "In the name of God the merciful and the compassionate. There is no God but God. He has neither son nor companion, nor does he have a partner in his domain."[32] One of the matters broached by Napoleon in the first proclamation was the fact that France had invaded Rome and destroyed the papal see, which had always urged Christians to make war against Islam.[33]

In his "Campagne d'Egypte et de Syrie," Napoleon accused the Copts of deceit and dishonesty. After the flight of the Turks from Egypt, many Copts assumed their positions in government and took advantage of the opportunity to enrich themselves. The French recruited for their service a legion of Copts. That caused, as is understandable, much resentment among the Moslems. They were seen as a fifth column. The Coptic Patriarch Marcus VIII (1798-1809) opposed the leading Copts who supported the French and attempted to restrict the recruiting. The serious consequences which the Copts had to suffer after the departure of the

134

French would later vindicate the fears of the patriarch. In the brief period of French rule, Christians and Jews were again permitted to ride on horses. Napoleon received complaints from the Moslems on this account and consequently again forced Copts and Jews to wear distinctive clothing.[34]

From a work of a Egyptian historian, 'Abd al-Rahman al-Jabarti (1753-1825/26), who witnessed the French invasion and occupation of Egypt, it is clear that the Moslems of the day did not allow themselves to be taken in by Napoleon's pro-Islamic proclamations. Al-Jabarti reported, among other things that:

Their Islam is deceit .... They are people who oppose both Christian and Moslem and hold to no religion. It is plain that they are materialists who deny all God's attributes, the hereafter and the resurrection, and reject both prophets and apostles.[35]

From the same description can be discerned that the French presence in Egypt did nothing to foster relations between Moslems and local Christians. For example, al-Jabarti told how the French recruited Copts to collect taxes. The Copts then went into the countryside as representatives of the government and using arrests, threats and violence, collected money, conducting themselves horribly among the Moslems. "Furthermore, the Copts terrorized Moslems with the threat of calling in French assistance if they did not quickly pay the requested amount. All this took place at the hands of Coptic swindlers," according to al-Jabarti.

Christians and Moslems in the Nineteenth Century

Under the rule of Muhammad 'Ali (1805-1849) the Copts, as well as the Greeks and Armenians, received many rights and high government positions. During his rule it was again permitted for Christians to ring their bells and to wear a cross in public. In the nineteenth century, the 'father of the Coptic reform (Renaissance)', Patriarch Kyrillos IV (1854-1861) began a educational and cultural movement. He established schools and founded a press. He dreamed of an ecumenical unity of the Greek, Russian and Anglican churches. The Copts view the reign of Khedive Isma'il (1863-1879) as their 'golden age'. He allowed Copts to assume high positions in government. Copts were found among the mayors, soldiers, officers, as well as in leading positions in the army and government.[36]

The head tax was abandoned in 1855, during the reign of Khedive Sa'id (1854-1863). Copts were allowed to take up military service.

Khedive Tawfiq Pasha (1879-1892) publicly proclaimed the principle of equality for all Egyptians, regardless of their ethnic origin or religion. This would also later be taken up into the constitution of 1922.[37]

In the summer of 1882, British troops landed near Isma'iliyya. At the battle of Tell al-Kebir they defeated the Egyptian troops led by fellah Ahmad 'Urabi (1839-1911) who emerged as a national leader: Egypt for the Egyptians (*Misr li'l Misriyin*). The Coptic Pope, Kyrillos V supported the nationalistic rebellion of 'Urabi Pasha as he usually is called. Consequently he was sent by the Khedive into the desert of Wadi Natrun. Nevertheless, there were many Copts who rejoiced at the coming of the British as a 'Christian nation'. The reason for the positive disposition of the Copts toward the British is connected with the fact that 'Urabi Pasha had declared that the increasing participation of the Copts in the regime of Isma'il Pasha brought the government into danger. Although under 'Urabi some spoke of resistance against 'the infidels' and used the expression like 'holy war', the fact remained that no Copts appeared among the victims of the bloody events. A clear distinction was made between foreigners (*nasara*)—i.e., British, Greeks, Syrians—and Copts (*aqbat*). According to W.S. Blunt (died 1922), the English poet who displayed warm sympathy for the Moslem national aspirations, the Copts supported the rebellion of 'Urabi Pasha.[38] The growing foreign influence accounted for the fact that an increasing number of foreigners held posts and offices, among which the Copts are strongly represented. Thus, the railroad administration and the ministry of finance fell into the hands of Europeans. The Minister of Finance in the government of Egypt gained notoriety for his hiring practices, by which foreigners were given preference over Egyptians. The Coptic magazine *al-Watan* carried on a campaign against this infringement upon what ought to have been the domain of the educated sons of the fatherland. When the English occupied Egypt in 1882, the Copts stood somewhat on the sidelines of the national movement while having at the same time little sympathy for the new rulers. Like the French, the British did not intend to favor the Copts on the basis of their religion. Their disposition was instead determined by power politics. Lord Cromer, the British Consul-General from 1883-1906 of Egypt, who ruled Egypt from behind the Egyptian throne after the occupation of Egypt in 1882, found the Copts to be just as 'backward' as the Moslems. In his view, the Copts were simply opportunists. He found the 'Syrians' (i.e. Christians) to be more modern, more emancipated, and closer to Europeans. He viewed them, along with the Armenians as the 'elite of the Orient'.[39]

The Copts enjoyed the protection of European consulates, who were, with the support of European Christian public opinion, continually ready to intervene on behalf of their fellow believers in this Islamic land. The subsequent phase of the struggle for independence bore Islamic and somewhat anti-Christian traits. As a result, the Copts remained rather reserved with respect to national independence.

That later changed. Another disposition is evident in the declaration of the *Wafd* politician, the Copt Makram 'Ubayd: "I am a Christian by religion, but a Moslem by nationality." The national leader, Mustafa Kamil (1874-1908), founder of the national party (*Hizb al-watani*) and the daily *Al-Liwa* (The Flag), beheld in the struggle with the West a type of cultural conflict. According to Mustafa Kamil, Copts and Moslems were "one people bound together by nationality, customs, character and way of life. We Egyptian Moslems and Copts speak of religion only when we are in the mosque or the church." In other words, his politics were directed toward solidarity with the threatened oriental community against the West.[40]

The Copts were outspoken opponents of friendship with the Turks because of the mass murders they had perpetrated against the Armenian Christians in 1884 and 1895. The Turks, in turn, often despised the Copts. They suspected the Copts of wanting to profit from the fact that the British were fellow-believers. This suspicion was strengthened for those who had been converted by Protestant missionaries. The Moslems had harbored similar suspicions already during the French occupation. In fact, the closer the contacts with the West, the greater was the fear of the Moslems that the Christian minority was collaborating. The well-known Islamic modernist, Muhammad 'Abduh (died 1905) said in this regard: "The Copts themselves bear responsibility for the persecutions later conducted against them."[41]

It was undeniable that the Copts hoped to gain strength with the support of Christian public opinion in England and the missionaries. A half-century after the lifting of the head tax, the Copts no longer cared to recognize Egypt as an Islamic nation nor to have Egypt designated as such. They regarded the new era from the perspective of liberation for the *dhimmi*s.

While in the eighteen-seventies the Copts allowed participation in the national movement to pass them by, they now consciously distanced themselves from it. The attempts of Mustafa Kamil to unite Copts and Moslems produced no immediate fruits. The Copts were afraid that inde-

137

pendence would again cause them to lose to the Islamic majority the improved status that they had gained under European power.[42]

Boutros Pasha Ghali, grandfather of Boutros Boutros Ghali, Minister of Foreign Affairs in Egypt for years and Secretary-General of the United Nations since 1992, was the most prominent politician during the British protectorate. He was Prime Minister when, on 20 February 1920, he was assassinated by a Moslem who admitted he had acted out of religious zeal.[43]

Nevertheless, inspired by the nationalistic sentiments of national leaders, Mustafa Kamil and later Sa'd Zaglul (1860-1927), who in 1918 led a delegation (*Wafd*) demanding independence from Britain, succeeded in uniting Copts and Moslems against the British government. For the first time the cross and crescent appeared on the same flag. Coptic priests and Islamic *'ulama* demonstrated arm in arm. For a while, Abuna Sargius, one of the most dynamic Coptic priests, preached in the Islamic bulwark in Cairo, al-Azhar. Copts and Moslems sat down together in the *Wafd* party.[44] Sa'd Zaglul, one of the leaders of the nationalistic party, is quoted as having said: "Egypt belongs both to the Copts and the Moslems. They have right to the same freedom and the same privileges." Two Copts took part in the government of Sa'd Zaglul, and that has remained the rule in Egypt until today.

The Islamic nationalistic historian Mohammed Sabri wrote in his book *Egyptian Revolution* that between 1919 and 1921, the Copts were "among the most ardent defenders of the national idea and the first victims to fall for the cause of independence."[45]

Copts in the Contemporary Moslem Environment

Numerically speaking, the largest church in the Middle East is in Egypt. Although official government figures quote a lower number, the Copts themselves speak of five or six million (or even more). One out of three Christians in the Middle East are Coptic. In light of the fact that they are currently thought to make up approximately 10-12 percent of the population, their number would actually be four or five million.[46] The lower official number mentioned above expresses something of what it means to be a Copt in an overwhelmingly Islamic land.

The Coptic church is currently lead by Patriarch Anba Shenuda III (born 1923). He is the 117th successor of the apostle Mark, who is thought to have been the first to bring the gospel to Egypt. After Mark's martyrdom, he was buried in Alexandria, but in 828, the Venetian merchants took his remains (except the head) to Venice. In June 1968, Pope Paul VI returned these relics to a delegation of the Coptic church, as a symbol of the improved relations between the Roman Catholic church and the church of Egypt. On the 25th of June 1968, together with President Nasser and Emperor Heile Selassie Kyrillos VI (1902-1971), he laid the foundation stone for the largest cathedral (at the time) in Africa to which the relics of St. Mark were brought. In 1973, the Coptic Patriarch Shenuda III travelled to Rome for a meeting with Pope Paul VI on the occasion of the sixteen-hundredth anniversary of the death of Athanasius of Alexandria.[47]

The Patriarch Shenuda III ascended to his throne in October 1971. In the previous year, president Sadat had taken over the government from the late President Nasser (died 1970). The election of the patriarch was carried out in accordance with an ancient custom whereby the name of three nominees are thrown into an urn from which, after prayer, one is removed by an eight-year-old boy. One of other names included in the urn was that of Anba Samuel, the bishop who was killed in the assault on President Sadat on 6 October 1981. Anba Shenuda had, like his predecessor Kyrillos VI, lived for years as a hermit in the desert. Kyrillos fell into conflict with the then president Nasser. That had to do, among other things, with the confiscation of monastery property by the Egyptian government. Out of protest, he retreated for a lengthy period into the desert. The dispute was later resolved when Nasser made a gift of 100,000 Egyptian pounds for the construction of the new cathedral of Saint Mark. The first stone was laid in the presence of Nasser on 24 July 1965. The inauguration of the cathedral took place on 25 June 1968 simultaneously with the return of the remains of Saint Mark.[48]

The current patriarch was once characterized by someone as follows: "He is the most intelligent man I have ever met *from the fourth century.*" This statement underscores the important role that tradition continues to play for the patriarch and his church. Anba Shenuda enjoys wide recognition and popularity among the Copts. Even before his election as Patriarch he was a proponent of spiritual renewal within the church. Thousands of people take part in the weekly gatherings in the cathedral of Cairo in which he answers questions posed from scripture, a type of popular catechism. Shenuda is a spirited defender of the rights of the Copts, who have the feeling during these times of rekindled Islamic fundamentalism that they have been relegated to second-class citizenship, not unlike the former *dhimmi* status of Christians in Islamic countries.

The measures instituted by the Egyptian government during the rule of Sadat, such as penalties for apostasy from Islam, were understood by the Copts as having been directed against them. When in 1977 the 'law of apostasy' was announced, the authorities of the Coptic church called for a voluntary 'fast of protest'. Thousands participated in the protest. It was, as the Coptic magazine noted, a peaceful gesture of protest in order to ask God to help those responsible to find a way to remove all barriers to national unity, to hinder all that unleashes confessional biases and feelings of belonging to a besieged minority.[49]

During the rule of Sadat the number of conflicts between Copts and Moslems increased. There were more, in any case, than had ever occurred under his predecessor. In September 1981, not long before his assassination, Sadat had the Coptic patriarch removed from his duties and sent to the Anba Bishoy monastery in Wadi Natrun, where he would spend two years in exile. The daily leadership of the church was placed in the hands of a number of bishops. This conflict displayed the increased tensions not only between the Copts and the government, or at least certain of the leaders, but also between Copts and Moslems in general.[50]

In Minyah, where twenty percent of the population is Christian, Islamic fundamentalists caused chaos in the spring of 1979, as well as in Assiut, another large city in Upper-Egypt where a relatively large part of the population is Christian. The Islamic students attempted to drive the Coptic students (more or less twenty percent of the 30,000 students in Assiut and of the 10,000 students in Minyah) from the university through intimidation, and impose on their fellow Islamic students sexual segregation. The situation was calmed by a visit from the president, but a year later, young Christians still could not live on campus nor attend classes except at their own risk.

The 'Abou Douhoun' or the 'bearded', as the Islamic fundamentalistic youths were called, checked identity cards in the university vans and refused transport to Copts. In one purely confessional incident someone shouted "Believers, defend yourselves! The infidels are attacking Islam!" The next day, they killed someone in the street and the houses of Coptic workers and store owners were attacked. A fundamentalist worship leader declared "The infidels worship a sheep and drink the blood of the messiah. Shenuda is a dog." It is evident from various publications that these fundamentalists were inspired by the revolution of ayatollah Khomeini in Iran (1979). One of the publications that was distributed was entitled: *What a Moslem Must Know about Christians and Evangelization*, a pamphlet written by a certain Ibrahim Slimane Gabhan and appearing for the first time in Saudi Arabia in 1977. In this pamphlet it is said that "The crusades have continued for eight hundred years and that 850,000 priests are preparing themselves to launch a campaign against the Islamic renaissance under the protection of the Americans and that the Copts in Assiut want to make it into a crusaders' city in a coalition with Israel against the Arabs."[51] Such comments were seen at the time as a reaction to the Lebanese conflict, among other things, improperly construed as a religious war between Moslems and Christians. The rise to power of the Falangists (during the civil war in Lebanon) and the late Major Haddad in South Lebanon, continually referred to as 'Christians', contributed strongly to this perception. One of the pamphlets called upon Moslems to kill Christians before they got the chance to gain positions, as Major Haddad had in South Lebanon. Such accusations in Egypt obviously had no substance, if one remembers that the Copts make up hardly twelve percent of the population and have not challenged central authority in Egypt since the year 831.[52]

The relations between Anba Shenuda and the Egyptian president deteriorated when Anba Shenuda apparently ruffled the feathers of the Egyptian president. Sadat held Shenuda responsible for the actions of a Coptic association in New Jersey (USA), under the direction of Shawqi Karas, which during the visit of Sadat to the United States in 1980 to meet with then President Carter published accusations in pamphlets and advertisements in such papers as *The New York Times*, regarding the "persecution of Christians in Egypt." In America and Canada, as well as in Australia, there are large groups of Coptic 'immigrants', who under the Nasser regime especially but also afterwards, left Egypt and still harbor a certain ill-will toward Egyptian leaders. Sadat took the accusations very seriously, especially because they were published outside the country and therefore tarnished the image of Egypt abroad.[53]

In an address delivered on 16 May 1980, President Sadat attacked the anti-Egyptian and anti-Islamic attitude of the high clergy of the Coptic church and accused them of having conspired with foreigners. In one of his tours of Egypt, Sadat said: "I am the Islamic president of an Islamic state; As a Moslem I rule an Islamic nation where Moslems and Christians live together. The Copts are trying to form a state within a state." Without naming Shenuda personally, he praised his predecessor, Kyrillos VI, who, he said, always tempered religious differences rather than aggravating them. Sadat wanted with these words to make clear to

Islamic fundamentalists that he had the Copts under his control, but at the same time to prevent 'fanatical Moslems' from abusing religious differences for their own ends.[54] Only the current Egyptian president, Hosni Mubarak, permitted the patriarch to resume his duties (4 January 1985 just in time for the Coptic Christmas celebration).

The estimates about the number of converts from Christianity to Islam ranges from a few hundred to less than a thousand per year. These estimates might not reflect the number of rural conversions. As reasons for conversion are mentioned "to find work, escape discrimination and obtain divorce".[55]

Coptic Customs

The Coptic language remained in use centuries after the Arab conquest. Since the tenth century, however, Arabic has been extensively used. Nevertheless, in the eighteenth century, a French consul found several villages in Upper Egypt where Coptic was still spoken. The same is still true of several remote villages to this day. Coptic is still also used, with Arabic, in the liturgy, yet it is becoming more and more a 'sacred tongue', which already in the twelfth century had been mastered only by the higher clergy, and with the exception of the outlying areas, had ceased to be the common language.[56]

At the insistence of the patriarchs, Arabic translations were made of Coptic liturgical books. There were eminent Coptic scholars, such as Ibn al-Assal and other members of his family, who were well versed in Coptic, Greek and Arabic. The first Copt to write several originally Arabic works (in the second half of the tenth century) was a monk and later Bishop of al-'Asmunain. He was known by the name Severus ibn al-Muqaffa'. In his work he followed the example of the Christians in Syrians, who had introduced Arabic as the language of Christian literature. His primary purpose in so doing was the instruction of all the people. His most important work was *The History of the Patriarchs*.[57]

If one visits a Coptic service today, one encounters a form of Christian worship and religious experience which appears to date back to New Testament times. The exorcism of demons from those who are possessed is a common practice. The hand cross worn by the Coptic priests is used for blessing and for exorcising demons. For centuries the Coptic church has continued the apostolic practice of healing and extreme unction is used not only for the dying, but also for the sick.[58] White ostrich eggs often are hung in the church as a symbol of continual vigilance, since the

142

ostrich stands at a distance from her eggs keeping watch over them with her eyes fixed on the spot.[59] Many Copts have tattooed a cross on the inside of their right wrist, often with the date of their pilgrimage to Jerusalem.[60] During the crusades the crusaders prevented the Copts from making the customary pilgrimage of Eastern Christianity to Jerusalem. That was a great blow to the pious Copts. In 1705, a costly Islamic legal decree (*fatwa*) was purchased from al-Azhar which permitted Copts to make the pilgrimage to Jerusalem for the first time in centuries.[61] In spite of the opening of the border between Egypt and Israel since the Camp David accords, the current patriarch has not permitted Copts to make the pilgrimage to Jerusalem yet, which for the Copts functions in much the same was as the pilgrimage (*hajj*) to Mecca does for Moslems.

There is also great honor paid to the Virgin Mary in the Coptic church. On 2 April 1968 the Virgin Mary appeared above one of the domes of the church in Zeitun, a suburb of Cairo, or so many Copts and even Moslems believe. The miracle was also officially recognized by the patriarch. The appearance was institutionalized with respect to worship and iconographically canonized.[62] Such appearances are "a normal phenomenon connected with times of personal and collective suffering and fear." At the time the apparition fulfilled the role of healer and comforter, and was connected with the crisis caused in part by the war of attrition which took place between Israel and Egypt along the Suez canal between 1968 and 1970 following the June War of 1967.[63]

Sometimes religious figures and practices from Pharaonic, Christian, and Islamic Egypt appear to be closely related to one another. This appears to be the case, for example, when a certain deity, martyr or shaykh seem to be found in each of the three under different names and titles. The Christian holy martyr or confessor took the place of a Pharaonic deity only later to be in turn replaced by an Islamic shaykh. The Egyptian god Horus, who harpooned the crocodile (the crocodile was one of the figures of Seth, the enemy of Osiris, the father of Horus), is not only the precursor of Saint George, who slew the dragon, but also of many other combative saints who are very popular among the Copts.[64]

Pilgrimages to *mawlids*, i.e. feasts of the birth of a saint were always an integral part of the Coptic piety. Healing miracles take place at *mawlids* and demons are exorcised. (*Post mortem*) miracles connected with the Coptic pope Kyrillos VI have occurred. Pilgrimages are made to the place where he lived as a hermit as well as to his grave site.[65]

The Ethiopian Church

The Ethiopian church came into existence in the fourth century through the evangelization of two brothers living in Tyre but originally from Alexandria: Frumentius and Aedesius (fourth century). They arrived there as a result of a shipwreck but were able to gain the confidence of the Negus in Aksum. Subsequently, nine Monophysite monks from Syria introduced monasticism in Ethiopia and produced a translation of the Bible in Ge'ez. Frumentius visited Alexandria (ca. 330) and was consecrated by Athanasius, thereby becoming the first Archbishop of Aksum. The Ethiopian church does not call itself Monophysite but Tawahedo, 'Unionite': meaning the union in Christ of the human and divine natures.

The Ethiopian church, which does not belong to the Arab world, recognizes the primacy of the Coptic Patriarch of Alexandria. Until 1951 all Ethiopian bishops were still appointed by Alexandria. The official title of the Coptic Patriarch is 'Pope of Alexandria and Patriarch of the See of St. Mark in Libya, the Five Cities of the West and the Lands of Egypt, Abyssinia and Nubia'. In the twentieth century, the Ethiopian church, whose membership was estimated in the mid-eighties at around twenty million, became independent of the Coptic church.[66]

One of the first achievements of Pope Kyrillos VI after his enthronement was to re-establish relations between the Coptic and Ethiopian churches.

The Coptic Catholic Church

On several occasions, the Roman Catholic church has attempted to 'reconcile' with the Coptic church. It was attempted, for example, at the Council of Ferrara-Florence in 1438-1445 (1442), albeit in vain. Another attempt was made in 1597 once again, however, without result. Actually, since the days of Saint Francis and then again in the sixteenth century, first Franciscans and later Jesuits tried to unite the Coptic church with the see of Rome. The first Coptic converts came through the efforts of Franciscans in the seventeenth century in the Holy Land. In 1741, the Coptic Bishop of Jerusalem, Athanasios, announced that he had become Catholic. The Pope of Rome appointed him overseer of the widely scattered Catholic Copts in Egypt, but he dared not go, leaving the work there to a vicar instead.

In 1775, the French entered Upper Egypt and the Jesuits established themselves in Cairo. Since the Catholic Copts had no church building of their own, they held services in the churches of the Franciscans. The Latin missionaries apparently gained more freedom during the French expedition to Egypt (1798-1801).

The introduction of Catholicism therefore appeared to have more to do with politics than with conviction. The Catholic mission stood under the protection of Venice and later Austria. The legal privileges granted to Austria by the so-called capitulations were therefore also extended to Catholic Copts. After the first unsuccessful attempts, the idea of union gained a foothold in Egypt in the nineteenth century. In 1824, a patriarchate was established but lasted only a short time. In 1829 permission was gained from the Ottoman sultan to build churches. The first Catholic Coptic Patriarch of Alexandria was appointed in 1895, when Kyrillos Macarius (Maqar) was promoted to Coptic papal nuncio of the entire diocese of Egypt. He was consecrated in 1899. He soon resigned, however, and became Greek Orthodox. In 1908, he returned to his original Coptic church, which he defended in polemical writings against Rome. In 1922 he died, once again as part of the 'uniate' church. The patriarchate was not occupied again until 1947 when Mark Khuzam (died 1958) was elected Patriarch. Since 1958, Stephanos I Sidarous has been the Coptic Catholic Patriarch of Alexandria, and became in 1965 a cardinal.[67] Stephanos II Ghattas became the new patriarch in 1986.

At this present time, the church numbers 100,000 members and is therefore numerically speaking the largest Catholic church in Egypt. There are seven dioceses—Alexandria (or Cairo), Minyah, Assiut, Thebes (or Luxor), Sohaq and Abadir (in the Delta)—with a total of two hundred priests.[68]

Copts and the Protestant Mission

The first Protestant missionaries arrived in Egypt in the mid-eighteenth century. Beginning in 1782, they worked for twelve years among the Copts, primarily in Cairo. At the beginning of the nineteenth century the first Anglicans came under the sponsorship of the *Church Missionary Society (C.M.S.)*. This young mission organization hoped to stimulate the Eastern churches to spread the Christian faith among the Moslems and heathens. It appears that they were able to maintain friendly relations with the Copts during their first visit. In 1815 William Jowett, a graduate of Cambridge, was sent to Egypt were he was warmly received by the Coptic patriarch. In 1825 the *C.M.S.* sent five additional missionaries. The Anglicans had no intention of establishing separate congregations. They distributed Bibles and tracts among the Christians and Moslems and established schools for the training of Coptic clergy. They also established hospitals and attempted primarily to reach Moslems. They did attract a handful of converts, among them also Copts. It is said about the Coptic Patriarch Kyrillos IV that before his consecration, he used to attend regularly the Bible lectures given by one of the *C.M.S.* missionaries, J.R.T. Lieder. It has been suggested that Kyrillos IV had iconoclastic tendencies as a result of his training by the English missionaries.[69]

The leading Protestant mission in Egypt, however, was that of the United Presbyterian Church of North America, which began mission work in 1854. The Coptic patriarch showed great appreciation for the Sunday school work that was set up by the missionaries and even once attended. In 1865, however, much to the chagrin of the Coptic patriarch, they began work in what was considered the capital city of the Copts, Assiut. He then began to perceive in their activities a great threat to the unity of the church and warned against Protestant propaganda.

Protestants were unable to gain the support of the vice-regent and later Khedive, Isma'il (1836-1879), or from Patriarch Demetrius (1862-1870), as they had from Kyrillos IV and Sa'id, who were seen by the American mission as patrons. Demetrius viewed the work of the American mission as a serious threat to the unity of his church. The patriarch had Protestants beaten or thrown in jail, according to one of the Protestant missionaries. He had a ban read in all the churches sharply warning Copts against Protestant propaganda. He prohibited his churches from selling land to Protestants. The government supported the measure taken by the Coptic church by laying obstacles in the way of the Protestant mission and hindering the construction of a prayer house.[70]

During the patriarchate of Demetrius there was a fairly widespread positive response to the Protestant mission (United Presbyterian U.S.A.) among the Copts in the Nile valley, especially in Assiut and Minyah. Many Copts joined the Protestant mission churches, because they were dissatisfied with the ecclesiastical laxity and political intrigues within the Coptic church. Demetrius, who saw in the Protestant mission the potential threat of rapid growth, excommunicated the members of the 'heretical' church.[71]

In 1875, in spite of persecution by the Copts and the civil authorities, there were approximately 600 Protestant church members from Alexandria to Assiut. In 1878 a secular head was appointed for the Protestants. In 1880 the new Protestant church had two Egyptian pastors, 161 associate workers and 985 communicant members. In 1895 the number of church members had grown to 4,554. This increase consisted almost entirely of Copts. The American mission also had a number of schools, the most important among them being the college in Assiut. In 1895 a presbytery was formed that was elevated in 1899 to a Synod with four presbyteries.[72]

With the British occupation of Egypt in 1882 and the new situation it brought about, the Anglicans of the *C.M.S.*, which had left Egypt in 1842, returned. This time, like the Americans, their objective was to establish new churches. In 1925 the *Episcopal Church* was established in Egypt.

Ninety-nine percent of Egyptian 'evangelicals' are former Copts. It has been said, with reason, that the mission efforts contributed to a reawakening of the Coptic church. Reform-minded young people viewed the Coptic clergy with contempt because of their ignorance and lack of education. The foreigners, in turn, were accused of wanting to split Coptic churches.[73] The Protestants, for their part, accused the Coptic church of being 'dormant', to which a Coptic priest once replied: "Do you call it love when you rob us of our children while we are sleeping?"

The Moslems too viewed the Coptic converts to the evangelical churches with suspicion since they thought that it was their intention to lend support to the occupying powers in order to provide them with a indigenous group other than the Moslems with which to do business.[74]

Once known as the *United Presbyterian Synod of the Nile*, whose first gathering took place in 1899, the evangelical Christians in Egypt gained ecclesiastical independence in 1957 with the establishment of the Coptic Evangelical church. In 1963 this church was accepted into the *World Council of Churches*.[75] Their membership is currently listed as 100,000.[76]

NOTES

1. Cf. Hitti, 1966, 344.

2. Meinardus, 1983, 68-91.

3. Meinardus, 1961, 285-87; Atiya, 23; Meinardus 1987, 58.

4. Atiya, 28,29; O'Leary 1957, 15, 20.

5. See Galey.

6. C.W. Griggs, *Early Egyptian Christianity: From Its Origins to 451 C.E.* Leiden etc. 1990, 229.

7. Meinardus, 1961, 26; Atiya, 43-45, 54.

8. Arberry I, 440.

9. Meinardus, 1983, *passim*.

10. Meinardus, 1961, 118, 161, 163, 173, 204; O'Leary, 27; Iris Habib el-Masri, 153-55.

11. Arberry I, 1969, 440.

12. Meinardus, 1961, 287, 384.

13. Waddell, 20, 22, 30, 31, 75; cf. Chitti.

14. Waddell, 127; Ward 1981, 10.

15. Waddell, 161. Cf. Micah 6:8

16. Ward, 1981, 12.

17. Ward, 1981, 12.

18. Schwarz-Bart.

19. Ward, 1981, 60.

20. Ward, 1987, 57, 58.

21. *E.I s.v.* Qibt; Müller, 123-25

22. Behrens, 7, 11.

23. Müller, 138.

24. Arberry I, 429; Meinardus, 1970, 345.

25. Meinardus, 1970, 347, 360, 364.

26. Atiya, 87-89; Müller, 165; Lane, 554; *E.I. s.v.* Al-Aziz and Al-Hakim; Browne, 61f.; Meinardus, 1970, 177.

27. Atiya, 96; Müller, 165.

28. Atiya, 94f.; Müller, 166; *E.I. s.v.* Saladin.

29. Atiya, 97; Müller, 168; Lane, 554-57.

30. Atiya, 99; *E.I..* Mamluks.

31. Benoist-Mechin.

32. For a reproduction of the Arabic text, cf. Moorehead, 74.

33. Moreh, 41.

34. Arberry I, 426; Behrens, 106; cf. Iris Habib el Misri, 495-89.

35. Al-Jabarti, 47.

36. Behrens, 7, 24f.; Arberry I, 1969, 427; cf. Iris Habib el Masri, 513-18.

37. *E.I. s.v.* Qibt.

38. Arberry I, 1969, 433; Behrens, 32.

39. Behrens, 35, 46f.

40. Behrens, 49-53.

41. Behrens, 82.

42. Behrens, 82.

43. Vatikiotis, 197.

44. Arberry I, 1969, 435; Behrens, 91.

45. Péroncel-Hugoz, 1983, 130.

46. Péronzel-Hugoz, 1983, 171; Horner, 1989, 104.

47. Atiya, 28; Meinardus, 1970, 177, 143; Betts, 129, 150.

48. *Proche Orient Chrétien* 18 (1968): 185-98.

49. *Al-watan-al- 'arabi*, no. 31 (16-23 September 1977): 18-21; *Etudes Arabes*, 49, 99; cf. Péroncel-Hugoz, 1983, 147-72.

50. *Le Monde*, 23/24 June 1980; cf. Péroncel-Hugoz, 1983, 162.

51. *Le Monde*, 21 June 1980.

52. *Le Monde*, 23/24 June 1980.

53. Cf. *The Copts, Christians in Egypt*.

54. *Le Monde*, 21 June 1980.

55. Carter, 241.

56. *E.I. s.v.* Qibt; Müller, 165.

57. Müller, 169.

58. Atiya, 112; Arberry, I, 1969, 450; Behrens, 37f.

59. Atiya, 127.

60. Atiya, 21.

61. Atiya, 93; Behrens, 5.

62. Meinardus, 1992, 107.

63. Meinardus, 1970, 264f.

64. O'Leary, 216f.; Meinardus, 1970, 1,4,6.

65. Meinardus, 1992, 102, 105, 106.

66. Greenfield, 24; Horner, 1989, 32; cf. Perham, 101-13.

67. Latourette, 25; Horner, 1989, 50f.; cf. Carter, 7-9.

68. Horner, 1989, 51; Valognes, 275.

69. Latourette, 25; Meinardus, 1970, 40; Behrens, 38.

70. Behrens, 39; cf. Iris Habib el Masri, 521f.

71. Arberry I, 430.

72. Behrens, 40; Latourette, 26.

73. Behrens, 40, 44; Müller, 234f.

74. Behrens, 68.

75. Arberry I, 1969, 449f.

76. Horner, 1989, 104.

VII. THE ARMENIANS: THE OLDEST CHRISTIAN KINGDOM

You have shown the way of Light to the Armenian people: the great Thaddaeus and Bartholomeus, the enlightened.

The Armenian Liturgy[1]

Introduction

After the story of the foundation of the Armenian church we will deal with the early response of the Armenians to the Moslems. The history of 'Little Armenia', as most relevant for the Armenians in the Middle East, is discussed as well as the position of the Armenians within the Ottoman Empire, including the role of the Protestant Mission and its consequences. Their present-day situation is described in particular in Lebanon.

The Founding of the Armenian Church

The history of the Armenian people can be traced back with certainty to the tenth century B.C. A pious legend locates the first proclamation of the gospel among the Armenians in the apostolic age. The apostle Judas Thaddaeus (44-63), together with the apostle Bartholomew, are said to have been responsible for the first Christianization—by the Syrian Orthodox—of Armenia. Thaddaeus was also then the first patriarch or catholicos (high bishop), as the Armenians refer to this dignitary. On the south side of Mount Ararat (where Noah's ark came to rest, according to Genesis 8:4) stands the Church of St. Thaddaeus, to which thousands of Armenians from Tehran and Tabriz make pilgrimages. The first recorded evidence of Christianity in Armenia is found in Eusebius, from about the year 250.

The actual founder of the Armenian church is Saint Gregory 'the Illuminator', who lived from 240-322. He is also named as the first real patriarch of this church, and his feast is celebrated on 30 September. For that reason it is sometimes referred to as the 'Gregorian' church. In the year 301, Gregory won King Tiridates III 'the Great' to the Christian faith. Thus Armenia became the first nation in which Christianity became the state religion. This occurred twelve years before the Edict of Milan (313), in which Constantine the Great gave recognition to Christianity in the Roman empire.

151

Within the lifetime of Gregory Armenia became a predominantly Christian nation. The first cathedral, in Echmiadzin, near Yerevan (the modern capital of what used to be the Soviet Republic of Armenia), was completed in 303. The church has been rebuilt several times, but always on the same site. By the time he died Gregory was able to leave behind a well organized church. In the year 365 the see of Echmiadzin would declare its independence from Constantinople. In the beginning years, Christianity was more a religion of the aristocracy than of the people. The catholicos was a militant prelate who customarily travelled about the land with a large entourage and a royal battalion. Both the patriarch and the bishop were in the first place ecclesiastical princes and feudal lords. Christian literature was initially inaccessible to the common folk because of the language. In the fifth century, the monk St. Mesrob (Mashtots) established an Armenian alphabet, however, and produced several translations. Before that time the Christian liturgy was available only in Greek or Syriac (Aramaic). These translations placed in the hands of the Armenians an instrument for the development of a separate identity and thus enabled them to withstand the cultural influence of both Persia and Byzantium. The Armenian translation of the Bible was finished in 406 while the definitive Armenian text of the Bible came in 433.[2]

Entangled in war, the Armenians were unable to attend the Council of Chalcedon in 451. At the Synod of Dvin in 506, however, they rejected the declarations of this decisive council. A half century later, they joined the Monophysites, and thereby retained communion with the Coptic and the Syrian Orthodox Churches, who like them had continued to hold to the christological confession of Cyril of Alexandria: the "one incarnate nature of the Word." As with the other Orthodox churches, there were political factors lying behind this 'theological' position. It resulted in resistance to both Rome and Byzantium, to whom they did not wish to submit. The Armenians begin their calendar with the year 522, the year in which they publicly distanced themselves from Byzantium.[3]

Armenians and Moslems

The Islamic conquest overtook the Armenians in 640, and the Armenians were subject to Islamic rule, even though they managed to preserve a measure of independence in the mountains. Arab-Islamic sovereignty remained until the eve of the crusades in 1071.[4]

In spite of Moslem opposition, the Armenians maintained their language, their national identity, and their faith. The famous Armenian Catholicos Hovhannes Otzun, called 'the philosopher' lived in the eighth century. He composed various theological works and introduced disciplinary reforms. He was known as an accomplished diplomat and was able to win various privileges for the Armenians. One frequently told story is that of a meeting with Caliph 'Umar II. Before meeting with the caliph, he dressed himself in the most beautiful ecclesiastical garments. When the caliph asked him if Christ had not taught his followers to dress simply, the catholicos asked to speak to him privately for a moment. He then showed him a tunic of goat's hair that he was wearing underneath his dazzling vestments. The caliph commented that "no human flesh can bear such sobriety without the will of God," and was then ready to grant him whatever he asked. In agreement with the terms of the so-called Treaty of 'Umar—which repealed certain of the discriminating regulations against Christians—'subject' communities were allowed to retain those religious buildings which were in existence at the time of the conquest, although they were required to refrain from building new churches or restoring the old. This standard was not, however, followed in Armenia.[5]

Little Armenia

In the second half of the ninth century the Armenian prince Ashott I (862-890) was granted permission by the 'Abbasids (ruled from 750-1258, with Baghdad as their capital) to establish a new dynasty in the Kingdom of Armenia. He ruled for twenty-five years as the 'prince of princes', and enjoyed the sympathy of both his subjects and the nobles. At the instigation of these nobles, he even received from the 'Abbasid caliph in Baghdad the title of king in 886. He maintained good relations with the caliph, but his kingdom later dissolved. Under the Seljuks (from the beginning of the eleventh century) the country was destroyed and Armenia's independent national existence came to an end. Many Armenians were put to flight by the Turkish Seljuks. They fled to the West, to Sis or Cilicia in the south of modern Turkey. They considered this place favorable for the establishment of a new nation, independent of Byzantium. A new principality was, therefore, established which would last for some three hundred years, until it fell before the Mamluks (1250-1517) in 1375. The new principality of Little Armenia was founded by a descendent of the first Armenian king in 1080. The prince had friendly relations with the crusaders and the nation was even organized somewhat along the lines of the French, semi-feudal example.[6] In Cicilia, the Armenians were prepared to lend troops to the crusader cause, to fight both

Greeks and Turks. The Armenians, became the staunchest allies of the Franks. During the period of the Crusades the Armenians settled in the cities of Syria and Lebanon. During the fourteenth century, many also emigrated to Europe.[7]

The Armenian church experienced periods of both prosperity and decline during the Middle Ages. One of those periods of prosperity was the tenth century, which was, however, immediately followed by a period of decline resulting from the attack of the Seljuks and the Mongolian invasion of Armenia which wrecked destruction on many of the intellectual centers. Some speak of a notable cultural revival of the Armenian kingdom of Cilicia. Cooperation with the crusaders also increased the influence of Latin Christianity. Already before the outbreak of the Crusades, an Armenian bishop was sent to Pope Gregory VII (1073-1085) to express sympathy for the 'holy war' (i.e., the crusade), and to assure him of the support of the Armenians and their church. In 1293 the see of the Catholicos was moved to Sis, in Little Armenia. In 1441, the monk Kirakos was chosen as Catholicos, and the see was once again, with much internal strife, moved to Echmiadzin, although Cilicia continued to possess a patriarchal seat. With him began the series of leaders bearing the title 'Catholicos of all the Armenians'. Echmiadzin means 'the only begotten has descended'. It forms the capital of Armenia and is for the Armenians a holy city. Relics of Gregory the Illuminator (parts of his right arm) are kept there.[8]

In the last decades of the fourteenth century, Armenia felt the destructive consequences of the Mongolian storm. The kingdom of Little Armenia met its demise and the Armenian church suffered heavy losses. During the conquest of the Ottoman sultans, Mehmed II (sultan from 1451 until 1481) and Selim I (sultan from 1512 until 1520), the Armenians endured much suffering as a result of the war between the Turks and the Persians. In 1461 Mehmed II appointed the Armenian Bishop of Bursa as Patriarch with authority over all the Armenians in the empire.[9]

During the time of the Crusades the Armenian Church came into contact with the Roman Catholics. When King Leo II was crowned in 1198 he made the Catholic confession.[10]

In connection with this contact with the pope, and thus with the Roman Catholic Church, in the fourteenth century, the Latin-Christian 'Society of Pilgrim Friars' succeeded in converting a few Armenians to the Roman Catholic Church. The founding of a separate church followed. The Catholic Patriarchate of Cicilia dates back to the appointment of

154

Abraham Ardzivean, the Catholic Bishop of Aleppo, as Catholicos of Sis on 26 March 1740. He later established his see in Bzumar in Lebanon, where the spiritual leadership of the Armenian Catholic church is still located.[11]

In 1960 the number of Armenian Catholics in the Middle East was estimated at 52,000. Today, the approximately 60,000 Armenian Catholics live primarily in the cities of Beirut, Aleppo, Damascus, Istanbul, Cairo, Baghdad and Tehran, as well as in such places as Anjar (Lebanon), Kesab (Syria), and New Julfa (Iran).[12] The current Armenian Catholic Patriarch (since 1976) is Jean Pierre XVII Gasparian.[13]

It was not until the eighteenth century that a renaissance was set in motion in the Armenian church. It began with the restoration of many monastic institutions in Armenia. The monk Mékhithar (Pierre Manouk), an Armenian theologian from Sebasta (died 1749) who had fled from the persecution of the Armenian Patriarch of Constantinople, established a monastery in Modon on the Morea river in 1706. Since he expected a Turkish invasion, he fled with his monks to Venice. There he established an order which became known, after his death in 1749, as the Mekhitarists. He copied scores of classical manuscripts and produced textbooks in grammar, logic, and various other subjects.[14]

Armenians in the Ottoman Empire

Until the beginning of the nineteenth century, the Armenians were known as one of the communities loyal to the Ottoman empire (*millet-i-sadaqa*). At that time Russia annexed Transcaucasia as far as the Arar River. This brought an important region of the former Greater Armenia, including the Armenian capital of Echmiadzin, within the realm of Russian Orthodox Christianity.[15]

The Armenians lived, like other Christian communities, under the *millet* system in the Ottoman empire, although with a greater measure of self-government. Further privileges were gained by the *Hatti-Sherif* of Gülhane in 1839 and through the constitution of 1863, which assured the Armenians of a semi-independent state within the framework and under the sovereignty of the Ottoman state. The Russian conquest of the Caucasus and the creation of Russian Armenia along the eastern border with Turkey brought about a change in this situation. In addition, new nationalistic and liberal ideas began to trickle in from Europe. These and several other factors gave tremendous impetus to the Armenian national movement. The Turks, however, viewed it as a deadly threat. They had al-

155

ready unwillingly surrendered large tracts to the Serbs, Bulgars, Albanians and Greeks. Unlike these, however, the Armenians did not live separately from the Turks, but among them in the same villages. For centuries they had peacefully coexisted.

In 1822, the *Basler Mission* began the work of evangelizing the Armenians in the city of Shusha, Turkey. This work was prohibited by the Armenian church in 1835. In 1831 the Congregationalist *American Board of Commissioners for Foreign Missions* initiated comprehensive work in Turkey—first in Istanbul, and later in the whole of Anatolia. They established schools and hospitals, produced literature, and founded a theological seminary. Their work in Turkey, Armenia, and Kurdistan began with the arrival of William Goodall (1792-1867) in Constantinople. The missionary H.G.O. Dwight (1803-1862) made a trip from Constantinople to East Turkey. He remained there in the capital city in order to work among the Armenians. On 9 June 1831 Goodall was transferred from Malta to Constantinople and the first mission post of the *American Board* was founded among the Armenians. At the time, the Armenian population in the capital stood at 100,000. Goodall was to begin his work as soon as the Armenian-Turkish version of the New Testament (written with Turkish and Armenian script) was published. The goal of the *American Mission* was "to bring the national Armenian or Gregorian Church to renewal, to deliver [it] from formalism and to accustom [it] to the preaching of the gospel." It was repeatedly declared by the *American Board*, that they had no intention of causing a split in the Church. As the secretary of the American Board, James L. Barton, stated:

In order that misunderstanding might be cleared up, it should be stated that missionaries to the Armenians and Greeks were not sent to divide the churches or to separate out those who should accept education and read from the Bible in the vernacular. Their one supreme endeavor was to help the Armenians and the Greeks carry out a quiet but genuine reform in their respective churches.

Goodall did not feel called to conduct an open attack on the Armenian church. His purpose was to place a leaven within the existing ecclesiastical organization in the knowledge that the movement toward a pure church would never arise from the church itself. The reformation of the entire Armenian Church appeared achievable to them. The Armenian laity were open to European progress and training. The scholarly priest Gregorius Peshtimalijian, called by some 'the Erasmus of the Armenian reformation', established a seminary in 1829. Many of his students were members of an evangelistic movement. Missionaries enjoyed cordial relations with the Armenian church structure. This situation soon changed,

156

however, perhaps because it was feared that the hierarchy would lose authority as a result. In 1843, an Armenian confessed, apparently 'under duress', to being a Turk, i.e., a Moslem. Later, however, he retracted this confession, and confessed once again his Christian faith. For reverting from Islam, he was put to death by the authorities, which at that time was an offense punishable by death. The British ambassador in Constantinople at the time, Sir Stratford Canning, raised the matter, and did not let it rest until he received on 22 March 1844 the promise that reverting would no longer be punishable by death.[16]

The mission was not fueled by the *American Board* alone, however. The Anglicans also played a role. Originally the Episcopalians, under Horatio Southgate, expressly did not wish to work among the Armenians in order to avoid interfering with the *American Mission*. This position changed, however, in 1844. The confessional lines of the Presbyterians and the Anglicans differed, even though they were in agreement with respect to social work and education. While the missionaries of the *American Mission* had as their objective to win proselytes among the Armenians, the Anglicans sought simply to reform the churches of the East. Southgate, who later did work among the Armenians, took upon himself the role of defender of the Armenian church and warned the Armenians against the evangelical Christian influence (i.e. that of the American Presbyterians). He pointed out to the Armenians that the evangelicals knew nothing of the traditional fasts, holy days, and historic Christian practices, and wanted nothing to do with that which the Eastern churches considered essential, such as bishops, confirmation and liturgy. On these latter considerations the Anglicans, in his opinion, stood in opposition to the Presbyterians.[17]

From 1841 on the Armenian Gregorian Church opposed its evangelical members. In 1839 a development occurred in Constantinople which left no doubt that there would be a split with the Protestant-minded Gregorian Christians. The first Armenian Evangelical Church among the Armenians separated and was established in Constantinople on 1 July 1846. Although 'Protestant' was not the name they chose for themselves, they were excommunicated by the mother church. The European ambassadors exercised an important degree of influence on the sultan on behalf of the Christians in the Ottoman empire. Sir Stratford Canning, who possessed great influence during the entire first half of the nineteenth century, went to great lengths to have the sultan recognize a separate Protestant *millet* in the Ottoman empire. Through the intervention of Lord Cowley, Canning's successor as British ambassador, the sultan granted

157

permission on 19 November 1847 for the creation of ecclesiastical independence for the Protestant Armenians. In 1850, a *firman* of the sultan placed Protestants on the same footing as other Christian bodies. In 1853 Christian subjects were given equality with Moslems and in 1856 the sultan granted full freedom of conscience and religious faith.[18]

Chapourian says with respect to this separation, that in spite of its perhaps original intent:

The clearer statement of their purposes to the Armenian Church might not have avoided the separation that came, but would have helped them not to think one thing and do another. ... The good they did would have been the same. In fact, a fair evaluation of the total work of the missionaries demonstrates that their contribution to the spiritual, intellectual, and social life of Armenians in the Ottoman Empire is incalculable.[19]

The struggle that would be ignited between Turks and Armenians, the nadir of which was the mass murders of 1915 and 1916, was actually "a struggle between two nations for the possession of a single land."[20]

By the time Sultan Abdul Hamid took power in 1876, the Armenian question had turned bitter. The sympathy that existed in Europe for the Armenians simply enraged the sultan all the more. With pronounced similarity to the events of the 1970's and 1980's, underground groups developed among Armenian youths in Armenia and abroad with the goal of bringing about an independent Armenia.[21]

The mass murders spread between 1894 and 1896. European intervention was counted on but never came. The Turkish authorities were also implicated in the Kurdish attack on the Armenians in the region around Diyarbakir (in modern Eastern Turkey). The Turkish army intervened, with the professed goal of putting an end to the fighting, but in fact assisted in the burning of various Armenian villages and the murder of their inhabitants. In 1895 the sultan gave permission for a bloody mass murder in which approximately 80,000 Armenians in Trebizond and the bordering provinces were killed. In response, the Ottoman bank in Istanbul was set ablaze by the Armenian underground movement in 1896. Innocent Armenians in secluded villages bore the fallout of this event. More than 6,000 Armenians lost their lives in two days. In 1905 another mass murder took place, this time in Cilicia, in which 20,000 Armenians died. From these incidents it is evident that the mass murders of 1915 and 1916 were but the final chapter in a much longer history of persecution.[22]

In 1908 the political movement within the Ottoman Empire known as the "Young Turks" took power. Initially a feeling of optimism and the

hope for new freedoms predominated, but the Young Turks quickly e-
volved into extreme nationalists. Their objective was to build a Turkish
nation in the ethnic sense of the word. The prerequisite, however, was
the extermination of the 'unassimilable minorities'. On 24 April 1915
254 Armenian intellectuals were arrested in Istanbul and nearly all of
them were executed. The events of 24 April and the ensuing days, which
were labelled 'genocide', were viewed as a contrived plot. On the face of
it, it was a relocation of the Armenian population to Aleppo in Syria.
Columns of women, children and the elderly were attacked. Only fifty
thousand Armenians arrived in Syria. The deportation resulted in approximately one million victims out of the 1,200,000 Armenians living in
the eastern provinces. Other Armenians fled to the Caucasus mountains.[23] Ankara never officially recognized the reality of the genocide
and explains it as a massive deportation of population for security reasons. A hundred thousand are thought to have died because of illnesses.

On paper, the American president Woodrow Wilson (1856-1924) and
the allies established a new Armenian republic between Trebizond and
Van. The Treaty of Sévres, signed on 10 August 1920, recognized Armenian independence. But this would prove to be of very short duration.
The future of Armenia was decided on the battlefield between the armies
of Russia and Turkey. The shortlived independence of Armenia (1919-
1921) was brought to an end in an offensive launched by Mustafa Kemal
Ataturk. The Soviet Union and Turkey divided Armenia between themselves. In the Treaty of Lausanne in 1923, at which this was arranged,
no mention was made of Armenian independence.[24]

Like the general population, the Patriarch of Cicilia was deported
during the First World War. In 1921 the Catholicos established his head-
quarters in Antelias, a little to the north of the Lebanese capital, Beirut.
That is the reason why there are two important patriarchates today, the
one having its center at Echmiadzin, and the other in Antelias. There are
also patriarchates which have been in existence for centuries in Istanbul
(since 1458, and especially since 1461) and Jerusalem (since 1311).[25]

After the mass murders of the Armenians in 1895/1896, an organization was founded in England called *Friends of Armenia*. At the same
time the *Deutsche Orientmission* of Dr. Lepsius was organized in Germany and was directed toward Islam. The mission was centered in Urfa,
formerly Edessa. The celebrated author, Franz Werfel, recounted for the
public at large the horror of the mass murders perpetrated against the
Armenians by the Turks in 1915 and 1916 in gripping fashion in the nov-

Armenians by the Turks in 1915 and 1916 in gripping fashion in the novel *The Forty Days of the Musa Dagh*. Franz Werfel is said to have based his book on the reports of Dr. Lepsius.

Aurora Mardiganian also related in her *Sold Souls* the indescribable atrocities:

Orders will soon come from Constantinople: you Christian dogs must leave; no man, woman or child who denies Mohammed may remain here. ... In Van they are about the slaughter: men, women and children are being hacked to pieces. The Kurds steal the little girls ....

Someone said that the sultan had commanded

that no Christian living in Turkey must remain alive and that he thought that the Sultan was right. ... One imam, or prayer reader, had come from Trebizonde for the express purpose of reading certain prayers that were composed precisely for such a great event as the beginning of a holy war or the massacre of Christians.[26]

The *Christoffel Blinden Mission* was established in Malatia, and later in Iran.

In 1922 Father Dr. Berron established *Action Chrétien en Orient* in Strasbourg for the Armenians and for the mission work in Syria. In France, the ACO again organized the Armenian Evangelical church among the Armenian refugees living there.[27] The ACO is still active in the Middle East.

The Present-Day Spread of the Armenians

When the Armenian patriarch was asked in the early eighties how many Armenians were still living in Turkey, he replied: "The deeper you dig, the more you find." What he meant by this was that since the massacres of 1915/1916, those Armenians who had neither died nor fled went 'underground', keeping their identity a secret by converting to Islam, changing their names, just as the Maran Jews in Spain once concealed their Jewish identity behind a Christian exterior. Armenians are today spread throughout the Middle East, for example, in Nicosia on the island of Cyprus.

It is very difficult to give any firm estimate as to the number of Armenians in Turkey. In a country where by the end of last century the percentage of Christians consisted of about 30% of the population (this included of course also the Greeks) divided among some fifteen denominations, there are some families to be found living in Anatolia, but only 3,000 at the most. In Istanbul they are more numerous, some 50,000 where they are organized and have churches, clergy and bishops as well as the patriarch. Statistics which are given for the whole of Turkey indicate 52,000 Armenian Gregorian Christians and 4,000 Armenian Catholic Christians.[28]

The Armenians in Iran can be found (besides in Tehran) in an Armenian quarter called New Julfa, near Isfahan, where they have lived since the seventeenth century when Shah 'Abbas the Great used them to help build the city of Isfahan. New Julfa, with a total of 210,000 members, is the largest Christian community (more or less three-fourths of the total) in Iran.[29] Armenians can also be found in Tabriz, the capital of Azerbaijan.

Armenian contacts with Egypt date back to the eleventh century, when an Armenian functioned as minister for the caliph. Today their number there is estimated at 12,000.[30] In Syria, the Armenians are found principally in Aleppo and Damascus. At the present time there are still some 100,000.[31]

In Iraq Armenians are to be found in Baghdad. According to recent statistics, there are 14,000 Armenians living there.[32] There is also an active Armenian community in Amman, the capital of Jordan.[33]

A small Armenian community still exists in Israel. In the old city of Jerusalem there is an Armenian quarter, concentrated around the Church and Monastery of St. James. Currently there are 1,200 and 2,600 Armenians respectively within the 1948 borders of Israel and the occupied territories.

In Lebanon Armenians today make up seven percent of the population, some 200,000 people. Numerically speaking, the Armenian community in Lebanon is comparable to that of the Druze and the Greek Orthodox.[34] Armenian refugees who had sought refuge in great numbers in Syria and Lebanon settled in the Beqa'a Valley in the city of Anjar. Most of the remainder of the Armenians live in the city of Beirut and in the Burj Hammoud suburb. The Armenians occupy seven parliamentary seats distributed over three parties, namely, the Dashnak (Social Democratic), Ramgavar (Liberal), and Hunschak (Socialist) parties. Until the outbreak of the Lebanese civil war in 1975, there were sixty Armenian elementary schools, high schools, and colleges in Lebanon, along with the so-called Haigazian college. There were also twenty Armenian churches, four Armenian newspapers, and more than a dozen Armenian weeklies, monthlies, and quarterlies. The Armenians play an important role, albeit from behind the scenes, in the business life of Beirut.

During the civil war of 1975 and the following years, the Armenians attempted to remain neutral. This was not viewed with favor, especially by the Maronite-dominated militia of the Falangists. This became apparent in an almost symbolic way at the end of October 1979, when an Armenian monument was blown up in the city of Ameriya, along the road to Bikfaya, the village where the founder of the Falangists, Pierre Jemayyil (father of the assassinated Bashir Jemayyil and of Amin Jemayyil, president of Lebanon from 1982 through 1988) made his residence. The sad part of this affair was that the monument had been dedicated as an expression of appreciation to Lebanon for its acceptance of the Armenians fleeing the mass murders in Turkey. On the base of the monument was inscribed: "As a sign of gratitude to Lebanon who received us after the Turkish mass murders of 1915." Pierre Jemayyil and his son Amin visited the Armenian Catholicos, Khoren I (died 1983), immediately after the incident in order to condemn the attack, at which time he again emphatically praised the Armenian contribution to Lebanon.

Today nearly six million Armenians live throughout the world. According to statistics from 1979 there were some 2,726,000 Armenians in Armenia and an additional 1,500,000 within the other former Soviet republics (Azerbijan, 650,000; Georgia, 600,000; Russia, 350,000). There are also some 500,000/600,000 Armenians living in the United States and 350,000 in France.[35]

The current number of members in a country like the Netherlands stands at 3,500. In this last country there were during the seventeenth century a few hundred Armenians as a result of trade with the Levant. From 1714 until 1856 there was an Armenian congregation and an Armenian church in Amsterdam on the Kromboomsloot (which was reopened on 26 November 1989). In 1660 an Armenian publishing press was founded in Amsterdam which published for 57 years and was 'free from Roman Catholic restrictions', unlike the state of affairs in the rest of Europe. In 1666 the first illustrated Armenian Bible was published in Amsterdam, a fact memorialized on a cornerstone of the church building on the Kromboogsloot.[36]

A Unique Contribution

Since its founding, the church has been both a refuge and a symbol for the Armenians, whether believers or unbelievers. The Armenian national identity is inextricably bound up with the church. The church continues to this day to be the single most important unifying factor for the Armenian people, more important than any political party or organization.[37]

The Armenians have always assumed a very unique place among the Orthodox churches of the Middle East. They have maintained their own language not only in the liturgy, but also in the literature and in their daily lives, even in Arab lands. They have their own style of church architecture, which makes them immediately recognizable as Armenian. While living in the diaspora, they have made an evident contribution to global culture in all areas, whether it be the literature of Henri Troyat or the well-known Armenian American author William Sorayan, or the music of the popular singer Charles Aznavour(ian).

It is not possible to review the frequently dramatic history of the Armenian church without making mention of what the current Catholicos in Antelias, Kerekin Sarkissian, is noted for having said, namely that martyrology has become another name for Armenian historiography.[38] Nor is it possible to experience the liturgy of the Armenian Church without detecting a moving echo of the centuries of suffering of this the first great Christian nation.

NOTES

1. Steck, 17.

2. Atiya, 312, 322; Carby, 225; Horner, 1989, 25.

3. Atiya, 326-34; Van Aalst, Macererian; Sanjian.

4. Atiya, 309, 329f.; Macererian, 89f.

5. Atiya, 309, 329f.; cf. Macererian, 89f.

6. Arberry I, 1969, 309f.; *E.I. s.v.* Armenia.

7. Arberry I, 1969, 258f.; Fiey 1975, 103.

8. Atiya, 332f., 335.

9. Jacob, 2.

10. *Kleines Wörterbuch des christlichen Orients.* (J. Assfalg, P. Krüger), 46.

11. Arberry I, 254; II, 519.

12. Horner, 1989, 46; Arberry II, 1969, 521.

13. Horner, 1989, 48.

14. Sanjian, 71f., 337 n.2.

15. Atiya, 310f.

16. Shaw, 34; Chopourian, 1.

17. Atiya, 339; Shaw, 46f., 69.

18. Atiya, 339f.; Shaw, 89; Kawerau, 326, 496f.; Barlett, 13; Chopourian, 118.

19. Chapourian, 47.

20. Lewis, 1968b, 356.

21. Atiya, 311.

22. Nobecourt; Atiya, 312; *Armenia*, 1984.

23. Nobecourt; Charby, 232; Macererian; Boyajian; cf. Jacob, 1994, 305.

24. Aitya, 335; Charby, 233; *Armenia* 1984; *Lexikon, s.v.* Christen.

25. Atiya, 335; *Lexikon, s.v.* Christen.

26. Mardiganian, 7f., 20,22.

27. *R.G.G. s.v.* Armenien III.

28. Jacob, 4, 5, 7.

29. Horner, 1979, 151f.; Horner, 1989, 105.

30. Horner, 1989, 104.

31. Horner, 1989, 115.

32. Horner, 1989, 106.

33. Horner, 1989, 108.

34. Sarkisian, 34.

35. Nobecourt; Horner, 1974; *Armenia* 1984.

36. Sanjian, 72, 338.

37. *Le Monde*, 6 March 1981.

38. Sarkissian, 34.

VIII. ALIENS AT HOME: THE ROLE OF MISSION FROM THE WEST

I am convinced that the missionary movement of the Church of Christ, for all its many defects and faults, has done more good to mankind than any other single movement in history.

Hassan Dehqani Tafti[1]

Introduction

It has frequently been the assumption of Protestant churches in the West that the Orthodox churches have not been 'mission' churches. Such an assumption overlooks the fact that over the centuries the Orthodox churches have been the source of extensive missionary activities. Already in the third and fourth centuries the 'mission' of the Orthodox churches had reached Persia and India. This expansion of the Christian faith through the mission of the Orthodox churches took not only an easterly, but also a westerly tack. The German tribes were initially evangelized by missionaries from Asia Minor and Byzantium. The same was true of the northerly routes, where the Slavic peoples were 'converted' by Byzantium.

Although the Protestants are not numerous in the Middle East it is worthwhile to discuss the role of the Protestant mission since it is very illustrative for the attitude the churches in the West took and quite often still take towards the churches in the Middle East as well as towards Islam. One can often notice a deep resentment on the part of the Orthodox towards the (Protestant) Christians from the West because of it.

In this chapter, we will explore more in depth the role which the Protestant mission from Europe and the United States have played in the Middle East—some of the Protestant churches have already been mentioned in other chapters—and will examine the impact that Protestants have had up to the present time. We will investigate how the Protestant missionaries in particular during the great missionary era ("The great century," as Scott Latourette called it) saw their mission. How did they judge the Orthodox churches at large and how did they evaluate Islam? What kind of theology of mission inspired them?

Within the context of the new domination of the West (in particular the United States) in the Middle East as became clear again during the

165

Gulf war (1991), it is essential to reflect on these positions from about one century ago because they are still very much with us today (history is repeating itself, as it were) and influence the approach of many Christians from the West until the present.

The predicament into which the Christian mission from Europe and the United States brought the Christians in the Middle East (its alienating function) can be exemplified with the case of Iran in particular. The question must be raised if the above quoted adagium of Hassan Dehqani Tafti can be fully maintained.

Protestant Missionaries

Through the efforts of Western Protestant missions during the last centuries, churches have arisen in various regions of Africa, Asia and Latin America. So too, Protestant missionaries appeared in the Middle East at the appointed time; yet they appeared in an area where the Church was not absent but had existed for centuries! While the goal of the Catholics coming from Europe was 'the reunification' of these Orthodox churches with the Roman Catholic Church (its role has already been reviewed in the treatment of the various Orthodox churches), the mission of the Protestants was directed, at least according to its original express purposes, toward the Christianization of the Moslems.

In the nineteenth century, interest in the East was inspired in no small part by the rebellion of the Greeks against the Turks. The rebellion generated much sympathy in Europe and the United States, and inspired a vision for mission work in the Middle East.

American Protestant missionaries saw the task of missions in relation to the work of divine providence. According to the American missionary Henry H. Jessup (1832-1910) there was a connection between two simultaneous historical events: the appearance of 'the Mohammedan religion'[2] on the one hand and the Christianization of the Saxon race in Great Britain on the other. In his *The Mohammedan Missionary Problem* Jessup attempted to demonstrate clearly how, according to God's plan, there was at that time and would be in the future a providential relation between the Anglo-Saxon Christian race and the Moslem world.[3] Jessup wanted to bring to the attention of both branches of this Anglo-Saxon Christian family, Great Britain and the United States, the fact that divine providence desired that they place their religious and educational resources in the service of the Christianization of the Moslem world.[4] That the Christianization of the Saxon race in Britain coincided precisely with the appearance of Islam was part of the divine plan: it was the remedy for the increasing moral chaos that he saw set in motion through the onset of Islam.[5]

'The Mohammedan Threat'

This negative approach to Islam as the instigator of 'moral chaos' was not unique to this American missionary but was prevalent in the Western attitude toward Islam. Even Sir William Muir, a well-known Scottish orientalist from the previous century, who wrote important groundbreaking studies on, among other things, the life of the prophet Mohammed, did not escape this bias that was so typical of the missionaries of his day: "The sword of Mohammed and the Koran are the most dogged enemies of civilization, freedom and truth that the world has ever known."[6] Pastor F. Würtz of the *Basler Mission* sounded the alarm in a pamphlet against the 'Mohammedan threat' to the indigenous church and to the many pagan areas of West Africa.[7]

It is perhaps worth our time to present some other views that Jessup held in more detail, since they give greater insight into the way in which many Protestant missionaries thought of Islam at the time. They also, unfortunately, can illustrate how in certain circles many still think today.[8] Jessup cited approvingly the British historian Edward Gibbon (1737-1794) who had said that the Islamic confession "There is no God but God and Mohammed is his apostle," contained an eternal truth and an eternal lie. The first problem that Jessup saw lay in the unity that existed in Islam between temporal and spiritual power. When Mohammed and his successors propagated the new faith, the scimitar was the precursor and supporter of the Koran. He viewed this alliance between religion and politics as it also existed in the Turkish empire as the letter and spirit of Islamic law and the fundamental obstacle to the evangelization of the Moslems. Yet according to him it can be said that:

... whatever in the Koran is true was taken from the Bible, and what is not from the Bible is either false or frivolous.
Islam is an intensely formal and ritual system, a religion of works—outward works, not affecting the heart or requiring transformation of the life. ... As their whole idea of *deen* or religion, refers to the outward and ceremonial, they have lost all conception of the spiritual nature of religion. ...

Another undesirable trait that he detects in Islam is the Ishmaelite intolerance. In his view, Mohammed gives people three options: Islam, slavery or death. "Whenever Islam holds the sword it uses it for the oppression and humiliation of all infidels, but when it loses the military control it submits with fatalistic sullenness."[9]

167

Another such feature that Jessup mentions is his belief that Islam destroys the family through polygamy and concubinage. He thought it permissible to judge a religion by its fruit in the life of the family and its treatment of women, and considered Islam a failure by this standard. Another negative trait mentioned was the falsehood of the Moslems. According to Jessup, before evangelical Christianity came to new life, a person who spoke the truth in the East was unheard of. In these days Moslems found an oath of even greater binding force than "by the beard of Mohammed"—namely "by the word of an Englishman" (sic!).

Jessup did not regard only Islam in such a negative way, however. He viewed the Orthodox Christians in the Middle East in the same way. For that reason it was his considered opinion that when the time came for Moslems to convert to Christianity, it would not be conversion to Latin or Greek (Orthodox) Christianity, but to "the simpler and purer form of Protestant evangelical faith."[10]

Religion and Politics

In the last decades insight has been gained into the ambivalent aspects of the relation between the missionary enterprise and colonialism.[11] Apparently, however, it escaped Jessup, as the secretary of the *American Board* said in a letter that in his time mission and colonialism often went hand in hand: "The American missionary has served his country no less than his Master."[12] That he was unaware of these aspects is all the more surprising when one considers that he was well aware of the dangerous aspects of a similar relation between religion and politics in Islam. In fact, when this subject arose with respect to Christianity, he even referred to this relation as something positive. Thus he considers it favorable that in his time there was talk of a dominant and growing influence of Christian nations in Moslem countries. Nearly a third of the Islamic world stood under the domination of what they themselves referred to as 'unbelievers'. Jessup predicted that "when the scimitar falls their confidence in their own system will fall."[13] In so doing he simply expressed the general feeling of superiority common to Westerners of that time. The statement made by the British governor of Egypt, Lord Cromer (from 1883 until 1906), at about the turn of the century is famous: "Reformed Islam is Islam no longer."

When it came to Christianity, Jessup viewed the relationship between religion and politics favorably. No matter how wide spread the Islamic religion might be, it was completely 'surrounded' by Anglo-Saxon, Christian politics and civil rule.[14]

168

The well-known American missionary in the Islamic world, Samuel M. Zwemer (1867-1952), spoke in the same spirit. In 1911 Zwemer noted that the Persian Gulf had practically become 'an English lake'. After all, British governance extended from Aden inland and British influence was great in Oman. He found those conditions very favorable for missions. Therefore he too acknowledged a close connection between politics and missions in the days of colonial expansion. In his view, the banner of the cross had to be unfurled over every province, and any delay would be fatal.[15]

Jessup contended that "more potent than the sermons or the tracts of missionaries has been the silent influence of British merchants." He said that he could give names of examples of those who preserved their integrity in the face of the temptations of commerce, dishonesty and duplicity of the native merchants and officials. For that reason he considered the extraordinary confidence that in his opinion had been placed in the English, along with the recently established British mandate over Asiatic Turkey (apparently referring to the Congress of Berlin; see chapter I) of the highest importance for the future relation between Christianity and Islam. As far as he was concerned, it was no simple coincidence that so many millions of people had given their trust to "the leading Christian colonizing and civilizing power of the world."[16]

'The Pure Gospel'

Protestant missionaries of the time were convinced that Protestant Christianity possessed the purest form of faith in the world. The people and rulers of the Islamic lands had confidence in the American missionaries, as he saw it. According to him, the missionaries had two things to offer the Moslems: the Bible and the Christian religion. There were two missionary tasks: to translate the Bible into Arabic and to establish a pure evangelical church in the Ottoman empire. In this way, the Christian religion could be displayed in all her purity to the Moslems, with a pure morality and religious practice free from idolatry and the worship of creatures. These two tasks were accordingly carried out. He referred to the Arabic Bible translation of Eli Smith (1801-1857) and Cornelis Van Dijck (1818-1895) of 1865. By the providence of God, the appearance of this revised translation of the Bible in the Ottoman empire occurred simultaneously with the signing of the Treaty of Berlin, in which freedom of conscience became law in the Turkish empire.[17] Jessup not only brought the events of the previous century into relation with the providence of God, he thought it possible to connect it with the Islamic religion

169

as well. After all, Moslems believed that in the last days, a universal falling away from Islam would occur. Then the 'true faith' would cease to exist. According to Jessup that meant that every new province that was snatched from Moslem control, every new defeat of Islamic weapons, every new demonstration of Christian superiority in civilization and in moral, intellectual and material progress, were equally potent demonstrations of the rapid approach of the inevitable fall of Islam awaited by Moslems themselves.[18]

Jessup also reflected on the problem of the conversion of Moslems to Christianity. Although the death penalty had in principle been removed, the sword of Damocles still hung over the heads of Islamic converts to Christianity. Jessup hoped, however, that once the last *firman* of the sultan was carried out and Christians were permitted into the army, this regime of terrorism and persecution would come to an end.[19]

At the end of his report, Jessup reminded his readers that when the European powers pledged themselves by treaty in 1856—he meant the peace conference of Paris following the Crimean war—not to interfere in the internal affairs of the Turkish empire, it led to a regime of suffering for the people of Turkey. With the new British policies, however, he saw a definitive end to noninterference. Reflecting in particular on the bloody confrontations in Syria and Lebanon in 1860, he declared that "no more Syrian massacres would take place, no more holocausts, no more human sacrifices in Hasbaya, Deyr al Qamar and Damascus." With the overwhelming defeat administered to the political position of Islam in the Russian-Turkish War and the British War of 1878-1881, Jessup saw the prestige and power of the Moslems quickly slipping away. In his view, Christian missions were being planted in and around the very citadels of Islam.[20]

The American Mission

In 1810, the *International American Board of Commissioners for Foreign Mission*, which was originally Congregationalist (Independent Protestant) and Presbyterian, and later exclusively Congregationalist, was founded in the United States. This *American Board* was composed of Congregational churches in New England along with a few other Protestant churches. In the nineteenth century the board developed a comprehensive missionary program in the Middle East. In the first period, Rufus Anderson, served as the competent and renowned secretary of the Board. The ultimate goal of the *American Board* in the Middle East and elsewhere was to win all peoples for the Kingdom of God. It was their view

170

that the conversion of the Moslem could not be hoped for until the Eastern churches could give an example of true Christianity. Thus a prior mission to the Eastern churches was a prerequisite to the conversion of the Moslems of Asia.[21] Two missionaries of the American Mission: Eli Smith, whom we have mentioned already and H.G.O. Dwight (1803-1862), came to the conclusion after an investigative trip in 1830 and 1831 that the Eastern churches, i.e., the Greek Orthodox, Armenian and Nestorian, would first have to be brought to life. Until such a time, according to them, nothing good would be accomplished for the non-Christians in the Near East.

In the first fifty years of the *American Board*, there were approximately eight mission posts established in Palestine, Syria, Greece, and among the Armenians in Turkey and Armenia, the Nestorians, the Assyrians in East Turkey and Iraq, the Jews and the Moslems. The greatest energies were indeed devoted to Eastern churches, the original goal being to initiate reform. But gradually the realization emerged that this would not occur without the formation of separate evangelical churches. In 1842 Anderson gave his report, and this thought was adopted as a resolution:

The great object of our missions to the Oriental Christian communities should be the revival of spiritual religion, the conversion of souls to Christ, the wide diffusion of the great regenerate idea of justification by faith alone, and not a controversy with the hierarchies of these communities about particular institutions, forms, and ceremonies. Whenever those Oriental churches, having had the Gospel fairly proposed to them, shall reject it, exscinding and casting out from their communion those who receive it, ... then it will be necessary for our missionary brethren to turn from them ... and to call on all God's children to come out from among them and not to be partakers.[22]

The attitude the American missionaries took towards the Orthodox churches and Christians was in fact not new. Christians in Europe had for centuries earlier looked down in similar fashion on their Orthodox brothers and sisters. They viewed them as a 'bedraggled lot' and saw themselves as the rescuers of the holy places. "They gave greater weight to the errors of the Byzantines than to the sins of the Moslems."[23]

The American Theology

If one seeks to understand why the American missionaries conducted themselves in the way they did with respect to the Orthodox churches in the Middle East, then one must be familiar with the theological views they held. The theologians of the *American Board* thought that the Christianity they possessed was pure and original. They did not view them-

171

selves as the adherents of one confession among many, but believed that their own truly 'catholic' confession stood above the rest. When the first missionaries departed for East Asia in 1812, it was impressed upon them that they were not to teach the commandments or dogmas of men, but the pure teaching of the gospel as derived directly from the Scriptures. In 1839 Rufus Anderson instructed the missionaries not to speak to people about holy days, fasts, rites and ceremonies, but to address them as lost sinners who were in need of a Savior. Jesus must be preached to them. He advised that they should do this after the true apostolic fashion of the pilgrims, Puritans and Protestants, who knew the gospel and were able to explain and teach it. Although it was obvious that he was dealing with (white) American missionaries from North America with a Protestant and Puritan background, they pretended and in fact were convinced that they were the truly 'catholic Christians'. According to another American missionary, Isaac Bird, who began work in Beirut in 1823, it had to be impressed upon Christians that they were not disciples of Luther or Calvin or any other human, but of Christ. They were not English Christians, but *evangelical* Christians.[24]

The Thousand Year Reign

A strongly millenarian mindset prevailed among the Christians of the *American Board*. It was hoped that the 'thousand year reign' would be brought closer through the work of missions. They were convinced that from the very first day that the settlers immigrated to New England, they had enjoyed the blessings of the Christian religion. The advantageous difference between the inhabitants of New England and the peoples who lived where 'heathen' influence prevailed was ascribed to the Christian faith. They considered the true biblical religion and American culture to be in essence one and the same, as two sides of the same coin. The spread of the Bible meant at the same time the spread of American institutions and way of life. The democratization and the evangelization of the world were one and the same. They viewed America as a tool in God's hand by which he would achieve his goal. They were the instrument through which God would evangelize the world of the heathen.

This worldview—"the new Jerusalem is impossible without American democracy"—in which the American missionaries were steeped and which gave them the confidence that America had the means by which to accomplish it, could be called a secular version of the millennial hope. It was once again evident to what extent the combination of Christian religion and politics had been positively accepted. Eli Smith warned in con-

172

nection with the millennium that no disobedient Jonah should be allowed to bring disaster down on the 'American Zion'. The efforts of the American churches to increase the number of preachers, establish new churches, or extend the benefits of Christian education, were viewed by him as preparing the way for the universal triumph of the gospel on earth and for the universal outpouring of the Holy Spirit.[25] Eli Smith invited American Christians to realize the final triumph of the gospel in the world, and thereby also the dawn of the millennium, by giving their daily efforts to earn money a new focus. Since mission was in compliance with the divine command, the riches of America would grow as a result. Was God not the provider of temporal prosperity? Was it not his blessing that enriched? In 1837, on the twenty-eighth anniversary of the *American Board*, a decision was taken with respect to the millennium. The Board pointed to the peace that prevailed, the spread of commerce and progress in geographic research throughout the earth as signs of the times: the long-awaited age when the gospel would be preached throughout the world had arrived.[26]

Missions and the Orthodox Churches

Although it may have been the original objective of the missions of both the Anglicans from Great Britain and the Americans to convert the Moslems, as soon as this appeared to be unsuccessful, they in fact turned to proselytizing members of the different Orthodox churches. The British and American missionaries encountered Orthodox churches along their way, but more and more they viewed these churches as obstacles standing in the way of the evangelization of the Islamic world. In any case, there were definite differences of opinion between the British and the Americans, or rather between the Anglican and non-Anglican Protestants (among them Americans) with respect to the task that lay before them.

The American missionary Jessup wrote negatively about all the Eastern churches without exception. Regardless of whether they were Orthodox or Catholic, Chalcedonian or non-Chalcedonian, Monophysite, Greek Orthodox, Maronites, Greek, Armenian or Abyssinian Catholic, or Latins, he regarded them all as 'papal' 'sects'. All these 'sects', he maintained, shared a common truth and a common error. In as much as they all still held to the teaching of transubstantiation, rebirth by baptism, priestly absolution, Mariolatry and the worship of saints, images and paintings (icons), auricular confession and prayers for the dead, they all were in need of reformation. Until that time, they formed an obstacle to the Christianization of the Islamic world.[27] Jessup remembered that the

173

first American missionaries who came to West Asia in 1819 in order to bring the gospel to Moslems were confronted with various Christian 'sects' that were ignorant, superstitious, idolatrous, and hated by the Moslems. The Armenian church was viewed as a fossil. Nevertheless, Jessup contended, these missionaries were given the task of concerning themselves with these Eastern churches, visiting their clergy and if possible convincing them of their errors, which were irreconcilable with the word of God. And so they devoted themselves to the task of instruction, distribution of the Bible and the production of literature.[28] Yet the mission to the Eastern Christians was increasingly seen as the presupposition for the Christianization of Islam. They wanted to convert Jews, Moslems and Christians to 'true Christianity' without distinction. They hoped to succeed in finding in the Orthodox churches those who were 'alive in Jesus Christ' and 'who could be awakened from their slumber and activated in the service of the good'. In their view, the many thousands of 'nominal' Christians in the Middle East lacked knowledge of God and had fallen into superstition and deception. As long as these 'nominal' Christians were not reformed, one could not expect the Moslems to convert to Christianity. It was agreed that the Christians were worse than the Turks. What Jessup meant here was that the conduct, ceremonies and superstition of the Eastern Christians had to inspire in the followers of the false prophet a disgust for the religion of the redeemer. Before the arrival of the Protestant missionaries, the Moslems had never had the opportunity to compare Islam with a form of Christianity that was exemplary enough to allow them to feel shame over their own religion (!). Eastern Christianity had only solicited feelings of contempt from its Islamic environment. He was even of the opinion that in that sense, Eastern Christianity bore the blame for the fact that Islam was still in existence. Eli Smith went one step further. He wondered how such an 'absurd and unclean religion' could emerge and spread itself over the same areas where the apostles had preached, martyrs had bled, and where Christianity had for so long been confessed. He attributed it finally to the fact that the peoples of those areas lacked the sword of the Spirit, the shield of faith. As soon as the religious life of the indigenous Christians was reformed, however, the cornerstone of Islam would fall. This was not Smith's personal conviction but the official view of the *American Board*. In 1838 Rufus Anderson wrote that the goal of the Eastern mission was to reach the Moslems through the revival of the Eastern churches. And he continued to hold to this view, for in 1872 he wrote that the conversion of the Moslem could not be hoped for until the Eastern churches gave them an example of true Christianity. In other words, he sought first a mission among the Eastern churches, and then a plan for the conversion of the Moslems in West Asia.[29]

With the reform of the Eastern churches was meant the transformation of the Eastern churches from the inside out. In 1838 Rufus Anderson declared that the goal of the mission to the Eastern churches was to reawaken the knowledge of the spirit of the gospel among them. They had to come to realize how 'miserable' they were; they had to be given living examples of the gospel, both in its spiritual nature and in its beneficial influence on individuals and nations. The intent of the Reformation was to bring the understanding to new life, not to transplant Congregationalism or Presbyterianism. The same church structures could remain in existence as long as the knowledge of the spirit of the gospel could be brought back to life. The intention was that the 'converted Christians' would remain in their own Orthodox churches. Only in those cases where they were excommunicated by their own churches, or for reasons of conscience could no longer belong to them, could they be accepted into the mission church. It was a question of saving souls, not of making proselytes for one's own confession.[30]

A similar intent was also expressed by the Archbishop of Canterbury in 1886 in a letter to the Greek Orthodox Patriarch in Antioch. In it he declared that the purpose of the mission of the two priests was not to lead the Assyrian Christians (= Nestorians) among whom they were working to the Anglican church, nor to attack the customs and ecclesiastical traditions, nor to bend certain confessed doctrines which are not in contradiction with the faith as taught by the councils of the undivided church. The purpose was, on the contrary, to encourage these Christians to improve their religious condition and to lend support to an ancient church which ignorance had consumed from within and persecution had attacked from without and thus prevented from maintaining itself alone.[31]

The proposal which the American missionaries had made regarding the missionary infiltration of the Eastern churches, however, would not succeed. The converted Eastern Christians found no occasion to work as leaven within the churches, since they were excommunicated by their respective churches. And so the work led not to reform and revival but to schism and separation. That resulted on the one hand in a weakening of the Eastern churches through loss of members, and on the other in changing the missionaries from 'friends and brotherly helpers' into open enemies of the ancient churches.[32]

A Separate Protestant Church

In September of 1835, the preachers Dr. Eli Smith and Dr. W.M. Thomson (1806-1894) and other missionaries assumed the following position in response to the request of a Greek Catholic priest from Akko to confess the Protestant faith:

1. It is not an object with us to draw individuals from other native Christian sects and thereby increase our own denomination.
2. Yet according to the principles of the churches who have sent us hither, when a member of any native sect, giving satisfactory evidence of piety, desires the sacraments of us, we cannot refuse his request, however it may interfere with his previous ecclesiastical relations.

On this basis individuals of the various Oriental churches, including bishops, priests, and others, were received to the Lord's table, together with baptized converts from the Druzes.[33] They requested a separate Protestant church, and this request was finally granted. The first Protestant church was constituted in 1848.[34]

The majority of the members of these Protestant congregations (at the end of the nineteenth century 175 parishes with 20,000 communicant members and nearly 100,000 baptized members) were undoubtedly from the Eastern churches. Jessup, as was mentioned earlier, pointed out that the Anglican churches had assumed a different position than the American Presbyterian missionaries. The Anglicans labelled the entire movement a mistake. They viewed it as proselytism and an attempt to build one church at the expense of another. Rather than responding to this charge, Jessup followed with a countercharge: "Et tu Brute?"[35] He maintained—and not without reason—that the Anglicans too had departed from their original stated purpose. Jessup correctly stated that the primary and ultimate goal of the mission work in West Asia was the conversion of the Moslems to the Christian faith, but since the Moslems were only familiar with the Eastern type of Christianity, they despised its immorality and idolatry, and protested against the worship of creatures and images (icons) in both the Greek Orthodox and the Latin churches. But no matter how much missionaries might protest and declare, it would do no good, Jessup contended, unless he was able to present to the Moslems a pure Christianity in doctrine and life, and to illustrate by means of living examples the biblical ideal of a Christian church.[36]

Just how negative and void of sympathy his view of the Orthodox churches was is evident from a description he once rendered of an Orthodox worship service, calling it a painful and nauseating spectacle of praying masses who burned incense, lit candles and bowed before "the dirty painted boards and then devoutly kissing them and crossing themselves." Jessup accused the Greek Orthodox church of divinizing the virgin Mary, thus justifying the charge of crass polytheism brought by Mohammed against the Christianity of his day. He called this Mariolatry of the Greek and Latin churches a rock of stumbling for the entire Islamic world. As he saw it, the Greek Orthodox church stood condemned as polytheistic, idolatrous and unscriptural by its own authority wielding symbols, and therefore deserved all the accusations leveled against the abominations of Rome by Huss, Luther, Wycliff and Knox. Jessup referred to the Protestants in the Middle East, the 20,000 confessing members of the Protestant churches in the Turkish empire, as "liberated prisoners," "the Sierra Leone and Free Town in this dark Africa of Eastern sacerdotalism." It was a joy for the Christian mission to be able to extend to such people a warm and brotherly welcome. He thought it imperative to make clear to the Moslems to what extent the Protestant churches differed from the "idolatrous Eastern churches." If a Protestant were to affiliate with such an "image-worshipping church," he would neutralize his influence among the Moslems. "Let Protestant Christianity keep her white garments free of the defilement of the unholy practices of these fallen and unspiritual systems of the East." According to Jessup, the Eastern churches had lost the necessary spirit for evangelizing the Moslems. The time had now come for this privilege to be taken from them and to be given to another, i.e., to the churches of the Reformation.[37]

Independent Churches and Converts

Protestant churches were formed already at an early stage of the mission, the first consisting primarily of missionaries and their family members. The Eastern churches were very impressed by the Sunday observance of the missionaries. As Eli Smith put it, they accused the missionaries of being Jews. Among the first Protestant converts were three Armenians (1827), two Greek Orthodox, one Greek Catholic, and two Maronites. The brothers As'ad and Faris al-Shidyaq were regarded as having been reborn in Christ. Of the two, As'ad al-Shidyaq (1797-1839) has become the better known. Isaac Bird dedicated a book to this 'martyr of Lebanon'.

As'ad al-Shidyaq was born in 1797 in Hadath (near Beirut), and was in the service of various Maronite patriarchs. In 1825 he wrote a response to an pamphlet published by the American missionaries, but in that same year he offered his services in Beirut to the missionaries as an Arabic instructor. Initially he was not accepted, but Jonas King (1792-1869) took him on as a Syriac instructor. When threatened with excommunication by the patriarch, he was forced to end his relationship with the missionaries. He was, however, plagued by conscience and returned to Beirut later in the year to remain in the service of Isaac Bird. When visiting the patriarch, he was held in confinement, fled, and was later again violently apprehended and returned to the patriarch, where he was not to be persuaded. In spite of abuse, he did not recant his Protestant faith. In October 1830 he died in his cell, according to reports, of fever.

At the beginning of 1844 Hashbaija, 35 kilometers to the southeast of Sidon was the backdrop for the establishment of the first indigenous Protestant congregation on West Asian soil. A half dozen members of the Greek Orthodox church separated themselves on 26 February 1844, declared themselves Protestants, and requested religious instruction from the *American Mission*. In 1848 the Pasha of Damascus gave the command to grant the Protestants free exercise of religion.

In 1851 a separate Protestant church was organized. The son of an Armenian convert, Gregor Wardapet, who had worked for three years already in Hashbaija, now became the pastor there. In 1851 the congregation numbered 25 members. To the first six Protestant congregations, which were established before May 1848, belonged Constantinople, Nicodemia, Ada, Basar, Trapezunt, 'Aintab and Beirut. The congregation in Beirut was established on 8 February 1848. At the end of 1849, the congregation numbered 27 members: 10 Greek Orthodox, 4 Greek Catholics, 4 Maronites, 5 Armenians, 3 Druzes and 1 Jacobite.[38]

Generally speaking, one must distinguish between the expectations attached to the efforts of the Protestant mission in general and its actual achievements, especially when it comes to converts. After in some cases a lifetime of work, there were still only a few thousand 'true Christians', as they were called, in contrast to millions of continuing 'nominal Christians' and Moslems. In that sense, the 'Syrian mission' did not meet with success.[39]

The Role of the Protestant Mission in Iran

The role of the Protestant mission of the last century two centuries—especially that of the British and Americans—and how it related to the political realm can be illustrated by means of the example of Iran.

Before the Islamic revolution of 1979, the number of Christians in Iran, excluding foreigners, was not even one percent of the population. The majority of Christians (210,000) were Armenians, who lived primarily in New Julfa, near Is-

178

fahan, and in Tehran. Other significant groups of Christians were the Nestorians or Assyrians, with a total of 15,000, and the Chaldeans, who are affiliated with Rome, numbering 1,500. The Protestants are primarily found in two churches: the evangelical Protestants with 3,000 and the Episcopalians (or Anglicans) with 2,600, the half of whom were foreigners before the Iranian revolution of 1978/79.[40]

It is worthwhile in this connection to give special attention to the insights of the Anglican Bishop Hassan Dehqani Tafti. When in the summer of 1979, after an Iranian Protestant pastor, himself a convert from Islam, was murdered, an attempt was made in that same fall to assassinate this Anglican bishop and his wife in Isfahan. Although they managed to escape with their lives, his secretary, Jean Waddel, was wounded in an attack on 1 May 1980, and on 24 May 1980 the son of the bishop, Bachram Dehqani Tafti was murdered after being kidnapped in Tehran.

In order to understand the nature of the problem of the mission in the Middle East in general and of the Presbyterian and Anglican Protestant missions to Persia in particular, it is important to reflect on the example of this bishop and his own analysis of the situation of his church in Iran. He now lives outside Iran and will not be able to return for the foreseeable future.

The church of Hassan Dehqani Tafti was the fruit of British Anglican mission work and was hindered for a long time in becoming a true indigenous church. When the first Synod of this church gathered in Yezd in 1933, all the delegates, with but one exception, were foreigners. It was not until 1963 that the leadership of this church passed into Iranian hands through the appointment of Hassan Dehqani Tafti. In that same year he was consecrated bishop in Jerusalem, to be crowned later in Isfahan.[41]

Eleven years later, in 1972, this bishop would be introduced to the Shah during the festivities surrounding the 2500th anniversary of the Persian monarchy. At the time this was seen as a sign that the Protestant churches had become part of the religious life of Iran.[42] But was that an accurate assessment?

Some thirty years ago, Hassan Dehqani Tafti, who had a Moslem father and a Christian mother, wrote a book about his conversion to the Christian faith entitled *Design of My World*. This title was inspired by one of the largest squares in the city of Isfahan, where he resided for years as bishop. His desire was to provide his readers with the pattern of the life and peace he had found through belief in Jesus Christ. Near the end of the book he remarks:

> The heart of Christianity is the cross of Jesus Christ; but this cross is often hidden in the clouds of hatred, suspicion, hardness of heart and pride, which prevail in the world among the sons of men. To dispel these clouds, and disclose the real cross, calls for more than preaching and teaching. It demands the bearing of the Cross in daily life. This is to go on loving when love seems impossible, and working when no result yet appears.[43]

Bishop Hassan was forced to live the words which he wrote at that time, and they have since become prophetic for his church as well.

In March 1981, he published another book entitled *The Hard Awakening*, in which he attempted with great honesty to weigh not only his own life, but also and especially that of his church and of the Protestant mission in Iran. The title of his book was derived from a poem by the well-known Persian poet Shams al-Din Muhammad Hafiz (ca. 1325-ca. 1390) entitled "Loves Awakening:"

> Love seemed at first an easy thing,
> But Ah! the hard awakening.

Hassan Dehqani Tafti relates how to be a Moslem and to be an Iranian are one and the same in Persia. A Christian may be Iranian, ethnically speaking, but because of his religion, he is a 'foreigner'—an Assyrian or Armenian. He relates an incident that is symbolic of the 'foreign' character of the church in the Persian context. It concerns an incident from the life of an English missionary, Henry Martyn (1781-1812), a celebrated figure in the history of Protestant missions. On 9 June 1811 this missionary arrived in Persia and began work in Shiraz. When he wanted to present his translation of the New Testament in Persian, which he had completed in the beginning of 1812, to the Persian prince Fat'hali, however, he was required to do so through the British ambassador at the court of the Shah.[44]

That meant that from the very beginning Christianity in its modern form in Iran was identified with a foreign government. When later, in the 'great century of missions' (the nineteenth century), American and British missionaries entered that nation, they originally worked among the Assyrians and the Armenians, where they were pioneers in medical care and established hospitals and schools. From this mission activity grew the beginnings of an indigenous Protestant church.

But right from the start that church had the stigma of being 'foreign'. Just as Henry Martyn could not have presented his New Testament to Fat'hali Shah without the help of the British Ambassador, so the American and British missionaries could not have built and run their hospitals and schools without the protection of their respective governments, particularly the prestige and influence of the British in the nineteenth century. Thus, ironically, the greatest obstacle in the way of the growth of the Church in Iran lay in the very cause of its existence.[45]

In spite of all this, however, Bishop Hassan pronounces this judgment out of deep loyalty toward the work of the British and other missionaries. He did not wish to speak derisively, as has become the fashion, of missionaries and mission movements, painting them with the single broad stroke of Western imperialism. Nor did he cast aspersions on their very existence: "I am convinced that the missionary movement of the Church of Christ, for all its many defects and faults, has done more good to mankind than any other movement of history."[46] And this was no hollow sentiment, coming as it did from a man who had almost lost his life, and whose son was murdered, because a century before missionaries were willing to leave their own countries to bring Christianity to Iran.[47]

Yet Hassan Dehqani Tafti went on to reflect on the history of the previous thirty years (1950-1980). He related how in 1940, at the dictatorial command of Reza Shah, the government confiscated the important mission schools and colleges and gave the Christian hospital in Isfahan six months to shut down. They had no choice but to obey. But then the government of Mossaddegh was toppled in 1953, and the Shah, who had gone into exile, returned. On the following day the department of health gave permission to the hospital to receive patients again.[48] It was also the opinion of Dehqani Tafti that the seeds that had been sown during the reign of Mossaddegh were reaped under the regime of Ayatollah Khomeini. After the fall of Mossaddegh, the English Anglican bishops were allowed to return from exile. Looking back thirty years after these events, Hassan Dehqani Tafti doubted whether the bishops did the right thing when they took the Anglican hospital back under their own control rather than allowing the hospital to be nationalized, as the American Presbyterians had done. They should have seen then the handwriting on the wall.[49]

Hassan Dehqani Tafti also illustrated the problem of alienation through his own experience. He had an Islamic background. By choosing Jesus Christ as a youth, he effectively cut himself off from his Islamic roots. Through his education he became alienated from his poor village background. He also took an English wife. "Whenever I visited Taft, my home village, it gave me a queer feeling of belonging and yet not belonging."[50]

In a period of one hundred years, Dehqani Tafti related, the Anglican church had baptized three thousand people, men, women and children. But the clinics and schools maintained by the church were an important expression of the presence of Christ in the Islamic environment. Without that additional aid, he stated, it would have been very difficult for a small Christian community, especially one consisting primarily of converts from Islam, to survive. But that entailed that the Christian institutions could exist and function only by the generosity of foreign support.[51]

Nevertheless, Bishop Hassan confessed, from the time he was a child that bothered him. When at the age of eighteen he considered becoming a priest, he was very disturbed by the involvement of foreigners in the local church. He was open to the criticism levelled by his compatriots, who suspected the Christians of complicity with foreigners. When he discussed this problem with the British Anglican bishop, the advice he received was sympathetic, but logical:

"If you really have a call from God to go and work separately for Christ like a dervish," he told me, "of course you are free to do so. But what will you do when you start making converts? Will you start a new church on your own, or will you join with the church that already exists?" I saw then that the first kind of church would not really be part of the Body of Christ because it would be an isolated, exclusive national body. The second option involved problems, but was the only true way to follow. I realized that the concept of a multi-national and multi-racial Christian community was too precious to be sacrificed, and I have upheld the idea ever since. I knew that one day we might have to pay heavily for this, and indeed we have done so; but is it possible to achieve anything sublime without sacrifice?[52]

It is beyond dispute that Bishop Hassan Dehqani Tafti and his church have had to pay dearly. In fact, the Western mission in general and the mission to Iran in particular have had to face the disturbing question of whether they, in addition to the undoubtedly impressive work that has been carried out by so many devoted Christians, have not also contributed to the alienation of converts from their own backgrounds, making it difficult for Christians to continue to feel at home in their own countries, Not only did they begin to see themselves as aliens but also felt pressure, both internal and external, to leave their country.

Protestantism in the Middle East

Today one encounters various Protestant churches in most of the nations of the Middle East. Nowhere were these churches founded before the beginning of the nineteenth century and there are some that did not come into existence until the twentieth century. The vast majority of their membership, and that applies to all the churches, has come from the Orthodox churches. Among the most important Protestant churches are those that stand in the Anglican tradition: the Episcopal church of the Middle East with five dioceses in Jerusalem (including Iraq and Cyprus); Iran and Egypt (including Libya and North Africa), Sudan (including Ethiopia), and Lebanon (including Jordan and Syria). They follow the 'low church' form of the Anglican tradition. The congregations of the Presbyterian and Reformed traditions together form the most widespread Protestant church in the area. To this category belong the Armenian Evangelical churches of the Middle East, which are most strongly represented in Lebanon and Syria, but are also present in Iran, Turkey, Greece, Cyprus and Egypt. The Coptic Evangelical church ('The Synod of the Nile') is by far and away the largest Protestant church in Egypt and the Middle East. The pastors of this church are trained at the Coptic Evangelical Seminary in Cairo. The National Evangelical Synod of Syria and Lebanon is the largest Protestant church in those nations, with approximately 25,000 members. There is a *Fellowship of Middle East Evangelical Churches (F.M.E.E.C)* which includes the churches of the Presbyterian, Anglican, Lutheran and Congregational traditions, i.e. all those who are also represented in the *Middle East Council of Churches M.E.C.C.).* The theological training for the various Protestant traditions is provided by the Near East School of Theology in Beirut, Lebanon.[53]

Not only Moslems, but also Orthodox Christians resisted the activities of the Protestant mission in the Middle East. Both Moslems and Orthodox were often anti-colonial, anti-Western, and anti-missionary (that is, against the Western mission) by disposition. Missionaries were equated with 'Western' Christians, against whom, according to the views of the 'Moslems brothers' *and* Eastern Christians, they should be on their guard.[54] The Lebanese journalist Farah Antoun (1874-1922) expended much effort in separating Eastern Christians from Western Christians and, even more so, from the European powers, who used religion to advance their political aims. "We must not forget the profit that we have derived from the missionaries, but let us not forget the political damage they have inflicted upon us. ... We are not responsible for what Western Christianity has done. Our loyalty is to the East."[55]

The Christians from the different Orthodox churches perceived in the Protestant mission a form of spiritual imperialism that sought to alienate Eastern Christianity from its own culture and church. That has led to continued tensions between the newly established Protestant churches and their Orthodox counterparts, from which the Protestants took most of their members. The 'politics' of the Presbyterians and Congregationalists from the United States on the one hand and the Anglicans from Great Britain (and the United States) on the other definitely differed, although there was agreement with regard to social work and education. Still, both ultimately lead to proselytism. According to the views of many missionaries, church history actually started with the sixteenth-century Reformation or even later with certain forms of (Anglican) pietism during the Great Awakening (in 1734/1735 and 1740-1742 in particular in New England and Massachusetts through the inspiration of the American theologian Jonathan Edwards (1703-1758) and George Whitefield (1714-1770), the most important preacher in the English/American Awakenings in the eighteenth century). The result was that many began to feel like 'Aliens at Home' (*Wanis Sema'an*) with the Protestants as well.

It is irrefutably true, and has not been contested by the Orthodox, that the activities of the mission delivered an enormous contribution in the area of education. The *Syrian Protestant College* (since 1920 the *American University of Beirut = A.U.B.*) is one of the better known examples.

George Sabra has said concerning the identity crisis in the churches of the Reformation in many parts of the Middle East that they are neither a colonial phenomenon nor a foreign (Western) transplant but "an extension of the Reformation and a communication of its essentially universal message."[56] In his opinion protestants should

first of all understand who they are in relation to this essential message of the Reformation, for, in the Middle East, many of them have alienated themselves from the Word of God either by dissolving it into some form of cultural Protestantism or by "koranizing" it, namely, equating the Bible with the Word of God, making God's revelation a revelation of texts rather than a revelation himself. ... Only by recovering the authentic traditions of the Reformation which revolve around the living and life-giving Word can Protestants come to terms with their identity and discover the way to an ecumenical witness in this part of the world.[57]

NOTES

1. 1981, 7.

2. It was customary until recently to use the word Mohammedan instead of the correct term 'Moslem'.

3. Jessup, 1879, 13f.; Barlett, 1.

4. Jessup, 1879, 22f.

5. Jessup, 1879, 23.

6. According to Zwemer, 1906, 82.

7. Zwemer, 1906, 84.

8. Cf. Marius Baar.

9. Jessup, 1879, 26-30, 34.

10. Jessup, 1879, 34, 36, 49, 51, 72.

11. Neill.

12. Barlett, 26.

13. Jessup, 1879, 75-77.

14. Jessup, 1879, 78.

15. Zwemer, 1911, 169.

16. Jessup, 1879, 85-87.

17. Jessup, 1879, 85-89, 100.

18. Jessup, 1879, 104-06.

19. Jessup, 1879, 115f.

20. Jessup, 1879, 126, 130, 135.

21. Van der Werff, 10, 103f.

22. Van der Werff, 108.

23. Mönnich, 1967, 438.

24. Kawerau, 200, 292-95.

25. Kawerau, 301f., 304, 306.

26. Kawerau, 623-25; cf. De Jong.

27. Jessup, 1891, 5; Hornus, 15-59.

28. Jessup, 1891, 6.

29. Kawerau, 305-10.

30. Kawerau, 323-25.

31. Reed, 19f.

32. Kawerau, 326.

33. Jessup, 1891, 7.

34. Jessup, 1891, 7f.

35. Jessup, 1891, 8.

36. Jessup, 1891, 9f.; cf. Cragg, 1969, 570-95.

37. Jessup, 1891, 18, 21f., 33, 36f., 40.

38. Kawerau, 483, 485, 488-90, 494f.

39. Kawerau, 608, 613-16.

40. Horner, 1989, 105.

41. Waterfield, 170, 175.

42. Waterfield, 175.

43. 1959, 79.

44. Waterfield, 92f., 95; Arberry, 574, 589.

45. Hassan Dehqani Tafti, 1981, 16f.

46. 1981, 17.

47. 1981, 19.

48. 1981, 20.

49. 1981, 20f.

50. 1981, 25, 27.

51. 1981, 30f.

52. 1981, 31.

53. Horner, 1974, 60, 64-67.

54. Mitchell, 231.

55. Hourani, 1962, 259.

56. Sabra, 38.

57. Sabra, 38, 39.

IX. DOES THE CHURCH STILL HAVE A FUTURE IN THE MIDDLE EAST?

Whoever does harm to a Christian or a Jew, against him will I myself [the prophet Mohammed] bring an accusation on the day of judgment.

(*Hadith* (tradition) of the Prophet Mohammed)

It may come to the point that the only possible way for the church to exist is liturgically. The church must then silently and patiently persevere in suffering.

Charles Malik[1]

Introduction

Do the churches in the Arab world still have a future? The previous chapters dealt with the history of the Eastern churches in the Middle East until today, their liturgy and theology, and their relationship to the predominately Moslem environment.

These churches flourished in the first millennium, just as the churches of Europe took center stage in the second millennium of the history of the church, and just as, according to Bühlmann, the center of church history may well shift to the Third World in the third millennium. But must this mean that the role of the churches in the Middle East will have already been played out by the third millennium, and that they will remain only as museum pieces?

Will it be possible in the future to speak of an 'Arab Christian' or a 'Christian Arab'?[2] One can imagine both a positive and a negative response to this question. If one asks what the future of the churches in the Arab East will be, one in fact poses a question that cannot be definitively answered.

1. Yet in order to attempt some kind of response, it is good to begin by referring to the situation in the Arab West, the *Maghreb*, during the early centuries as well as the nineteenth and early twentieth centuries. By asking what lessons can be drawn from that history, light can be shed on the present and future situation in the Arab East (*Mashrik*).

2. It is often assumed that over the centuries the Arab world has harbored the same kind of anti-Semitism that left such a bloody trail through European 'Christian' history. It is therefore frequently contended that Christian and Moslem resistance in the Arab world today to the Israeli

state is just another expression of this same anti-Semitism. What is the specific situation of the Arab Christians in the state of Israel and what is their attitude towards the Jews?

3. We will then ask to what extent a confrontation between Christians and Moslems is inevitable, after which we will consider the situation of Christians in view of the appearance of what in the last decade has been called the 'revival of Islamic fundamentalism'. For that purpose we will illustrate, on the basis of some literary examples both from Christians and Moslems, how socio-political conflicts have been and are presented as religious conflicts.

4. We will then pay attention to the effects of fundamentalism on the mutual relationships between Moslems and Christians. By comparing the periods of the crusades and of colonialism with the present-day situation one can discover a phenomenon similar to the one today: the *fundamentalization* of religion and the polarization of the relationship between Christians and Moslems. Will the future bring the further isolation of Christians or will a renewed interaction with the Moslem environment be possible?

1. *The Arab West*

Although one can at least speak of authentic, indigenous and viable Christian communities in the Arab East (*Mashrik*), one can no longer say the same of the Christian churches in the Arab West (*Maghreb*). The indigenous element there has practically disappeared. The remaining churches consist primarily of foreigners—French (or in the case of Libya, Italian) expatriates, who remained behind after the independence of Libya (1952), Morocco (1956), Tunisia (1956) and Algeria (1962). Some 'foreigners' even took on the nationality of their respective countries of residence. The number of Moslems who have converted to Christianity is very small.

A book published by a Tunisian tourist organization several years ago, called *Early Christian Tunesia*, relates how Christianity penetrated that part of Africa through Carthage, the capital of the Roman province of Africa. The first Christian mission may have begun already during the persecution that took place under the Roman emperor Nero in A.D. 64 or near the end of the first century. From *Africa Vetus* the gospel spread toward the West, as far as Mauritania. The percentage of Christians at that time was the highest of any province in Africa. This church soon had a well established hierarchy, which, already during the episcopate of Cyprian (died 258), consisted of 59 bishops. Cyprian died in 258 as the first martyr bishop in Africa. Carthage, called the 'queen of the provinces of the entire Roman world', played an important role. It was also called 'Rome in Africa' or 'the rival of Constantinople'. Christian literature was produced in Latin in Carthage before it was produced in Rome. Tertullian (ca. 150/155-ca. 220) was the first in a long series of great 'Church Fathers', which contains the names of people like Cyprian and Augustine.

Of the once great North African church, only the literature, which has had a lasting impact on the Church throughout the world, and the ruins of churches and various other structures, noted for their early Christian mosaics, remain. Mosaics decorating flat slabs covering graves are frequent. They typically contain scripture texts and symbols of the Christian faith. Because of their number, their elaborate decoration and their widespread presence throughout Tunisia, they today represent the greatest store of Christian art remaining in the land. Among the symbols are the cross, the fish, the shell, and the peacock. The anchor is the symbol of the Christian Church and the dolphin represents the 'faithful Christian'.[3]

What caused the church to disappear in the *Maghreb*? Why has nothing remained of the church that gave rise to such church fathers like Tertullian, Cyprian, and Augustine (354-430), apart from a few ruins, like those at Hippo near Carthage in modern Tunisia? The decline of the church in North Africa is usually attributed to the arrival of Islam. But before we consider this explanation further, we must ask to what extent the church in North Africa had become indigenous before the spread of Islam to that part of the world. In North Africa, it was primarily the provinces of Africa and Numidia—which more or less correspond to the modern nations of Tunisia and Algeria—where the Christians became a sizable minority. The number of Christians in Mauritania, modern Morocco, was much smaller.[4]

St. Augustine

F. van der Meer, in his biography of Augustine, described the situation in the following way:

Two hundred and fifty years after the death of Augustine, Islam arrived: Sidi Oqba founded the first of Cairo's beautiful mosques. He came in the name of God, but without secrets, without rites and without many demands; tolerant of superstition and with lax morals, but intolerant of other religions. We would still hear for some time of a few bishops, of a courageous Berber queen Kahena, a

Jewess, who resisted them; of the Christian hero Koçeila who twice became a renegade. And then it became dark in the ancient land of churches. Indigenous African Christianity with five hundred dioceses disappeared so quickly from the earth that we can hardly believe our eyes at the ever-increasing number of ruins that are uncovered. The riddle of this decline is not yet solved. But whoever may have been to blame, it was not the indefatigable Bishop of Hippo, who in the farthest reaches of his diocese appointed priests and bishops, who although having been schooled in Latin, could still speak Punic. The African church had produced an incomparable elite, but not a Christian people; the barbarians and the divisions left her no time. But if she today is unforgettable, it is primarily because of Augustine. ... He and those like him found no time to transform the poor Berbers into independent Christians! When after his death the Roman ecclesiastical structure fell apart because the barbarian Vandals banished the bishops, murdered the clerics, burned the basilicas in the interior, confiscated their possessions, occupied or closed the churches in the large cities for decades, and dispersed or rebaptized the Latin speaking population as Arians, the natives retained nothing ....[5]

In other words, the church in the *Maghreb* was in the process of decline already before the arrival of Islam. Of the more than 700 North African dioceses in Augustine's time, only some 35 remained at the time of the Arab conquest. Most of these disappeared by the end of the eighth century. The remaining Christians were then included in the Patriarchate of Alexandria. In the year 411, five-hundred and sixty-five North African bishops gathered at a synod in Carthage in order to put an end to the Donatist controversy. The Donatists were typically called 'provincials', native North Africans, who bore a basic hatred for Rome and all its works.[6]

One could to a certain extent differ with Van der Meer's assessment regarding the causes of the decline of the church in North Africa, since he also attributes it in part to the arrival of Islam. The description which he gives of Islam contains some elements which correspond to the usual (biased) picture that Christians in the West had and still have of Islam, For example, according to Van der Meer, Islam is an 'easy religion', with 'lax morals' and 'without secrets' (sacraments), all of which would have made it easy for Christians and others to accept, thereby suggesting that Christianity had to give way to Islam. The entire medieval assessment of Islam in Europe was fraught with such caricatures.[7]

The true explanation must, however, be sought at a deeper level and is not to be traced to specific individuals, and least of all Augustine. And yet it is important to seek causes, since this can perhaps shed some light

191

on the question regarding what kind of future the church in the Arab East, humanly speaking, can expect.

In light of the consequences of the war with the Vandals, the 'riddle' of the disappearance of the church in that part of North Africa could well have something to do with the fact that the church recruited her followers for the most part from the Romanized part of the population. Punic (Phoenician) was spoken in some places (Carthage was probably founded in the ninth century B.C. by inhabitants of the city of Tyre (Lebanon)) and even some of the Christian priests were able to speak it. But this language, like Latin, was an 'import'. It left the inhabitants of the villages and the deserts, who were of Berber descent and spoke Berber, beyond the reach of the church. Although Augustine was himself a Berber, his education was in Latin. The church of North Africa was a Latin-speaking church, concentrated in and around cities and already in decline due to the controversy with the Donatists long before the arrival of Islam. In rural areas the church had made no significant advances. Even the monastic communities were established in the cities and made little effort to Christianize 'heathen territory'.[8] For example, the Bible was never translated into Berber.[9] "The indigenous church, as a transcultural entity did not represent a solid religious opposition to the Moslem invaders, in spite of the fact that the Christians probably made up the largest element of the population, at least in *Ifriqiya*."[10]

With the arrival of Islam, then, an almost universal 'falling away' took place. Norman Horner gives two reasons for the 'failure' of the church in that part of North Africa. In the first place, the church never became indigenous. And in the second place, the church never effectively reached the masses who lived beyond the 'imported' Roman culture.[11]

One can clearly, therefore, speak of a decline in the church in that part of North Africa already before the arrival of Islam. In the year of Augustine's death (430), there were six to seven hundred bishops; in 488 the number had decreased to 470, and in 536 there were only 220. By the time of the Arab conquest that number was down to forty, and in 1053 probably not more than five. But by then there was talk of an 'immigrant' church, not unlike today, which no longer bore any relation to the 'African Christianity' of the past. In 1076, Pope Gregory VII (pope from 1072 until 1085) complained that in North Africa he could no longer find the three men necessary for an appointment. He had to have the nominated priest brought to Rome before his appointment. Christianity did not simply disappear with the Arab conquest. "The Berbers quickly and without regret yielded what Rome had brought to them in terms of intellectual method and social organization. A certain number of them remained faithful."[12]

It was not therefore a question of the sudden collapse of the church in the wake of the arrival of Islam. The demise took place over the course of half of a millennium. Apparently, Christianity had taken root primarily in the more Romanized circles. It was a Latin or Greek Christianity, the language and culture of the 'rulers'. They were cut off from Latin and Byzantine Christianity after the Islamic conquest, and so became 'isolated'. Whatever remained of the Christian church would, however, several centuries later, suffer greatly under the regime of the Almohads (= *al- muwahidun*, literally, 'those who confess the unity'). Under the government of the Almohads in Spain and North Africa, a dynasty arose from an Islamic sect that had been founded and inspired by Muhammad ibn Tumart (ca. 1078-1129), Christians were open to accusation due to their belief in the Trinity.[13] In 1160, Africa (*Ifriqiya*) was conquered by an Almohad prince and Carthage fell. Many Christians were killed. In the same year, Mahdiya (Tunisia) fell and the soldiers of the Almohads put an end to the last remains of the church in the *Maghreb*.[14] Jean Corbon expresses the fate of the church in the *Maghreb* thus:

The drama of the church in the Maghreb is not that evangelization took place at the same time as Romanization, but that the Romanization remained so superficial and the coexistence of these two blocks (the Berbers and those who had been Latinized) did not evolve into an original symbiosis. The vital and normal development would have caused the Romanized group to be absorbed into a cultural interpenetration, an example of which is displayed for us on the other side of the banks of the empire.[15]

North Africa at the Turn of the Century

In the nineteenth century France conquered Algeria and Tunisia. The borders of French authority were continually pushed to the south, where, in 1881 and 1883, French protectorates were established. Once again, as in the time of Augustine, the Christian presence was an immigrant presence, primarily Roman Catholic (from France), but also, to a certain extent, Protestant Christianity. In this context, Charles Martila Allemand Lavigerie (1825-1892) gained notoriety. He would later be promoted to cardinal. In 1884, after French authority was extended over Tunisia, he received the title of Archbishop of Carthage and the Primate of Africa. In this way 'Rome' attempted to dramatize the 'reconquest' of an area where Islam had once triumphed. Lavigerie was actively involved in the attempt to bring Tunisia under the authority of France. In his mind, the French *pied à terre* in North Africa was an open door for the evangelization of the entire African continent and founded the order of the *White Fathers*. The *White Fathers* gained a few converts among the Kabyle people, who primarily sought (successfully) to gain naturalization as French citizens.[16] In a letter, dated 18 September 1874, to the missionaries concerning their rule, Lavigerie wrote:

Only a few years ago, not only did your little association not exist, but even the conditions, which were created for us here in Algeria, appeared impossible. How can we dream of making our colony the center for a mission penetrating into the depths of Africa when the apostolate of Algeria itself could not be practiced. But 'God wills it'.

He meant here that this conquest, the last by a strongly Christian king of France (Louis Philippe), was also the last crusade, which should be brought to its completion by the true apostolic weapons—love and martyrdom. He wanted new apostles to participate on these banks where the holiest of the kings (Louis IX, 'the saint', 1214-1270) had died [he lost his life in Tunisia].[17]

As the Moslems saw it, the activities of the mission in North Africa (and the Middle East) were directed against Islam. They reacted against it in the 'colonial era'. In response to a well-publicized mission conference that took place in Jerusalem in 1928 (at that time under the British mandate in Palestine), the Arab press wrote:

This conference was held in the heart of the Islamic world in order to find a means of promoting the success of the propaganda of the mission. All over the world people are going to great lengths in order to make Moslems in particular Christians.

The Moslems were disturbed by the fact that missionaries had been sent to Egypt, Syria, Palestine and Iraq, "where no heathenism exists, but rather, a noble religion. We wish that the Europeans and Americans understood that the sending of missionaries to attack Islamic lands is an absurdity and a scandal."[18]

But just as in the time of Augustine, Christianity remained for the most part a foreign affair in the 'French era'. In the time of Augustine, the church suffered in the struggle with the Donatists. This group is usually known as a movement that was battled and condemned as a 'heresy'. Yet in retrospect one might well ask whether it might not have been a group that already in that time promoted the cause of a unique African i-

*dentity. It does not seem impossible to view it as comparable to the con-
temporary phenomenon of the so-called 'independent African churches',
which arose out of resistance to the imposed Western church structure
and theology of the so-called 'mission churches'. One could imagine that
a lack of contextualization, as it is called today, or perhaps, as Van der
Meer says, a lack of time for it, contributed more than anything to the
rapid spread of Islam in that part of North Africa and the virtual disappearance of Christianity. As evidence that one should search in such a direction, the example of the Coptic church could be cited. It is true that
countless Copts, in a process that lasted centuries and continues until
today, were converted to Islam. Yet, in spite of that, the Egyptian church
appears to have taken root in Egyptian soil and to be well established.
Although it may have been weakened through conversions to Islam and,
more recently, through continual emigrations, it remains the largest
Christian church in the Arab world. One could well ask whether they
have not remained because they took their own context more seriously
than the churches of the Maghreb did or could in their time.*

2. Arabs and Jews

What about the relationship of the Arabs in general and the Arab
Christians in particular towards the Jews? The positive attitude of the
Jews toward their position *vis à vis* the Moslems can be illustrated by a
statement by a German Jew in the second half of the fifteenth century.
Writing to his brothers in Germany and Italy from Adrianople, in an at-
tempt to convince them to come and live in the Ottoman empire, he said:
"Under Ishmael everyone lives safely under his own vine and fig tree.
That is not the case in Germany and the surrounding lands. No Jew is
required to wear green or red in any of the cities there [in Turkey]."[19]
The great Hungarian Jewish Islamic scholar, Ignaz Goldziher, who lived
and worked around the turn of the century, wrote to one of his Arab
students shortly before his death: "I have lived for your people and mine.
When you return to your land, tell that to your brothers."[20]

It is important to remember that positive statements on the relation
of the Moslems to the Jews (for example, how good the Moslems were
towards the Jews in the Middle Ages—a fact that is generally not contested) were made and disseminated by Jews in the nineteenth century. It
was used primarily as a rebuke to Christians. In our time the reverse occurs: many Arabs and Moslems use the same argument, but now against
the Jews.[21]

195

One can generally assume that the Jews, like other minority groups, were *tolerated*. That is not the same, however, as full political freedom. They were in fact second-class citizens in the sense that their rights were restricted and determined by the Moslem majority. Jews, like Christians, could at various times attain to high and even very high political and economic positions, for example, in the Umayyad and the Abbasid dynasties, as well as the Ottoman empire (from 1517 until the First World War; see above ch. I). According to Bernard Lewis, the status which the *dhimmis*, both Jews and Christians, enjoyed has been idealized by some writers, and the tolerance displayed by Moslem governments in the granting of full equality, which certainly existed, has been glorified. He states that they were second-class citizens, paid higher taxes, suffered under certain social unpleasantries, and in a limited number of cases were subject to open persecution. But in general they enjoyed the free exercise of religion and at times attained to high positions. They were accepted into the artisan guilds, where they sometimes predominated. But as Lewis says, they were never forced to undergo martyrdom for their belief.[22] This same well-known Jewish scholar of Islam states that if by religious tolerance one means the absence of persecution, then classical Islamic society was indeed tolerant toward its Jewish and Christians subjects. By this he means, however, that tolerance in Spain was perhaps greater than in the East and "incomparably greater than medieval Christendom." It is almost universally held that the situation of the Jews in the Arab world was more favorable than that of the Jews in Christian Europe during the Middle Ages.[23] But Lewis does conclude that "if tolerance means the absence of discrimination, then Islam was never tolerant, nor did it claim to be. On the contrary, Islam clung to the privileged superiority of the true believer both in this world and in the world to come."[24]

Two 'Arab' Jews on the Arab/Jewish Relationship

The difficulty with much of the literature dealing with the Jews in the Arab world is that it is one-sided. Either it is assumed that the anti-Semitism of the past and present are of the same sort (i.e. anti-Zionism = anti-Semitism) or the past situation of the Jewish community in the Arab world is idealized. In support of both these positions a series of 'facts' are marshalled which are supposed to legitimate the one position or the other. Both positions are also defended by Jews.

The well-known Tunisian Jewish writer, Albert Memmi (born 1920), is of the opinion that the Jews in the Arab world were exposed to the same types of pogroms, persecutions and discrimination as the Jews in Europe. He wrote a book which is highly autobiographical and bears the title *Pillar of Salt* (1953). The title plays on the story of Lot's wife, who together with Lot and their daughters fled Sodom which faced imminent destruction. The messengers of God had warned them not to look back at Sodom as they fled, "But Lot's wife behind him looked back, and she became a pillar of salt" (Genesis 19:26). Although Albert Memmi especially wants to put the impoverished past in the Jewish ghetto of Tunisia (an Arab land under French colonial rule) where he spent his youth behind him, the book seems to suggest that he looks back on the entire Arab world that he left behind as though looking back at Sodom. Memmi thinks that "those too are bound to their actions who are not able to free themselves from the past, in which colonial rule, exploitation and intolerance dominated."[25]

This book narrates the life of a Tunisian Jew with a French education for whom it has become impossible to define himself in any way. His culture is French and in his class he is the only student who understands the French tragic poet Jean Racine (1639-1699) as he should be understood. Herein lies the dilemma in which many of the writers from the *Maghreb* still find themselves. Educated in French schools, they have not mastered Arabic, so that they must, consequently, have their works published in Paris. The majority of their compatriots therefore read them with difficulty, if at all.

"The neighborhood *(hara)*," writes Memmi, "was inhabited by the poor who earned just enough to buy bread for the day, and a little meat once a week. ... But even those poor taught me that every human being, even the most miserable, there is something holy". He describes the neighborhood as a place both of fear and refuge, where one could still, in spite of its difficulties, protect oneself from the inhuman reality of the French colonial regime. Yet Memmi makes it clear that one had to break out of this neighborhood. In spite of his achievements, he remained for the French a bourgeois and an outsider.[26] His dilemma is clearly expressed in the following quotation:

I belong to French culture, but I am a Tunisian. ... I am a Tunisian, but a Jew, in political and social terms an outcast, since I speak the national language with a strange accent. ... Jew I am, but one who has broken with the religion and the ghetto, who does not know Jewish culture, but who at the same time despises unbelieving Jews. Finally, I am poor and I have had the ardent desire to cast off poverty, but did not want to do what was necessary to that end. I will not join the Western world. I will no longer have anything to do with the Western world. I have rejected the East, and the Western world turned me back. What must I then be? I am neither Jew, nor oriental, nor poor, I do not belong to my family nor to my religion. ... This time nothing hinders my self analysis. I have broken with the alley, since it was but a child's dream. With father and mother, since I was ashamed for them, for the community and its goals, because they were out-moded, and I was ashamed of my ambition and bourgeois mentality because they were unwarranted and deceitful ....[27]

At the end of his book, Albert Memmi himself weighs all things in the balance, so to speak, and turns his eye on himself:

I discovered a long time ago that I am dying because I have turned to look back at myself. It is forbidden to look at oneself, but I have finally recognized myself. Can I continue to live after having looked back, like Lot's wife whom God changed into a pillar of salt?[28]

In contrast to the thoughts of this Tunisian Jew stands the thought of André Chouraqui, an Algerian Jew who emigrated to the state of Israel and wrote that the periodic outbursts of violence against Jews in North Africa are not only occasioned by the attitude toward non-Moslems in general, but also by the horrifying misery into which feudalism had plunged the entire population of the region. According to him, there never was a philosophy and tradition of anti-Semitism in the Arab world like that of Europe.[29]

Anti-Semitism and Anti-Zionism

Since the establishment of the state of Israel in 1948, which was cre-ated not as a result of waves of anti-Semitism in the Arab world, but, in part, as a result of the anti-Semitism of Europe, which culminated in the Holocaust, the majority of Jewish communities in the Arab world have disappeared or been greatly reduced. Most Jews in the Arab world emi-grated to Europe or to the United States or to the state of Israel. The creation of the state of Israel made them potential citizens of that state according to 'the law of return', and therefore suspect to the govern-ments of the various Arab nations. Especially in the wake of the several wars between Israel and its Arab neighbors, in particular the war of 1956, the Jewish community in Egypt decreased greatly in numbers.

In N.A. Stillmann's comprehensive study on the Jewish communities in Arab countries, one sees countless images of Jewish men and women and families (for example, during a Jewish wedding), which occasion a sort of melancholy, since the communities have for the most part defin-itely disappeared from Arab countries.[30]

To contend that one can hear no echoes of anti-Semitism in the modern developments of the last decades would do violence to the truth. Hitler's *Mein Kampf* can be found in Arab translation. In 1927, the *Protocols of the Elders of Zion*, the infamous anti-Semitic forgery, was translated into Arabic. It is especially striking that in a time of political crises, anti-Jewish sentiments are brought to light, primarily in fundamentalistic Moslem circles. Under the influence of the so-called 'revival of Islam', there has undoubtedly been an increase in fundamentalistic Islamic circles of anti-Jewish statements, both oral and written.

A few statements from an obviously dated document from the 'traditional' university in Cairo, al-Azhar serve well to illustrate this increase. It is a report of a conference of religious leaders that took place in 1968. This date itself speaks volumes, since the report was filed after the defeat of the Arab nations (Egypt, Jordan and Syria) in the 1967 Six-Day War (starting 5 June), in which East Jerusalem, the West Bank, the Gaza Strip and the Golan Heights were all occupied by Israel.

The mufti of Lebanon, Hasan Khalid, a political-religious dignitary of the Sunni Moslems in Lebanon (the same who later would be killed in an attack during the civil war in Lebanon), spoke of the obligation of Moslems and Arabs to wage a *jihad* for the liberation of the land (Palestine), to retain their honor, to regain the al-Aqsa mosque (in Jerusalem), as well as to purify the 'Church of the Resurrection' (the Church of the Holy Sepulchre), the birthplace of prophecy, the seat of revelation and the meeting place of the prophets from the hands of Zionism, the enemy of humanity, truth and justice, and the enemy of God.[31] Someone at the conference spoke of the malevolent conduct of the Jews, whose evil was incurable, unless they were subdued by force. No good could be expected from them, unless they lived under the aegis of Islam, as loyal and obedient subjects. The Moslem community would treat them nobly and tolerantly, just as they always had.[32] Another speaker referred to the Jews as a blight and as a plague, who were cursed like Satan, who had been banished beyond the reach of God's grace.[33] A verse from the Koran was quoted in which it is said that against the Jews God would send peoples who would exact a heavy punishment from them until the day of resurrection.[34] The explanation that accompanied the quotation was that God would occasionally send people to harm, scatter and persecute the Jews. This verse purportedly also revealed the evil nature of the Jews, which caused them to twist the words of God, not to believe in Him, to kill the prophets without reason and to perpetrate evil in the land. Their evil deeds knew no bounds. The evil Jewish nature would never change and the history of Israel and Palestine would reek of blood.[35]

This little 'anthology' makes clear that anti-Jewish, not simply anti-Zionist, sentiments can be found in the Arab world. It is especially damning that in this report the Koranic passages that speak positively of the Jews, quoted earlier in the first chapter, did not form any counterbalance. One of the speakers at the conference even addressed the contention that the passages should be explained away.[36] One can hardly consider the terms 'noble' and 'tolerant' apropos once the subject of the 'incurable evil' of the Jews has been broached.[37]

Not as an excuse but perhaps as a clarification, one could mention that such statements usually coincide with situations of conflict. As was frequently the case in the past, economic and political crises give rise to the occurrence or resurgence—especially in fundamentalistic circles—of such anti-Jewish statements, just as conflicts with the 'Christian' colonial governments gave and give rise to anti-Christian sentiments. Thus a direct line can be drawn between the events surrounding the very humiliating defeat in the 1967 Six Day War and the statements cited above. Usually, as soon as the political or military tension abates, for example, after the 1973 Yom Kippur War, when the Arabs felt that they had regained their honor, such attitudes are much less frequently expressed.

In a country such as Saudi Arabia, however, one could speak of a more or less dogmatic anti-Semitism, that has no equal in other Arab countries, except perhaps in the circles of the Moslem Brothers of Egypt, Syria, and Jordan. In such instances hostility is expressed not only toward Zionism, but toward Jews, who are called enemies of humanity and are accused of having been out to destroy Islam since the time of Mohammed. The Jewish state thus supposedly has the destruction of Islam as its aim, which demands in return that Moslems participate in the struggle against Israel.[38]

In spite of these vituperative views, one must be careful to place these anti-Jewish expressions in the same category with the anti-Semitism that appeared in Europe. It was primarily political considerations that gave rise to the use, or rather, misuse of religion. Therefore it is unjust to equate any Arab resistance to the state of Israel with anti-Semitism, or to explain it in those terms, although the resistance to the state of Israel and Zionism undoubtedly sometimes issues into anti-Semitism.

Ultimately, however, the question of anti-Semitism in the Middle East is very complicated and ambiguous. Although the conflict in the

Middle East is not about theological matters, but rather at the most elementary level must be explained in terms of political, economic and cultural as well as psychological factors, it is nevertheless undeniable that on the popular level the religious factor does indeed play a role. The 'fundamentalistic' preaching of the mosque in times of crisis undoubtedly plays on the religious sentiments of the masses and exploits them with dangerous consequences. When religion and state (politics), *din wa dawla*, are so closely interwoven, as they are, for example, for orthodox fundamentalistic Moslems, it is very difficult to distinguish clearly between the political and religious factors.

There is no denying that anti-Semitism can easily arise and indeed frequently flows from opposition to the state of Israel and Zionism. There are undeniably expressions of hatred of the Jews in the Middle East. Yet it is an oversimplification to equate the situations of the past or present in Europe and the Arab world.

Arab Christians and the Jews

There are less than 200,000 Christians living in the state of Israel, of whom 70,000 to 100,000 reside in Israel and 50,000 in the so-called occupied territories. The official number given is in Israel 120,000 and 50,000 in the occupied territories (35,000 in the West Bank and Gaza and 14,000 in Jerusalem. The Arab Christians (in particular Melchites) are mainly found in Galilee (Nazareth).[39]

It is maintained by some that religious anti-Semitism in the Arab world is not of Islamic but of Christian origin. Bernard Lewis once commented that "Arabs are not anti-Semites because they are for the most part not Christians." The suggestion is made that anti-Semitism appears in the Arab world precisely where Western Christian influence is traceable. In this instance, the influence of French anti-Semitism is referred to. Morroe Berger says that when swastikas began to appear again in various European cities in the sixties, Beirut was the only city in the Middle East where anything similar occurred, because, he adds by way of explanation, this was the only city with a high percentage of Christians.[40] He does not, however, offer any evidence for his contention, and his opinion therefore remains, in our view, just that.

Whatever the case may be, one can point in this connection to the fact that at the time Arab Catholic bishops from some of the Catholic churches opposed, albeit in vain, the acceptance of the declaration on the Jews of the Second Vatican Council. Certain Coptic Catholics explained: "Because the Jews martyred and crucified Christ, they bear from genera-

201

tion to generation the burden of the responsibility for this brutal crime."
Such an explanation, which is shared by other Orthodox Christians, cannot be explained simply in terms of the adaptation of the Christians to the political situation in Egypt, but cuts rather to the heart of a religiously based anti-Semitism, according to Otto Meinardus.[41]

In any case, it cannot be denied that the attitude of the Arab Christians toward the Jews has been influenced in our time by the political climate that has prevailed since the establishment of the state of Israel in 1948. Thus, the Greek Orthodox Patriarch of Syria/Lebanon, at an Islamic conference held in February 1975 in Lahore, Pakistan, spoke of Jerusalem as the city of Moslems and Christians but made no mention of Jews. A few months later, when he visited King Khalid of Saudi Arabia in Jiddah, the first time that such a visit took place, he spoke of the rights of the Moslems and Christians to Jerusalem, and of the Jews as 'guests'. No matter how much one might wish to give to this word 'guest' a positive content, it is no guarantee of hospitality or rights.

On the basis of the Bible (the Old Testament particularly), much is said in the West, especially by Protestants, regarding the relation toward Israel and Judaism based on the Bible. Western Christians are able to speak rather abstractly and informally about biblical interpretation in connection with Israel. Kenneth Cragg, a well-known Middle East scholar, points out in his book, *This Year in Jerusalem*, how Arab Christians too, as *Christians*, recognize that they are bound to the unity of the Bible, the Old and New Testaments, and therefore also to the Jewish antecedents of the gospel. But as Arabs, they share with the entire Arab world the tragedy formed in their experience by the state of Israel. But there is also, in Cragg's words, the tension between the Israel of the prophets and the Israel of Premier Menachim Begin. This creates tremendous stress when, for example, the 'Song of Zechariah' (Luke 1:67-79) is sung in the liturgy.

It has become unsingable in the painful stresses of contemporary Arab Christianity: "Blessed be the Lord God of Israel", it opens, celebrating his 'redeemed people'. But which Israel? What redemption? Zachariah's words ended with a vision of peace: ... "to give light to them that sit in darkness and to guide our feet into the way of peace, a vision which is quite disqualified if, for Israel one has to read your own farms occupied, your fathers' villages alienated and their graves in strangers' custody. The sentiment of the *Benedictus* of Zachariah, at it may be sung in some English Cathedral or in the remoteness of America's Middle West is one thing. It is another for Arab Christians in the pains of the Middle East. ... If we turn to the Psalms in general similar tensions arise. So often in them the enemies of the Lord and the enemies of the state are assumed to be the same. Many Psalms rejoice at the discomfiture of the Canaanites who were driven out in order that so that 'the people of God' might be planted in .... Today Palestinians are counterparts of the Philistines of old and their unwillingness to forego their homeland is therefore resistance to God.[42]

It is worthwhile to listen to the voice of the Palestinian Christians within the state of Israel. There has been a development in Israel of what first took place in Latin America, i.e., 'Liberation Theology'. One even speaks of the development of 'Uprising Theology' (*Lahut al-intifada*).[43] (9 December 1987 marks the beginning of what soon came to be called the *intifada*). This theology "came to embody the reality of the commitment of the local church, and the Christian communities, to the Palestinian people."[44]

In 1989 a book entitled *Justice and Only Justice; A Palestinian Theology of Liberation* appeared written by the Palestinian theologian Na'im Ateek, an Anglican canon in (East) Jerusalem. Ateek belongs to a Palestinian family that remained in Israel/Palestine after 1948. He possesses Israeli citizenship. His family was expelled from Beyt Shean in Galilee in 1948. He expressly refers to himself as a Christian, Palestinian, an Arab and a Israeli—in that order.[45] His book makes clear that Arabs cannot escape the reality of the Holocaust, which forms such a dominant background for the Israeli Jews. Although it may be true that the Holocaust was not a Middle Eastern phenomenon, nevertheless, in his opinion, Palestinians must learn to understand the severity of its trauma for the Jews. As hosts, the Palestinians must accept the fact that the best part of Palestine (West Palestine) has been given to the Jews, not because they have any right to it, nor because of the Balfour declaration, and not even because of anti-Semitism, but because of the Holocaust.[46]

In André Elias Mazawi's article "Palestinian Local Theology and the Issue of Islamo-Christian Dialogue: An Appraisal," he states that

orthodox theology did not address the question of the reality of Islam on the one hand, nor of the Israeli-Palestinian/Arab conflict on the other. It was therefore an impetus for the creation of a genuine local Palestinian theology. ... Palestinian local theology remains limited in its contribution as to the relevance of Islam for the faith of the Palestinian Christian. In general, the contribution of Palestinian local theology remains on the symbolic socio-political level.[47]

After 'The Handshake'

After the handshake between Israeli Prime Minister Israel Yitshaq Rabin and Yasser Arafat, the chairman of the Palestine Liberation Organization, on 13 September 1993 in Washington, graffiti with the word "Imagine" appeared on one of the walls in Jericho. Indeed, who could have imagined only a few weeks previously that the two archenemies would shake hands before the eyes of the whole world? Some twenty years earlier another Israeli Prime Minister, Golda Meir, had completely denied that Palestinians existed. For several decades Israel had refused to recognize the PLO as a representative body of the Palestinians or to talk with their members. All of a sudden this had changed. Secret talks in Norway had brought the two parties closer to each other so that both were prepared to recognize each other and to take at least the first step to establish autonomy in the 'occupied territories, first in Jericho and Gaza.

Indeed, imagine! But is it really so unimaginable that Jews and Arabs (both Moslems and Christians) could come closer to each other? It is not so strange if one is aware of their history. It is a fact that for many centuries most of the Jews did not live in 'Christian' Europe but in the Arab world. Jews were much better of under Moslem rule than in medieval Christian Europe.

With S.D. Goitein one can distinguish different periods in the relationship between Arabs and Jews: namely a) 500-1300, b) 1300-1900, and c) 1900 until now.

a. One of the most important events in that period for what is now called the Arab world was the emergence of Islam in the seventh century S.D. Goitein refers to the origin and early development of Islam in its Jewish environment and calls Islam "an Arab recast of Israel's religion."[48] Islam, like Christianity, cannot be understood without awareness of its Jewish roots.

But Arab culture and Islam became very significant for the Jews as well. Arab culture influenced Jewish thought and the Hebrew language was influenced by Arab language and literature.

There were two main centers where Jews lived in the Arab world: in the East, particularly in (of all places!) Baghdad and in the West, particularly in Spain. Of course that meant Spain during Moslem rule. The Arabs called the country al-Andalus. Arabs (both Moslems and Christians) as well as Jews shared the same culture which knew periods of great flourishing. Philosophy as well as medicine was studied together. Jews used the Arab language, wrote philosophical works and poems in Arabic (Judah Halevi ca.1085-ca.1141) and took part in the Arab culture. In many respects Jews made valuable contributions to Arab civilization.

The Spanish Jewish philosopher and Hebrew poet, Ibn Gabirol (1021-1052), was influenced by Arab poetics.[49] The Hellenistic heritage which was transmitted by Christians in the East to Moslems was passed on by the Arabs to the West. For most of his life, the Jewish philosopher and physician Maimonides, born in Spain (1135), worked in Cairo where he died in 1204. Maimonides' main philosophical work, *The Guide of the Perplexed*, "is a great monument of Jewish-Arab symbiosis, not merely because it is written in Arabic by an original Jewish thinker and was studied by Arabs [i.e., Moslems *and* Christians], but because it developed and conveyed to large sections of the Jewish people ideas which had so long occupied the Arab mind".[50] The Moslems were also fascinated by Maimonides.[51] The work of the famous Roman Catholic 'angelic theologian' Thomas Aquinas is unthinkable without the influence of the Arab philosopher Ibn Rush (Averroes). Goitein spoke in this connection about a 'creative symbiosis' between Jews and Arabs.[52] This means that there was a fruitful interaction between them.

Maimonides' example could be followed today, in whom David Hartman sees a basis for a Judeo-Islamic accord.

Maimonides, who lived with Islam, wrote a response about Islam not being paganism, and had a very high regard for Islamic monotheism. So there is a very interesting tradition in which Jewish philosophers, in which Maimonides, the greatest Jewish Halakhist philosopher of Jewish history, lives with intense dialogue and respect for Islamic philosophy. So there is a precedent now for a rich intercultural, spiritual theme.[53]

b. The period from 1300-1900 was one of decline for Arab culture. Baghdad was destroyed by the Mongols in 1258. Arab disappeared as it where from the world stage. Something similar can be said about the oriental Jews. As the Arabs 'faded out' from world history, so the oriental Jews 'faded' from Jewish history. Both knew a common history of suffering.[54]

c. From about the year 1900 onwards there have been both Jewish and Arab revivals. With respect to the Arabs, one can mention the Arab Awakening (George Antonius), the literary renaissance (*nahda*), followed later by Arab nationalism and Arab socialism (*istirakiyya*). As far as the Jews are concerned, one may indicate the emergence and development since the 1890's of Jewish nationalism in the form of a more politically oriented Zionism (Theodor Herzl). These two nationalism 'met', or rather confronted, each other in Palestine. The Jews were seen as a Western intrusion into the East and the Jewish immigrants for the Arab countries (after the creation of the state of Israel in 1948) as well as the Arab citizens of Israel as an Eastern intrusion into a Western society.[55]

The question that inevitably rises today is: in which direction will these developments go—after the 'handshake'. Are we living on the eve of a new confrontation or are we entering a new period of a creative symbiosis?

Thomas Friedman, a well-known American Jewish journalist who wrote a fascinating book on the Lebanese civil war and Israeli politics in the eighties, *From Beirut to Jerusalem*, related the following anecdote in *New York Times* article after the 'handshake' had occurred. In the past he always began his talks on the Middle East with this anecdote.

For years I have explained the longevity of the Arab-Israeli conflict with a joke about a very religious Jew named Goldberg who wanted to win the lottery. He would go to synagogue every Sabbath and pray: "God, I have been such a pious man all my life. What would be so bad if I won the lottery?" And the lottery would come, and Goldberg would not win.

This went on week after week, month after month. Finally, one Sabbath, Goldberg couldn't take it anymore, and said to the Almighty: "God, I have been so good, so observant. What do I have to do to win the lottery?"

And suddenly the heavens parted and the voice of God boomed out: "Goldberg, give me a chance. Buy a ticket."

Thomas Friedman's conclusion is that "Yasser Arafat and Yitzhak Rabin at least finally bought a ticket."

In this context Gabriel Habib, General Secretary of the *M.E.C.C.* until 1994, declared:

We view the present PLO/Israeli agreement in Washington as a sign of hope and a turning point in the history of the Middle East and particularly in the Palestinian-Israeli relationship. At the same time, it is only a significant beginning of the process of liberation of the Palestinian people and of the implementation of its legitimate political and human rights. It is also an encouraging indication of the Israeli willingness to withdraw from all occupied Arab territories in view of a comprehensive peace in the whole Middle East region.

Moreover, as we witness the miracle of transformation from a past of fear and war into a future of possible mutual trust for peace, we wish to affirm once again the centrality of Jerusalem for all peoples and religious communities concerned. In this regard we reject all attempts for exclusive control over the city by any religious or political entity and long for genuine partnership between Judaism, Christianity and Islam in defining the destiny of the Holy City of peace.[56]

Here is not the place to speculate as to what could or will happen. Undoubtedly there are still many obstacles to be overcome before a definite solution can be reached. The massacre in the mosque of Abraham (al-Haram al-Ibrahimi) in Hebron (in Arabic called Khalil, 'friend', i.e., the friend of God—Abraham) on 25 February 1994 is such a set-back). But that does not alter the fact that together they took the first step necessary, according to a Chinese proverb, for undertaking the journey of a thousand miles. At least a beginning has been made in drawing the sting out of the conflict that has plagued the relationship between Jews, Christian and Muslims not only in the Middle East but worldwide. The success of the agreement could become a way of proving those on both side who oppose the settlement wrong. A successful implementation economically as well could help exorcise the reality and fear of the so-called fundamentalism (on both sides) since bad social conditions prove again and again a breeding ground for extremism (Hizbollah, Hamas). It could help to overcome the danger of the 'Islamization' of the Arab-Israeli and Palestinian conflicts.[57] The Jewish philosopher David Hartman said: "Unless fundamentalism gets healed, unless pluralism becomes a spiritual value, I don't see any future in the Middle East".[58]

It could well be that if a more lasting solution is found the Jews and Arabs (both Moslems and Christians!) might open up new perspectives for a fruitful and creative symbiosis. That could set an example for the world in other regions as well (Bosnia, for instance).

The peace of Jerusalem for all people appears to be farther away than ever. Several communities, from Israeli Jews and Palestinians to Moslems and Christians, feel their own existence and identity threatened. Najib Azuri, the Maronite said in his book *Réveil de nation arabe* (The Arab Awakening) (1905) that two important phenomena of the same nature and yet opposite had manifested themselves in Turkey. On the one side, there was the Awakening of the Arab nation and, on the other, the efforts of Judaism to reestablish on a broad scale the old monarchy of Israel. It was his opinion that these two movements were destined to struggle continually with each other until one became the master. He saw the fate of the entire world hanging in the balance of this struggle.[59] The state of Israel came into existence less than a half century after Najib Azuri wrote these words. Yet as we approach the end of the twentieth century, the ultimate outcome of the struggle and peace for Jerusalem is not yet in view.

3. Is a Confrontation of Christians with the Moslems Unavoidable?

This partly rhetorical question places squarely before us the fundamental issue of the relation of the Christian churches to their increasingly (since the seventh century) Islamic environment. When referring to the weakness or disappearance of these churches, is it not logical, one could ask, in the search for guilty or responsible parties, to consider Islam as well, which has hindered and even made the survival of the churches impossible and will no doubt continue to do so?

All three of the major religions trace their spiritual heritage back to Abraham. Pious Moslems, who turn five times a day toward Mecca in ritual prayer, believe that the 'house of God' there, the Ka'ba, was built by Abraham together with his son Ishmael.[60] Their spiritual ancestry is traced back to this 'father of all believers', whom the Jews and Christians also view as their own. Jews, Christians and Moslems belong to one spiritual family, but perhaps precisely for that reason their conflicts have become just that much more intense.

The cleft between Jews and Christians, and Moslems is sometimes related to the two sons of Abraham: Ishmael and Isaac. Jews view themselves as descendants of Isaac, whereas Arabs and Moslems see themselves as descending from Ishmael, who, according to the biblical account was made second to Isaac. At times the conflict is thought to be anchored precisely in these two figures.

After speaking of his objections to Islam at a missions conference held in 1890 at Middelburg (The Netherlands), the renowned Calvinist, Abraham Kuyper, (died 1920), added that the mission of the churches should also build on the "true elements that have remained in their [i.e. Islam's] confession of Moses and the Christ." In his opinion, one should honor and acknowledge the line "by which the Mohammadens are linked to Abraham. Ishmael was born of Abraham and was circumcised by Abraham. Christ saved Ishmael's life and indicated the refreshing spring. Mohammedanism has the worldwide call to be a bulwark against heathenism."[61]

Once at a gathering of followers of various religions the comment was made by a Christian that "Jews, Christians and Moslems have much in common, since all three of them are adherents of monotheistic religion, thus, all three believe in one God." An Indian in the group then commented, "Indeed, you Jews, Christians and Moslems have much in common, you are all three *fanatics*." To this very day, Moslems and Christians make each other out to be 'fanatics'. Voltaire used the word fanaticism in the title of a play about Mohammed: *Fanatisme ou Mahomet le prophète*. In the last decades events in such places as Libya (Qadhafi's seizure of power in 1969); Pakistan (Ziya ul-Haqq's seizure of power in 1977), Iran (the Iranian revolution of 1978/79), Iraq (Saddam Hussein and the invasion of Kuwait on 2 August 1990); the (re-)introduction of 'Islamic penalties' in such lands as Pakistan, Saudi Arabia and Sudan (the last with frequent appeals to Islamic law). For Westerners, who share this evaluation of Islam as fanaticism, these events appear to confirm and establish their views.

Moslems, however, frequently accuse the West of fanaticism, making little distinction between the West and Christianity. Ayatollah Khomeini, in particular, depicted the United States as the great Satan, and saw in the United States the incarnation of evil and the devil. In the repeated call to 'holy war' in 1990, the Iraqi leader, Saddam Hussein, mentioned the United States, Saudi Arabia and the Zionists in one breath.

A Lethal Chess Match?

There is a drawing found in a Christian manuscript from the thirteenth century, when Islamic power was in rapid and catastrophic decline in Spain, a period of confrontation comparable to our own, in which a Christian and a Moslem are playing chess together. The accompanying text reads: "There is something symbolic in the game between the two opponents. The one respects the other and learns from him, but they are inevitably driven to the final, absolute confrontation."[62]

This is indeed what took place in Spain (*al-Andalus*). The essential question for Christians in the West, but also in the East (in Lebanon, Sudan, Egypt, and as far as East Asia, as in the Philippines and Indonesia) is whether such a confrontation is inevitable, a *jihad* ('holy war') for the one and a crusade for the other?

One must deal cautiously with historiography, however. It appears that the ubiquitous animosity is very often in the eye of the beholder. That becomes apparent when one examines some of the conflicts of the past. On closer inspection it often appears that the conflict was not religious in nature, even though it was and is presented as such. In the case of the Iberian peninsula during the Moorish occupation, it appears that both Moslems and Christians gave little thought to religious differences. There was little enthusiasm displayed for the Catholic faith.

209

The eighth and ninth centuries saw little demonstration of a deep religious consciousness. Many Moslems and Christians had family members who belonged to the other faith. Until late into the tenth century, Moslems and Christians shared a common culture. Secular elements predominated over religious elements. The growth of a specifically religious enthusiasm among Christians was connected with the cult of St. James (Santiago) of Compostela.[63]

The apostle James and his shrine in Galicia glitter at the head of Spanish Christianity in the Middle Ages. We do not know if there are any traces of such a cult previous to the Moslem invasion, but it was certainly the Moslem invasion which gave it vitality and the aspect of a palladium and a shield of the Christian faith in the Iberian Peninsula.[64]

Not until the eleventh century was there more or less conscious mention of an identification between the spread of the *northern kingdoms* and the spread of *Christianity*. Not long thereafter the Moslems became conscious defenders of the territories under Islamic rule.[65]

It is striking that precisely at that time the first polemical writings appeared in Spain. Ibn Hazm (993-1064), whose grandfather was a Christian, became a Moslem. It is to him that the first polemical treatment from Moslem Spain can be ascribed. Ibn Hazm himself took the initiative in his anti-Christian polemic, while many other polemical treatments were occasioned by similar attacks by Christians, to which Moslems reacted. Ibn Hazm's work has been seen as a sign of the state of tension which overtook the Moslem community in Spain at that time. He is viewed in the West as the father or master of polemic, and his method of analyzing the Bible, especially his listing of contradictions in the gospels, was taken over by later authors.[66]

In general, the 'Spanish' Islamic polemic consisted of four aspects: 1) the Christian belief in the Trinity (in contradiction to the one and only God) and the incarnation of Christ are absurd and cannot be justified by the scriptures; 2) the scriptures confirm the prophetic character of Mohammed; 3) the miracles and prophecies of Mohammed also confirm him as does the preeminent truth of his religion; 4) Christian worship and practice is just as false as Christian belief.[67]

The way in which a political conflict can be presented and described as a religious conflict can be illustrated by means of the epic poems, which were usually written long after the events they narrate. We will examine the examples of the *Chanson de Roland* and *El Poema del Cid*.

Chanson de Roland

The famous *Chanson de Roland* appeared in the eleventh century. It narrates an expedition of Charlemagne (768-814) to Saragossa in the year 788. This expedition was, militarily speaking, an insignificant victory achieved by a rear flank of his army in Roncesvalles. Charlemagne appeared to have no interest in further conquests in Spain. He had simply taken advantage of an internal Arab dispute in order to extend French control. Yet in the *Chanson de Roland* it immediately becomes an entirely different matter. There the struggle becomes part of a broader strategy for the *reconquista* (reconquest) of the Iberian peninsula from the Moslems. This epic poem depicts the ideal Frankish knight who confronts the Saracens. In fact, however, during the reign of Charlemagne, relations with the Moslems were not that bad, especially if we are to believe that he maintained contact with Harun al-Rashid, who has been immortalized in *The Thousand and One Nights*.[68] The religious twist to the story was not given until the eleventh century.[69]

El Poema del Cid

El Poema del Cid is a comparable example, a tale of similar contours that grew around the person of a Spanish knight from Castile, Rodrigo Diaz de Vivar (1043-1099). Vivar, or Bivar, was situated near Burgos, North Spain. Originally, this Spanish knight was made governor in 1065 under a Castilian king, but was banished after plundering Toledo in 1081. In the wake of his dispute with the Christian King Alfonsus VI, he offered his services to the Moorish king of Saragossa, Al-Muqtadir, who was at war with the Moorish king of Valencia. El Cid took the city of Valencia in 1094 and died in 1099 as an independent prince of that Islamic city. Because of his bravery he was given the name el Cid ('my master') which is derived from the Arabic *sayyid(i)*.

His history, however, was spun into a legend, which inspired a writer in 1140 to compose *El Poema del Cid*. The poem describes his last years. In the poem, however, the Spanish knight el Cid becomes the *campeador* ('warrior') and the model of knightly honor, the great champion of Christianity.

On the Moslem side of the ledger a similar phenomenon occurs. That which is political in nature is described, explained, and experienced in terms of the religious. That will be obvious several times over to any Western observer of the Islamic world.

In 1965 I had a conversation with a former Egyptian officer who had fought in Yemen in the early sixties. He related how he had walked through a battlefield in which a young soldier lay wounded. "Why are we here?" the dying youth had asked. The officer, who had earlier confided to me that he had never understood the efforts of the Egyptian President Gamal 'Abd al Nasser to support the revolutionary government of Yemen in Sana', said to the boy, apparently in an effort to comfort him, "Because of Islam." The dying youth replied "Al-Hamdulillah [thank God], then I am going to Paradise."

For centuries Moslems and Christians have engaged in warfare. In many of those cases, religion is used as a justification and comfort. For a Moslem, to be killed in a 'holy war' (jihad) means to attain Paradise. In the Middle Ages, Christians undertook crusades against the Moslems with the motto: 'God wills it' (Deus le volt). Many participated as a form of penance and to earn indulgences. The idea that, if killed, one would die as a martyr, apparently did not initially exist but soon developed under the influence of the Islamic jihad. When Pope Urbanus II called for the first crusade, he did not make reference to the hope of martyrdom, yet he was certain that those who died would be 'saved'.[70]

Heraclius: The Battle of Mohammed against the Christians

Like the two examples of European literature cited above, in which a political struggle was depicted as a religious struggle after the fact, examples can be cited within Islamic literature as well. There is an epic poem in Swahili, the language spoken in large areas of East Africa, which is sometimes called the first epic poem in any African language. The title reads: Heraclius: The Battle of Mohammed against the Christians.[71]

Heraclius (610-641) is the name of the Christian Byzantine emperor who was a contemporary of Mohammed. In reality, Mohammed never went to battle against this Byzantine emperor. Although near the end of Mohammed's life, the first skirmishes took place on the northern border of the Arabian peninsula between Arab Moslems and Byzantine troops, not until 1453 did Byzantium, the great center of the Byzantine empire, fall. And it fell, not to Arabs, but to Turks.

Actually, according to general Islamic understanding, war may not be conducted against Christians at all, since they, like the Jews, are 'people of the book' *(ahl al-kitab)*. If Christians submit themselves to Islamic political authority, they must be tolerated and respected in the exercise of their religious obligations, even though discriminating restrictions may be placed upon them.

In this poem, however, there is no doubt over the legitimacy of conducting war against Christians. Christians are idolaters (who, according to the Koran, may be fought), because they worship saints and images. They are also labelled drunkards. This has become a rewarding subject in the Islamic polemic against Christians, since Moslems are considered abstainers. To put it in the words of the poem itself:

> This was the army of men [the Byzantines],
> The image of God formed from dust,
> There were thirteen in all,
> All of them drunken men. (114)

And with regard to the Byzantine soldiers it is said:

> And they had little images,
> of many colors on their breast;
> each of them had one,
> each of the ten thousand men.
>
> When the Greeks underestimated them,
> and the judgment befell them,
> they called: "Ave Maria!
> She is the greatest of all the images." (106)

When reading this last line, one cannot help but think of the members of the Maronite (Falangist) militias, who adorned their chests, and even their tanks, with crosses, crucifixes and images of Mary during the Lebanese civil war in the seventies. The term 'crusade' was derived, after all, from the fact that the crusaders had the custom of affixing a red cross to their right shoulder.

In the poem Christianity is depicted as a religion of weakness, and is contrasted with Islam as a religion of power. The latter's success was seen as a sign of God's favor.

> Jesus the prophet never
> preached a powerful faith,
> but only to follow the man
> with the large bell and tricks. (138)

'The large bell' apparently means church bells, whose sound frequently (even today) irritated the Moslems, in much the same way that the loudspeakers used by mosques disturb Christians (and Moslems?). At times the Moslems and Christians seem to compete with each other in seeing how much noise their respective bells and loudspeakers perched on minarets during the five daily calls to prayer can produce, preferably built next to one another. The 'tricks' would then refer to the dishonesty of the Christians in contrast to the Moslems.

But, as the poem narrates, the emperor's knights surrender themselves. The Christians are introduced as saying the following:

> We maintain that ever since Jesus
> no prophet has ever been like him,
> no one who acted like he acted,
> no one who ever has done what he did!
> A belief in predestination is absolutely unacceptable,
> a command of glories
> he certainly has not sent.
>
> It is the call of Satan,
> with the sabre in his hands!
> we will never confess, you hear?
> We will not convert. (130)

It is obvious that these epic poems were not intended to promote Moslem-Christian dialogue. They contain typical biases and prejudices. But that which is true of the 'Christian' *Chanson de Roland* and *El Poema del Cid* is also true, *mutatis mutandis*, of the 'Moslem' epic *Heraclius*.

It should also be pointed out that the Moslem epic was written in reaction to the *Portuguese* colonial occupation, which explains its voracity towards Christians. It is said that the epic was intended to serve as propaganda against the Christians in order to incite lukewarm Moslems.[72] The Swahilis, who inhabit the East African coast, the region from which this work derives, are known as a very tolerant people. As one writer notes, "By failing to emphasize that the Epic of Heraclius relates the struggle of Mohammed against the Christians with an eye toward Portuguese rule, the way is paved for the misunderstanding of Islam as an exceptionally aggressive religion."[73]

4. *The Role of Islamic Fundamentalism*

Currently in Europe and the West much is being said with respect to the phenomenon of the renaissance or revival of 'fundamentalistic' Islam. Even in Islamic circles use is made of such words as 'renaissance' (*nahda*) or 'revival' (*ihya*), but in a positive sense, while in the West they are usually used in connection with Islam in a negative sense. After the Iranian revolution in 1978/1979, books and articles appeared with

214

titles such as *Militant Islam* (G.H. Jansen), "Militant Revival" (*Time*, 17 April 1979) or "Islam Attacks" (*Der Spiegel*, 12 February 1979). Edward Said, in his book *Covering Islam*, gives countless examples of how events in the Islamic world are reported in the United States, and could easily have expanded these examples to include Europe. In addition to the fact that such complex events were reported in simplistic fashion, the use of the term 'fundamentalism' is disturbing for other reasons. It derives from a specific American *Protestant* context, where it referred at the beginning of the century to a return to the 'fundamentals' of the Christian faith. A series of pamphlets appeared in 1910 and for several years following under the title, *The Fundamentals: A Testimony of Faith.* The primary issues were the inerrancy of the scriptures and the physical resurrection of Jesus Christ. Oddly enough, this phenomenon of Islamic fundamentalism was described in French by the word *integrisme*, which derives from a Catholic context. It originally designated a 'rightist' Catholicism and stood in contrast to the progressives on the left. Although suggestions have been made for other designations (for example, Detlev Khalid proposed the term *Islamiyya* (Islamism))[74]—one must now take into account the fact that this has become part of popular parlance.

Yet, no matter what name is chosen for this phenomenon, one must be conscious of the fact that (to state it somewhat cynically) fundamentalism is an ecumenical phenomenon. Islam is not the only religion in which it is manifest. In the Middle East, it appears in Jewish circles (the French newspaper, *Le Monde* referred at about the same time to movements such as the *Gush Emunim*, or the 'block of the faithful believers', as the 'Jewish Khomeinism') as well as in Christian circles (such as the fundamentalistic movement among the 'Christian forces' in Lebanon.

A comparison between our own times and two previous eras in history (those of the crusades (especially the period from 1095 until 1291) and of colonialism (especially the nineteenth century and the first half of the twentieth century)) can be very instructive in understanding developments in our own time. Although the actual causes of the confrontations between East and West during the crusades and the colonial era were primarily of a social, economic and political nature, they had a tendency in the experience of the masses to take on religious characteristics. In both periods, subsequent to the confrontations, the same phenomenon, which could be called 'fundamentalism' is present. Another phenomenon which accompanies that of 'fundamentalism' is the polarization of relations between local Christians (one can think here of Maronites, Armenians, Copts and even the Greek Orthodox) *and* Moslems, resulting in harassment, persecution and ending in the emigration of many Christians from the Middle East.

4a. *Fundamentalism and Polarization Subsequent to the Crusades*

Although the crusades were represented as issuing from the will of God, the actual motives of the crusades were closely related to politics and commerce. It was not religious sentiment or piety that prompted the Genovese to offer their ships for the transportation of the crusaders but rather their own commercial interests, which were at the time in a state of decline. They saw many prospects in renewed contact with the Levant, and the presence of Western Christians did indeed produce much profit for such medieval commercial cities as Genoa, Pisa, Venice and Marseille.[75] As W.M. Watt so cautiously understates, "On the religious side there was the idea of the pilgrimage par excellence. On the secular side the commercial ambitions of several Italian cities may have played a part."[76] Both Moslems and Christians respectively exploited the call to holy war and to take up the cross to mask ulterior motives. In the twelfth and thirteenth centuries both the holy war and the cross played the same role as political ideology plays today. A few centuries later, when later the religious motives for a crusade were present, the call went unheeded, because the political and economic conditions were absent. Indeed, Pope Pius II (1458-1464) had planned a crusade against the Turks, but it remained just that—a plan. It was no longer possible to muster the necessary enthusiasm among the commerce-oriented Italian republics, as had been the case a few centuries earlier. The Genovese merchants assumed a neutral position during the siege of Constantinople in 1453. Already on 2 June 1453 they signed an agreement with Sultan Mehmed II (1451-1481), in which they received guarantees regarding life, property, and the undisturbed exercise of religion and freedom of trade, in exchange for payment. In 1454 a similar treaty was signed with Venice.[77] Among Moslems, the crusades were presented as a threat to Islam. "The most enduring results of the crusades was the vehement reaction of the Islamic polity to the continued aggression of Western Christendom against Moslem territory for three centuries."[78] As a result of the European attacks against the Middle East, a religious/political reaction was manifest which, as was said, could be designated by the name 'fundamentalism'. Moslems wanted to defend Islamic identity, which they thought to be at risk as a result of these European invasions.[79] The work of the Arab

216

theologian and jurist Ibn Taymiyya (1263-1328), who saw the end of the crusades during his lifetime, is in a certain sense an illustration of just such a 'fundamentalistic' reaction. He could be regarded a representative of fundamentalistic political ideology. During the rule of al-Malik, al-Mansur Lajin (1291-97) was appointed to motivate believers to *jihad* during the campaign against Asia Minor. By means of pamphlets he inveighed against the maintenance and construction of synagogues and churches.[80]

The fundamentalistic ideology of Ibn Taymiyya would later inspire the Syrian Muhammad Rashid Rida (died 1935), one of the three representatives of the reformist (*salafiyya*) movement in the Middle East, along with the renowned Persian Jamal al-Din al Afghani (died 1897), sometimes called the 'Great Awakener', and the Egyptian reformer Muhammad 'Abduh (died 1905). It comes then as no surprise that Ibn Taymiyya's work is very popular in fundamentalist circles today.

During the period of the crusades as well there was evidence of the accompanying phenomenon of polarization of Moslem-Christian relations. Christians and Christian churches in the Middle East were also victims of the crusades. This was the case when the fourth crusade (1202-1204) led not only to the occupation and plundering of Constantinople, but also to the rise of the Ottoman empire in Asia Minor. During the time of Saladin Armenians were persecuted, to be sure, not on religious, but political grounds.[81] When Constantinople fell in 1453, "the full extent of the guilt of the crusaders" was revealed.[82] Christians were forced to pay for their collaboration, or supposed collaboration, with their Christian brothers from the West. In 1268, in the Islamic reconquest of Antioch, for example, the Latin Patriarch was put to death by the Mamluk sultan Baibar (1233-1277) on the altar, "less as a martyr than as a servant of the crusaders."[83] Christians were persecuted, became more and more isolated, and fled. A large number either willingly or forcibly left for the other side of the Byzantine border.[84] Maronites removed to Cyprus in great numbers, while Nubian Christianity received the *coup de grâce* from the Moslems as a consequence of the crusaders' actions.

4b. *Fundamentalism and Polarization in the Colonial Period*

In a certain sense, history repeated itself at the end of the nineteenth century and the beginning of the twentieth. In the colonial period, the same phenomena of fundamentalism and polarization which resulted from the crusades could again be witnessed. Napoleon's expedition to Egypt in

217

1797 is regarded by some as the beginning of the modern era for the Arab world. The well-known French author François René Chateaubriand (1768-1848), who published a report of a trip around the Mediterranean Sea, *L'itineraire de Paris à Jerusalem* (1811), described Napoleon as the 'last crusader'.[85] One may not be inclined currently to think of the colonial era as an era of crusades, but as appears from this citation, it was so perceived at that time. It is said that after conquering Damascus during the First World War, the French general, Henri-Joseph-Eugéne Gouraud, who served from 1919 to 1923 as High Commissioner of Syria, went to the grave of Saladin, the famous Ayyubid prince, who defeated the crusaders in 1187 at Hattin. When he approached the grave, Gouraud is reported to have said: "Me voilà, Saladin" (Here I am, Saladin).

A similar statement is attributed to the English general, Edmond Henry Hynman Allenby, who from 1919 to 1925 served as High Commissioner of Egypt. He is reported to have said, upon entering the temple square after the conquest of Jerusalem in 1917, and is cited in Arab periodicals to this day, "Today the crusades have ended." The taking of Jerusalem by the allied forces on 8 December 1917 did indeed signal the reinitiation of the crusades for many.[86] Many mosques were destroyed during the Greek campaign in Turkey. When the Greek king, Constantine I (1868-1923) landed at Smyrna in 1919, he was saluted by the Greek Orthodox metropolitan, Chrysostomos, as a crusader. As counterpart to the destruction of mosques stood the destruction of churches. After the First World War, an exchange of population took place. Between 1923 and 1930 one and a quarter million Greeks were repatriated to Greece and a smaller number of Turks were returned to Turkey. In fact, the exchange was one of Greek Orthodox for Moslems.[87] In 1920, Istanbul possessed a population that was 80% Christian, made up primarily of Greek Orthodox. Today there are little more than three thousand Greek Orthodox remaining in a population of six million.[88]

Islamic 'fundamentalists' also viewed the colonial ventures as a renewal or continuation of the crusades, even though they were primarily motivated by economic concerns. In the popular mind, however, it again became a religious conflict. The polarization of relations between Christians and Moslems, which in this period also accompanied the phenomenon of fundamentalism, had disastrous consequences for the Christian communities in the Middle East. Although the massacre of Armenians in Turkey in 1915 had other causes (cf. ch. VII), it must be seen in part in

connection with the consequences of colonialism. It led to the further isolation of Christians and their continued emigration from the Middle East.
After the massacre of the Armenians in 1915, Christians still had to suffer for several decades: in the twenties in Turkey and Iraq, and in the
forties in Iran it was again the Eastern Christians who were sacrificed to
the interests of the superpowers in their pursuit of the oil of Kurdistan.[89]

4c. *Fundamentalism and Polarization in the Contemporary Period*

Where does this comparison with earlier eras leave us? An understanding of these two periods can shed light on the events following
World War Two. The conflict between Europe and the West on the one
hand and the Middle East on the other has again manifested the two phenomena of fundamentalism and polarization.

Our current age could be characterized as neocolonial. This comes
to expression especially in the disposition of the United States (as well as
other European countries) since the fifties toward such nations as Iran. It
is now public knowledge that when the Iranian nationalist movement of
Prime Minister Mohammed Hedayat Mosaddegh (1888-1967) attempted
to nationalize the Iranian oil industry and the Shah was ousted, the Shah
was returned to power and Mosaddegh was toppled through the intervention of the American Central Intelligence Agency (CIA) and the British
Secret Service. This act brought in its wake a manifestation of fundamentalism and polarization. The frustration of these Iranian nationalist
aspirations was a direct cause of the 'fundamentalistic' reaction, which
would reach its zenith in the ascent to power of Ayatollah Khomeini in
1979. The consequences for local Christians ensuing from Iranian fundamentalism was discussed in connection with the example of the Iranian
bishop Hasan Deqhani Tafti and the history of his church (ch. VIII).

At issue is the fact that fundamentalism was in part provoked by a
specific type of Western policy and by a failure to tackle and resolve
social and economic problems. Nor does it hurt to repeat that the religious issues were not *per se* the primary causes of the conflict. Rather, it
was for the most part social, economic and political tensions that led to a
polarization in the relation between Christians and Moslems. One could
also assert that when foreign missionaries were banned from Sudan and
the indigenous Christian church and (African) Christians in the south of
that country were exposed to persecution in 1964, it was again a result of

a political struggle and not of 'a holy war'.[90] Nevertheless, the negative consequences for Christians were soon apparent.

A similar 'Islamism' is manifesting itself in such countries as Algeria (*FIS* or Salvation Front), Tunisia, Jordan and Lebanon. Where Lebanon is concerned, one can immediately think of the fundamentalist Shi-'ite movement Hizbollah, the 'Party of God'. The Hamas movement in the occupied territories of Israel is another example.

In Egypt, one could point to the activities of Islamic fundamentalists in Minyah, Abu Kurkas (July 1990) or Assiut (April 1990). During Passover 1990 riots erupted in the Fayoum oasis, which since 1988 has grown to become a fundamentalist bulwark,[91] when the rumor spread that a Christian storeowner had raped a Moslem girl. Assiut, the home town of Nasser and once known as a leftist 'Nasserite' stronghold, has a relatively large Christian population. There too incidents took place when an anti-Christian pamphlet was distributed by *Gama'at Islamiyya* spreading the rumor that a 'crusader' (a common fundamentalist designation for Christians) had slept with a Moslem girl. Near the end of March 1990, fundamentalists in Assiut fired on two churches and a Coptic youth center.

When President Anwar al-Sadat (died 1981) came to power in 1970, he freed many of the leaders of the Moslem Brothers, whom his predecessor, Nasser, had imprisoned. A book appeared at the time, written by Muhammad 'Abd al-Salam Farag, entitled *Farida al-Ga'iba*, "The Hidden Imperative," in which a fundamentalist ideology was defended and a 'sixth pillar', that of *jihad*, (besides the five pillars of Islam) was viewed as obligatory.[92] Therefore, he has in mind not only 'enemies of Islam' but also native regimes that are viewed as betraying the Islamic cause.[93] In the view of such fundamentalists, local Christians are not only accused of being part of the worldwide crusade against Islam but are also held accountable for economic exploitation, social diseases and moral decay. The result of these and similar fundamentalistic beliefs is that many Copts are attempting to emigrate to the West. And while Islamism creates pressure on wealthier Copts to pursue this route, poorer Copts are pressured to convert. Nawal al-Saadawi, the well-known Egyptian feminist writer, says that the strategy of these groups is to destabilize the Egyptian state in order to pave the way for an Islamic republic in Egypt.[94]

For centuries Christians in the West have lived in a situation that has continued more or less without interruption since Constantine (ca. 280-337) recognized Christianity in 312, a recognition which entailed a marriage of sorts between church and state. The churches of the East, with the exception of the Byzantine Church (which later followed suit), soon found themselves subject to Islamic rule. To be sure, the Islamic state was not always hostile, but it certainly was not an extension of the church. Nestorians hoped in the Middle Ages to gain the political support of the Mongols. Maronites and Armenians have to a certain extent managed to maintain a certain degree of political independence over against their political environment, not wishing to allow themselves to be subjected to *dhimmi* status, as was generally the case for many of the other churches. That is the reason why the Armenians and Maronites have historically assumed a more militant attitude toward their Islamic surroundings. One could say that the image of Saint Vartan, an Armenian national hero of the faith, who is often depicted with a sword embellished with a cross, is representative for that reason. Certain Maronite groups would also recognize themselves in such descriptions as that of the celebrated Romanian author of *The Twenty-fifth Hour* (1949), Constantin Virgil Georghiu (1916-1992), who at the beginning of the Lebanese civil war stated it thus:

The Maronite monks defend Christ, just as Saint Peter, as an apostle, manifested the same excessive zeal (when he cut off the ear of Malchus, John 18:10). They know that Christ will one day repair the damage cause by the excessive love of those who defend him. As a church, the Maronites are cut off from the rest of Christianity. Between them and other Christian nations stand the walls of the mountain fortresses as well as the oceans of conquerors who surround them on all sides. The Maronite church was as an island lost in the Moslem world.[95]

Yet one must avoid giving the impression that fundamentalism dominates the Islamic world today. In fact, nowhere in the Islamic world (possibly with the exception of Iran) do Moslem fundamentalists form a majority, even though the attention they receive in the media and the chaos they sometimes occasion might lead one to that conclusion. Anti-fundamentalist plays, such as *Akhlan Ya' Bakaat* ("Welcome, Sir") and *Inkilab* ("The Coup") attracted, so it was reported, enthusiastic crowds in Cairo (1989).

It is also of great importance to remain conscious of the fact that a Moslem is not necessarily a fundamentalist. That is an objection that can be levelled against the well-known book of V.S. Naipaul, *Among Believers*, in which he describes several groups of fanatics in such countries

221

as Iran, Pakistan, Malaysia and Indonesia. Such fanatics are indeed to be found in these countries, but the injustice is that the title seems to suggest that it deals with Moslem believers in general.

The trouble is that it's highly selective truth, a novelist's truth masquerading as objective reality. Take Iran: no hint in these pages that in the new Islam there is a good deal more than Khomeinism, or that mullocracy's hold on the people is actually very fragile. Naipaul never mentions the Mujahideen-e-Khalq, whose leader Rajavi is committed to a 'multi-party democratic system of government'; but the Mujahideen are certainly 'believers'.[96]

Moslems by nature are no more fanatic than Jews or Christians are, nor is the Islamic religion any more predisposed to fanaticism. The question must always be asked as to what causes a person to become fanatic. Who and what are responsible for fanaticism? It is also of importance to point out that this phenomenon is more of a political than a religious nature. Islamic fundamentalism is properly understood as a reaction movement. In a certain sense 'fundamentalism' is not 'born' but 'made', namely, by difficult social and economic circumstances. In the end one finds social and political factors combined with the instability factor hidden within fundamentalism.

4d. *The Consequences of Fundamentalism? 'A Third Crusader Era'?*

Should we expect that the same phenomena—fundamentalism and polarization—which manifested themselves at the time of the crusades and colonialism era will manifest themselves again as a result of the Gulf War? Obviously, the intention of the West in the Gulf War to defend its interests by all available means had nothing directly to do with religion. There was, however, abundant evidence both during the Gulf crisis (August 1990-January 1991) and the Gulf War (January-April 1991) that Islamic fundamentalist sentiments were aroused, whether with government sponsorship or not. For example, in August 1990 a mufti in Amman (Jordan) declared that the arrival of American soldiers was the beginning of a third crusader era!

Stephen Neill once wrote regarding the crusader era that "the moral temperature of Christianity fell."[97] In order to answer the question regarding the future of the churches in the modern Middle East—especially after the Gulf War—it is important to inquire after the moral temperature of the West. For years the West, including the former Soviet Union, have had few scruples when it came to delivering weapons to various regimes in the region, including Iraq. In spite of the long list of United Nations resolutions, the occupation of the north of Cyprus in 1974 by Turkey, that of Lebanon by Syria in 1976 and the following years, and the occupation of the West Bank (and East Jerusalem) which has already gone on for decades, the Gaza Strip and the Golan Heights, no armed coalition of Western or Middle Eastern nations to implement those resolutions has been formed. In August of 1990 this changed completely, not least because of the changed East-West relations. Russia was no longer an ally of Syria, for instance. It is difficult to deny that the rapidity of the response was in some way connected with the direct economic interests of the West which were at risk.

Of course there is little reason to call Saddam Hussein's invasion of Kuwait and his campaign against Saudi Arabia, the United States and the Zionists a holy war (jihad), as the Iraqi president claimed it was. It is commonly known how this Iraqi president came to power and how much blood he has shed in order to maintain that power. He has deported his own people, especially the Kurds, in great numbers and after the first Gulf War (between Iraq and Iran from September 1980 until 1988) he attempted to eliminate Kurds with poisonous gas.[98]

In the aftermath of the Gulf War large numbers of the Kurds fled from their region in the northern Iraq. Christians who live in the same area suffer as well. They also become victims because of the ongoing international sanctions against Iraq. They, most of whom are illiterate farmers, have either fled to the 'safer' cities or are living in sheds. Because of their, to say the least, complex relationship with the Kurds, Christians face more difficulties in regaining their villages and resettling in their homes, which have often been occupied by Kurdish people.[99]

Listing these problems (the Lebanese and Palestinian problem) is also relevant to the question posed at the beginning of this chapter regarding the future of the Christian churches in the Middle East. The West especially must be aware that intervention in the Middle East has led in the past to fundamentalism and the polarization of relations between Christians and Moslems. The failure to confront and resolve the social and political problems of Israel and Palestine, Lebanon and the rest, might provoke fundamentalist reactions in the future that will have very negative consequences, as it has in the past, for the Christian church in the Arab East.

What precisely the consequences of the conflicts between the West and the Middle East before and after the latest Gulf War for Christians will be cannot be predicted. Yet, when seen against the historical back-drop, it is not unreasonable to assume that despite the fact that this (basically neither the Lebanese civil war, the Palestinian problem, nor the Gulf War) was not in the first place a religious conflict, it could have serious consequences for Christian minorities. This can be illustrated even in a nation like Iraq, which is not ruled by a fundamentalistic ideology. The socialist Ba'th party has held power in Iraq (as it has in Syria) for several decades. As already noted, this party was founded by Michel Aflaq, a Greek Orthodox Christian from Syria. When Aflaq died in Paris in 1989, he was buried in Baghdad. The rumor was then spread that he had became a Moslem shortly before his death. For the founder of such an important political party to be a Christian seemed to be too much. One could also perhaps think of the example of the now well-known former Iraqi Minister of Foreign Affairs, Tareq (Hannah) Aziz, who is a (Chaldean) Christian. Is it entirely coincidental that the 'Christian' name, Hannah, which would make his religious identity plain to the Arab world, is often omitted? In other words, is there a potential difficulty even in the socialist, and therefore not fundamentalist, climate of Iraq in publicly stating that Tareq Aziz is a Christian and in recognizing that the founder of the Ba'th party was and remained a Christian until his death?

It is important to indicate that both in the East and in the West there are other voices to which we must attend who have in the past attempted to resist polarization. In 1965 the Archbishop of Cologne made a wing of the cathedral available for prayer to Moslem workers in Germany. "Approximately fifteen hundred Turks prayed in the same place from which in 1147 the abbot Bernard of Clairvaux (1090-1153), with the authorization of the pope, called for the second crusade against Islam."[100]

Regarding developments related to the Gulf war, the Archbishop of Algeria, Henry Teissier, pointed out that "certain Islamic circles in the Maghreb had attempted to give a confessional slant to the [Gulf] conflict by depicting it as some sort of Jewish-Christian crusade against the Moslems. ... Fortunately, the intervention of the Holy See has called for a halt to this manipulation of history."[101] As is well-known, Pope John Paul II in his Christmas address in 1990 referred to the war as "an adventure from which there is no return." He consistently spoke out against it. That his actions were not completely without effect may be gathered from an interview given by the leader of the Lebanese Shi'ite 'fundamentalist' movement, Hizbollah, Sheikh Fadlallah. When asked what the

224

repercussions of the Gulf War would be for the relations between East and West, and between Islam and Christianity, he said:

I make a distinction between Christianity and the West. The politic of the West with respect to the Third World does not represent the work of Christianity in that region. We do not hold Christianity accountable for all the problems that we Arabs face as Moslems and peoples of the third world. After all, there are many nations in Latin America, in Africa and the Middle East where Christians live alongside Moslems and undergo the same persecution as the Moslems as a result of imperialism. ... The presence of Western armies in a region considered holy by Moslems has numerous consequences. But not for the relation between Islam and Christianity, in light of the fact that the pope has called for peace and has condemned the war.[102]

4e. *Isolation or Interaction*

The effects of the call to introduce Islamic law (*shari'a*) in various countries spreads fear and anxiety among Christians. This is so, for example, in Sudan where it occurred in the last years of the regime of Muhammad Ja'far al-Numayri (born 1930) and afterwards as well (July 1990). Under the government of the current prime minister, El-Bashir, the call of the fundamentalist Moslems for the introduction of the *shari'a* is being heard once again and the green flag (green is the color of Islam) of the national front is again being seen.

As this situation of increasing fundamentalism, caused in part and strengthened by neocolonial influence, gathers impetus, it will bring in its wake a continuing marginalization, even a self-marginalization, and, in the case of the Maronites in Lebanon, a continuing militant ghettoization at least for some time (with all its accompanying dangers) and a further catalyst for the emigration of Christians from the region (in 1990 they left Lebanon by the tens of thousands!). Being threatened or feeling threatened, and belonging to an increasingly smaller minority with all its psychological implications, many Christians flee to Europe and even more to the United States, with the result that the churches are being continually robbed of active members.[103] Throughout this century there has been a steady stream of Christians departing from such nations as Iraq, Syria, Jordan, Egypt and Israel.[104] "Arab Christians: an 'endangered species' of the West Bank."[105] The question is whether Christians can continue to be "the stars in the Islamic universe," as the tenth century Islamic historian, al-Mas'udi (died 956) once described them.

For many Christians the ultimate fear is the fall or disappearance of Christianity and the Christians faith from the Arab East, as it was expressed by Grégoire Haddad.[106] A similar sentiment was expressed in Iraq approximately a decade ago, in spite of the various measures taken by President Saddam Hussein in favor of Christians. The churches had lent the Iraqi authorities various services in exchange for which they received a considerable amount of material support for the building of churches and the restoration of monasteries.[107] Nevertheless, the head of one of the Christian families said, "We appreciate all that, but we still want to emigrate in order to raise our children as we please."[108] In 1979, according to the same article, 2,500 people, both the poor and the well-educated, the majority of them Christians, received exit visas. In certain families of Armenian, Nestorian and Chaldean descent three successive generations have experienced three migrations or deportations. To find a place where one's children can be free, and be Christians, and live in peace is the right of every person.[109]

A similar situation confronts Christians within the state of Israel. In 1922, during the British mandate, 14,699 of the 28,607 inhabitants of Jerusalem were Christian, or 51.4% of the total population. In 1978, according to official Israeli figures, 10,191 of the 93,509 people living in East Jerusalem were Christian, or 9.3% of the population. The current number is not more than 7,000, or approximately 6% of the population.[110] Amos Elon wrote that Jerusalem would soon become a museum for tourists, robbed of any vital form of Christianity. The number of Christians in Jerusalem is estimated to be a third of the number present in 1948.[111] While at the end of the nineteenth century about 30% of the population of Turkey was Christian, today it amounts to a maximum of 90,000 persons. Christians now constitute only 0,15% of the total population of sixty million.[112]

Speaking about the situation of the Christians in Lebanon, the Maronite Archbishop, Youssef Khoury, said that nothing less than the survival of the Maronite people is at stake. Or, to state the case more broadly, "The very survival of Christianity is at stake."[113]

In a talk at Christmas 1993 Pope Shenouda III opposed the idea of a creation of a Christian political party in Egypt "in order not to increase the isolation of Copts in the Society." On the contrary, he appealed to the Copts to participate in political life in order to become incorporated in society. He added: "It is not the church which pushes the Copts into isolation but rather those who keep them away from political activity." In this way he implicitly criticized the government, which rarely nominates Copts to high positions.[114]

226

A 1989 meeting of the executive committee of the *Middle East Council of Churches* dealt with a working paper on the sensitive and alarming issue of Christian emigration from the Middle East. According to the paper, the resulting decline in the number of Christians in the region presents the churches with three options:

They can become a militant ghetto (cf. Lebanon), they can become a docile ghetto, or they can seek to adopt an open Christianity which acknowledges the legitimacy of the Islamic revival, but which also searches for its own role in current events.[115]

More insight into what role that might be is given by the Lebanese sociologist and Greek Orthodox Christian, Tareq Mitri. Christians in the West have little understanding of the fact that modern Arab Christians put a great deal of emphasis on simple 'survival', according to Tareq Mitri. The faith and religious views of Arab Christians are permeated with the pursuit of a continued existence. Many Arab Christians point to the virtue of survival in such difficult, or at least unfavorable circumstances. They think it unfair that they are expected to direct their faith and religious practice toward expansion and mission when this more basic requirement looms before them. Tareq Mitri further points out that this pursuit of self-maintenance is more a psychological than a theological problem, even though it may be a psychological problem with theological implications. Many Arab Christians who pose the question of survival are of the opinion that the Islamic revival, or political Islam, is a threat to Christianity. This is not always objectively ascertained and often exaggerated conclusions are drawn.

Tareq Mitri also goes on to discuss those Christians who are concerned primarily with the survival of their own social group, including its political interests and or rights, and who lay claim to a para-national identity. Here he no doubt has in mind Christians with a mentality like that of the Falangists or 'the Christian military forces' in Lebanon. These Christians see the church primarily as an instrument for ideological mobilization and as a medium for conveying cultural identity or rather for toning cultural particularism. The primary objective is the struggle for the rights of Christian minorities. Therefore, they do not encourage political pluralism within the Christian community. When survival is at stake, so they think, as Christians they must close ranks. According to Tareq Mitri, such an attitude is only strengthened in the face of the revival of fundamentalistic Islam.[116]

Jean Corbon is of the opinion that Arab Christians and Christians in the Arab world today face the choice of becoming the 'church of the

227

Arabs' or disappearing. However, because of their fear they do not per ceive this choice clearly. They are afraid of the Islamic majority. The cause of the mass emigration is no longer economic, as it was in the pre vious century, but essentially has become the pervasive feeling of uncer tainty.[117] According to Paul Balta, the question regarding the future o Christians in the Middle East will depend on the Moslem response to two questions: Do you regard Christians as brothers, as fellow believers? O do you perceive Christians as infidels and therefore betrayers? If th answer to the first question is positive, a symbiosis of sorts will b possible. If a positive answer is given to the second question, it will ult imately mean the end of Arab Christians in the Arab world.[118] Will i be possible for the two communities to coexist, or will the Lebanese prove true: you cannot hold two watermelons in one hand? Western Christians must not take these problems lightly. An Algerian Christian once remarked concerning this point:

In your Western churches you speak at length about Exodus and self-surrender to others. But you are not forced to it. Your ghetto is still intact. You can always return to its security. We live daily in self-surrender, whether we want to or not Because our ghetto has been disrupted. We suffer and are paying for it.[119]

Will the day come when nothing but a handful of Christians remain in the Middle East, like the handful of Samaritans in Nablus?[120] Is the time approaching when the 'living stones' of the church of Jerusalem will disappear, as Pope Paul VI (1897-1978) once expressed his fear? Will the day soon arrive when no more Christians are to be found in the Mid dle East, but only the ruins of Christian churches, as is the case in Tunisia, or the ones near Aleppo in northern Syria, where the ruins o the beautiful church and the pillar of Simon the Stylite, through which so many Iraqis became Christians, now stand?

If a church is to remain in the Arab world, according to Corbon then it must become "the community of God and Arabs." It is the mys tery of communion that will form the unique contribution of the church to the building of a more humane world.[121] If this comes to pass, then there is still hope that one will be able to speak in the third millennium of both 'Arab and Christian'.

NOTES

1. According to Schoen, 1976, 165.

2. Betts, 224.

228

3. *Early Christian Tunesia*; cf. Horner, 1980.

4. Mönnich, 1967, 115.

5. Van der Meer II, 270, 269.

6. Ritter, 35; Mönnich, 111.

7. Daniel.

8. Horner, 1980.

9. Neill, 38.

10. Speight, 78.

11. Horner, 1980.

12. Courtois, 36f.

13. Cuoq, 174, 176, 178.

14. Corbon, 1958, 2.

15. Corbon, 1958, 2.

16. Latourette, 9f., 13-16.

17. Lavigerie, 131. I owe this reference to Maurice Borrmans.

18. Wessels, 1972, 44f. and the literature cited there.

19. Lewis, 1968, 137.

20. Lewis, 1968, 137.

21. Lewis, 1968, 135.

22. Lewis, 1968, 94.

23. Goitein, 84.

24. Lewis, 1968, 135.

25. According to Hans Jürgen Hartmann, in a postscript to the German edition of Memmi's book, 1978, 322.

26. Memmi, 1978, 324-26.

27. Memmi, 1953, 209, 298, 311.

28. Memmi, 1978, 91.

29. Chouraqi, 1968.

229

30. Stillmann.

31. *Arab Theology*, 12.

32. *Arab Theology*, 13.

33. *Arab Theology*, 38.

34. Koran 7:167.

35. *Arab Theology*, 14, 16.

36. *Arab Theology*, 63.

37. *Arab Theology*, 13.

38. Carré, 1982, 235f.

39. Valognes, 566, 572, 573, 580, 838.

40. Berger, 241.

41. 1979, 450f.

42. Cragg, 1982, 101-03.

43. Mazawi, 105.

44. Mazawi, 105.

45. Ateek, ch.1.

46. 206f. Cf. Mazawi.

47. Mazawi, 93.

48. Goitein, 11.

49. Watt, 1965, 157.

50. Goitein, 1964, 145, 146.

51. Ahmed, 64, "Maimonides fascinates Muslims; see Calamus Foundation Lecture, London 21 January 1991, of Prince Hassan of Jordan: Pluralism in Muslim culture: the example of Maimonindes".

52. Goitein, 11.

53. Skipler, 1986, 367.

54. Goitein, 1964, 11.

55. Goitein, 1964, 12.

56. *MEEC News Reports* (September/October 1993).

57. Tibi, 183.

58. Shipler, 138.

59. Hourani, 1962, 279.

60. Koran 2:125 (119), 127 (121).

61. Kuyper, 1940, 10.

62. Lewis, 1977, 245.

63. Watt, 1972, 46f.

64. Schacht, 1974, 90.

65. Watt, 1965, 170.

66. Elpalza, 1971, 99-101; *E.I. s.v.* Ibn Hazm.

67. Elpalza, 103.

68. Watt, 1965, 34,,159; Watt, 1972, 45, 56.

69. Watt, 1972, 13, 45, 56.

70. *Lexikon s.v.* Kreuzzuge.

71. Knappert.

72. Knappert, 14.

73. Haafkens, Thesis 3 of his dissertation on J. Knappert.

74. D. Khalid, 1982.

75. Wisniewski, 17.

76. Watt, 1972, 55.

77. Rodinson, 1966, 216f.; *E.I. s.v.* Imtiyaz.

78. Atiya, 1975, 662.

79. Watt, 1972, 56.

80. *E.I. s.v.* Ibn Taymiyya.

81. Sivan, 1968, 188.

82. Neill, 114.

83. Strothmann, 34.

84. Browne, 49.

85. According to Said, 171.

86. Hajjar, 1974, 187f.

87. Strothmann, 37, 48; Lewis, 1968, 354f.

88. *Time*, 23 April 1990, 44.

89. Balta, 65.

90. Robert O. Collings, 351.

91. Cf. the activities of the blind fundamentalist preacher, 'Umar 'Abd al Rahman.

92. Islam has only five pillars: confession, ritual prayer (*salat*), alms (*zakat*), fasting during the month of Ramadan (*sawm*), and the pilgrimage to Mecca (*hajj*).

93. Jansen.

94. *Nieuwe Rotterdamse Courant*, 4 June 1990.

95. Gheorghiu, 117f.

96. Rushdy, 374.

97. Neill, 115.

98. Cf. Miller and Mylroie.

99. *Courier Oecumenique du Moyen Orient* 19 (I-1993), 13.

100. Abdullah, 71.

101. *Le Monde*, 7 March 1991.

102. *La Croix*, 1 January 1991.

103. Lyko, 130.

104. Corbon, 1977, 234.

105. Mazawi, 100, n. 21 where one finds more references such "emigration and extinction of many families from Bethlehem".

106. 1975, 234.

107. *Le Monde*, 29 August 1990.

108. *Le Monde*, 12 August 1980.

109. Corbon, 127.

110. *Middle East Council of Churches, Perspectives* (July 1990), 4.

111. *Time*, 23 April 1990, 44.

112. Jacob, 1, 3.

113. *Time*, 23 April 1990, 44.

114. *Courier Oecumenique du Moyen Orient* 19 (1-1993), 12.

115. *MECC News Report*, Vol. 2/5, July/August 1989, 3. Cf. *The Emigration Problem*, edited by the Center for Religious and Heritage Studies in the Holy Land, Jerusalem, 1990. Also published in: *Al-Liqa' Journal* Volume 2 (December, 1992). This book draws the attention of all concerned people to the enormity and gravity of the drain of emigration, according to a reviewer of this report in: *Al-Liqa'*, Vol 1 (May) 1992, 113.

116. *MECC*, 1986. A. Maqdisi speaks in the same vein. He points out how much the progressive movements of the 1950's kept the *Nahda* perspectives alive, whereas the pre_ent renewal of integrist and fundamentalist ideologies put in jeopardy what had been gained, including the very principles themselves, in the name of various narrow and dangerous sectarisms. In his article he proposes a program intended to revive the spirit of the *Nahda*. *Islamochristiana* XIV (1988).

117. Corbon, 211.

118. Balta, 179.

119. As quoted by Schoen, 164.

120. Corbon, 123f.

121. Corbon, 127.

BIBLIOGRAPHY

Adnan, E. *Sitt Marie Rose*. Paris, 1977.

Ahmad, A. *History of Islamic Sicily*. Edinburgh, 1975.

Ahmad, Ibrahim Khalil. *Al-mustashriqun wa'l-mubashirun fi'l 'alam al-islami (Orientalists and Missionaries in the Islamic World)*. Cairo, 1964.

Ahmed, Akbar S. *Postmodernism and Promise*. London/New York, 1992.

Al-Liqa' Journal, since 1992.

Anderson, R. *History of the Missions of the American Board of Commissioners for Foreign Missions: The Oriental Churches in Two Volumes*. Vol. III-IV. Boston, 1875.

Andrae, T. *Les origines de l'islam en le christianisme*. Paris, 1955; Germ. tr. *Der Ursprung des Islams und das Christentums*. Uppsala, 1926.

Antonius, G. *The Arab Awakening*. Beirut, rpt. 1969.

Arab Theologians: the Fourth Conference of the Academy of Islamic Research. Geneva, 1971.

Arberry, A.J. *Tales from the Masnavi*. London, 2nd ed., 1968.

―――. *Religion in the Middle East: Three Religions in Concord and Conflict*. Cambridge, 1969.

―――. *Armenia: The Continuing Tragedy*. Geneva, 1984.

Assad, M. and H. Zbinden. *Islam und Abendland: Begegnung zweier Welten*. Olten and Freiburg in Breslau, 1958/59.

Ateek, Naim. *Justice and Only Justice: A Palestinian Theology of Liberation*. New York, 1989.

Atiya, A.S. *A History of Eastern Christianity*. London, 1968, 1976.

Awwad, Tawfiq Yusuf. *Death in Beirut*. London, 1976.

Balta, P. *L'islam dans le monde*. Paris, 1986.

Barlett, S.C. *Historical Sketch of the Missions of the American Board*. 1872.

Barret, D.B., (ed.). *World Christian Encyclopedia*. New York, 1982.

Behrens-Abouseif, D. *Die Kopten in der ägyptischen Gesellschaft von Mitte des 19 Jahrhunderts bis 1923*. Freiburg in Breslau.

Bell, R. *The Origin of Islam in Its Christian Environment*. London, rpt. 1968.

Benoist-Méchin. *Bonaparte en Egypte ou le réve inassouvi*. Lausanne, 1966.

Benz. E. *Geist und Leben der Ostkirche*. Hamburg, 1957.

Berger, M. *The Arab World Today*. New York, 1964.

Berkouwer, G.C. *The Person of Christ*. Grand Rapids, 1961.

Betts, R.B. *Christians in the Arab East*. London, 1978.

Binder, L., (ed.). *Politics in Lebanon*. New York, 1966.

Borrmans, M. "Jérusalem dans la tradition religieuse musulmane." *Islamo-christiana* VII (1981): 1-18.

234

Boyajian, D. *Armenia: The Case for the Forgotten Genocide.* Westwood, New Jersey, 1972.

Browne, E.G. *The Eclipse of Christianity in Asia.* New York, 1967.

Bühlman, W. *The Coming of the Third Church.* New York, 1978.

Bijlefeld, W.A. *De Islam als na-christelijke religie.* Den Haag, 1959.

Carter, B.L. *The Copts in Egyptian Politics.* London, 1986.

C.E. See *Christelijke Encyclopedie.*

Cemam Reports: *Religion, State and Ideology.* Beirut, 1976.

Charby, L. and A. Charby. *Politique et minoritées au proche-orient; Les raisons d'une explosion.* Paris, 1984.

Chamussy, R. *Chronique d'une guerre.* Lebanon, 1975-1977, 1978.

Chitty, D.J. *The Desert a City: An Introduction to the Study of Egyptian and Palestinian Monasticism under the Christian Empire.* New York, 1966.

Chopourian, G.H. *The Armenian Evangelical Reformation: Causes and Effects.* New York, 1972.

Chouraqui, A. *Leven voor Jerusalem.* Hilversum, 1979; Fr. tr. *Jérusalem: une métropole spirituelle.* Paris, 1981.

Christelijke Encyclopedie. Eds. F.W. Grosheide and G.P. van Itterzon. Kampen, 1958.

Churchill, C. *The Druzes and the Maronites.* London, 1862. New York, rpt. 1973.

The Copts: Christians of Egypt. Jersey City: The American and Canadian Coptic Association.

Corbon, J. *L'église des arabes.* Paris, 1977.

———. "Reflections sur la mort d'une église." *Proche orient chrétien* 8 (1958): 197-226.

Corm, G.C. *L'art phénicien: petit répertoire.* Beirut, 1966.

———. *Contributions á l'étude des sociétés multiconfessionelles: Effect socio-juridiques et politiques du pluralisme religieux.* Paris, 1971.

———. *Le Proche orient éclaté.* Paris, 1983.

Courier oecumenique du moyen-orient. Cyprus: MECC Liaision Office Limassol.

Courtois, C. "Gregoire VII en l'Afrique du Nord: Remarques sur les communautés chrétiennes d'Afrique au XIe siécle." *Revue Historique* (1945): 107-25.

Cragg, K. "The Anglican Church." Ed. A.J. Arberry. *Religion in the Middle East.* Cambridge, 1969. Pp.570-95.

———. *The Christian Arab: A History in the Middle East.* London, 1991.

———. *This Year in Jerusalem: Israel in Experience.* London, 1982.

Crawford, R.W. "William of Tyre and the Maronites." *Speculum* 3 (1955): 222-28.

Cuoq, J. *L'église d'Afrique du Nord du IIe an XII siécle.* Paris, 1984.

Dadrian, V.N. "Genocide as a Problem of National and International Law." *Yale Journal of International Law.* 1989.

Daniel, N. *Islam and the West: The Making of an Image.* Edinburgh, 1960, 1993.

Dauvillier, J. "L'espansion de l'église syrienne en Asie central et en extremeorient." *L'Orient Syrien* (1958): 76-87.

De Epalza, M. "Notes pour une historie des polémiques anti-chrétiennes dans l'occident musulman." *Arabica* 18 (1971): 100-03.

Dehqani Tafti, H. *Design of My World.* London, 1959.

———. *The Hard Awakening.* London, 1981.

De Jong, J.A. *As the Waters Cover the Sea: Millenial Expectations in the Rise of Anglo-American Missions.* Kampen, 1970.

Dib, P. *La perpétuelle orthodoxie des Maronites.* Ars, 1896.

"Dossier les Arabes Chrétiens." *France Pays Arabes* 105 (1980): 34-50.

Du Bourquet, P. *Coptic Art.* London, 1967.

Duclier, A. *Les Byzantines.* Paris, 1963.

Early Christian Tunesia. Tunis, 1973.

Edelby, N. "L'origine des jurisdictions confessionelles en terre d'islam." *Proche Orient Chrétien* 1 (1951): 192-208.

E.I., or, *The Encyclopedia of Islam.* New Edition. Leiden, since 1960.

Entelis, I. *Pluralism and Party Transformation in Lebanon: al-Kata'ib 1936-1970.* Leiden, 1974.

Evdokimov, P. *La théologie de l'Icone.* Bruges, 1970.

Every, G. *Understanding Orthodox Christianity.* London, 1980.

Farrukh, Khalidi U. *Al-Tabshir wa'l istimar fi'l bilad al-'arabiyah.* Evangelization and Imperialism in the Arab Coruntries: an Exposition of the Activities of Missionaries which Aimed at Subjecting the East to Western Imperialism. Beirut, 1952.

Faris, N.A. "Lebanon: 'Land of Light'." Eds. J. Kritzeck and R. Bayly Winder. *The World of Islam.* London, 1960.

Fattal, A. *Le statut Légal des non-musulmans en pays d'islam.* Beirut, 1958.

Feddan, R. *Syria and Lebanon.* London, 1963.

Fiey, J.M. *Ahwal al-nasari fi khilafati bani al-'abbasi.* Beirut, 1990.

———. *Assyrie Chrétienne (Bét Garmaï, Bét Aramayé, Maison Nestorien).* Beirut, 1968.

———. *Chrétiens syriaques sous les Abbasssides surtout á Bagdad (749-1258).* Louvain, 1980.

———. *Chrétiens syriaques sous les Mongols (Il-Khanat de Perse, XIIIe-XIVe siécle).* Louvain, 1975.

———. *Communautés syriaques en Iran et Irak des origines á 1552.* London, rpt. 1979.

———. *Jalons pour une histoire de l'église en Iraq.* Louvain, 1970.

236

————. *Mossoul chrétienne: Essai sur l'histoire, l'archéologie et l'état actuel des monuments chrétiens de la ville de Mossoul*. Beirut.

Fisher, E.J. "The Holy See and the State of Israel: The Evolution of Attitudes and Policies." *Journal of Ecumenical Studies* 24 (1987): 191-211.

Fisk, R. *Pity the Nation: Lebanon at War*. Oxford, 1991.

Friedman, T. *From Beirut to Jerusalem*. Glasgow, 1990.

Fück, J. *Die arabischen Studien in Europa bis in der Anfang des 20. Jahrhunderts*. Leipzig, 1955.

Galey, J. *Sinai and the Monastery of St. Catherine*. Israel, 1980.

Gardet, L. *De Islam: Godsdienst en gemeenschap*. Roermond, 1964.

Gemayel, N. *Les échanges culturels entre les Maronites et l'Europe (1584-1789)*. Kaslik, Lebanon, 1984.

Gheorghiu, V. *Christ au Liban de Moïse aux Palestiniens*. Paris, 1978.

Goitein, S.D. *Jews and Arabs: Their Contacts Through the Ages*. New York, 1964.

Grant, A. *The Nestorians of the Lost Tribes*. New York, 1841.

Greenfield, R. *Ethiopa: A New Political History*. London, 1965.

Griggs, C.W. *Early Egyptian Christianity: From its Origins to 451 C.E.* Leiden, 1990.

Gülcan, E. "The Renewal of Monastic Life for Women in a Monastery in Tur Abdin." *Sobernost* (1977): 288-97.

Guillaume, A. *The Life of Muhammad: A Translation of Ishaq's Sirat Rasul Allah*. London, 1967.

Haafkens, H. *Chants Musulmans in Peuil*. Leiden, 1983.

Habachi, R. *Jeunesse culture et engagement. Liban I*. Paris, 1970.

————. *Sociologie et développement. Liban II*. Paris, 1971.

Haddad, G. *Libére le Christ et l'homme*. Beirut, 1975.

Haim, S.C. *Arab Nationalism*. Los Angeles, 1964.

Hajjar, J. *Le Christianisme en Orient: Etudes d'historie contemporaine (1684-1968)*. Beirut, 1971.

————. *L'Europe et les destinées du Proche-Orient: Napoléon III et ses visées orientales (1871-1882)*. Vol. 1-2. Damas, 1990.

————. "De oosterse kerken van de Krim-oorlog." *Geschiedenis van de kerk*. Vol. X. Bussum, 1974. Pp.363-69.

Hartmann, K.P. *Untersuchungen zur Sozialgeographie christlicher Minderheiten im Vorderen Orient*. Wiesbaden, 1980.

Hayek, M. *Les Arabes ou le baptéme des larmes*. Paris, 1972.

Hazim, I. *La résurrection et l'homme d'aujourd'hui*.

Heussi, K. *Kompendium der Kirchengeschichte*. Tübingen, 1933 (8).

Hintlian, K. *History of the Armenians in the Holy Land*. Jerusalem, 1989.

Hisham, Ibn. See Guillaume, A.

Hitti, P.K. *Lebanon in History: From the Earliest Times to the Present.* 3rd ed. New York, 1967.

———. *The Origins of the Islamic State.* Beirut, rpt. 1966.

Holl, K. *Gesammelte Ausätze zur Kirchengeschichte.* Vol. 2. *Der Osten.* Darmstadt, 1964.

Horner, N.A. "Christianity in North Africa Today." *Occasional Bulletin* 4/2 (1980): 9.

———. *A Guide to Christian Churches in the Middle East: Present Day Christianity in the Middle East and North Africa.* Elkart, Indiana, 1989.

———. "Is Christianity at Home in Iran?" *Occasional Bulletin* 3/4 (1979): 151f.

———. "Present-Day Christianity in the Gulf States of the Arabian Peninsula." *Occasional Bulletin* 2/2 (1978): 53-60.

———. *Rediscovering Christianity Where it Began.* Beirut, 1974.

Hornus, J.M. "Contacts entre l'église orientale et le protestantisme continental avant le debut de l'ére missionaire." *Le Monde non-chrétien* 73 (1965): 15-59.

Hourani, A. *Arabic Thought in the Liberal Age, 1789-1939.* London, 1962.

———. *Minorities in the Arab World.* London, 1947.

———. *A Vision of History.* Beirut, 1961.

Hudson, M.C. "The Lebanese Crisis and the Limits of the Consociational Democracy." *Journal of Palestine Studies* 19/20 (1976): 109-22.

———. *The Precarious Republic: Political Modernization in Lebanon.* New York, 1968.

Jacob, Xavier. "Christians in Turkey and their Relations with Islam." *Studies in Interreligious Dialogue* 4 1994/1.

Jessup, H.H. *The Greek Church and the Protestant Mission: Mission of the Oriental Churches.* Beirut, 1891.

———. *The Mohammedan Missionary Problem.* Philadelphia, 1879.

Johnson, N. *Islam and Politics of Meaning in Palestinian Nationalism.* London, 1982.

Joseph, J. *The Nestorians and Their Muslim Neighbours: A Study of Western Influence in Their Relations.* Princeton, New Jersey, 1961.

Juynboll, T.W. *Handbuch des islamischen Gesetzes.* Leiden, 1910.

Kawerau, P. *Amerika und die orientalischen Kirchen: Ursprung und Anfang der amerikanischen Mission unter den Nationalkirchen Westasiens.* Berlin, 1958.

Kedar, Benjamin Z. *Crusade and Mission: European Approaches toward the Muslims.* Princeton, 1984.

Keiser, K., *et al.*, (eds.). *Lexikon der islamischen Welt.* Stuttgart, 1974.

Khalaf, T. "The Phalange and the Maronite Community." *From Lebanonism to Maronism: Essays on the Crisis in Lebanon.* Ed. R. Owen. London, 1976.

Khodr, G. "L'Arabie." *Pentalogie islamo-chrétienne.* Ed. Y. Moubarac. Vol. 5. *Palestine et Arabité.* Beirut, 1973. Pp.185-99.

———— et al. *Al-kanisa fi'l 'alam (Church in the World)*. Beirut, 1973.

Kleines Wörterbuch des christlichen Orients. Eds. Julius Assfalg and Paul Krüger. Wiesbaden, 1975.

Kleyn, H.G. *Jacobus Baradaeüs, de stichter der syrische monophysietische kerk*. Leiden, 1882.

Klijn, A.F.J. *Edessa, de stad van de apostel Thomas*. Baarn, 1962.

Knappert, J. *Het epos van Heraklios*. Amsterdam. 1977.

Kramer, G. *Minderheit, millet nation? Die Juden in ägypten 1914-1952*. Eng. tr. I.B. Taurus. Wiesbaden, 1982

Kreutz, A. *Vatican Policy on the Palestinian/Israeli Conflict: The Struggle for the Holy Land*. New York, 1990.

Kuyper, A. *Historische Document*. Utrecht, 1940.

Lamy, T.M. *S.Ephraemi Syri Hymni*. Vol. 1-4. 1882-1902.

Lane, E.W. *Manners and Customs of the Modern Egyptians*. London, 1895.

Laroui, A. *L'idéologie contemporaine: essai critique*. Paris, 1967.

Latourette, K. Scott. *The Great Century: A.D. 1800-A.D. 1914 in Northern Africa and Asia*. London, 1947.

Laurens, H. "Le Vatican mise sur l'Etat d'Israël." *Le Monde Diplomatique*. March 1994.

Lavigerie, Cardinal Charles Martial Allemand. *Ecrits d'Afrique*. Ed. A. Hampnan. Paris, 1966.

Lazarus-Yafeh, H. *Intertwined Worlds: Medieval Islam and Bible Criticism*. Princeton, 1992.

Leroy, J. *Monks and Monasteries of the Near East*. London, 1963.

Lewis, B. *The Arabs in History*. London, rpt. 1968.

————. *The Emergence of Modern Turkey*. London, 1968.

————, (ed.). *The World of Islam: Faith, People, Culture*. London, 1976.

Lexikon. See Keiser.

Liban 1975-1976: Qu'avons-nous fait et que faire? 6 (1976).

Lossky, V. *In the Image and Likeness of God*. London, 1974.

————. *The Mystical Theology of the Eastern Church*. London, 1957.

Luiks, A.G. *Cathedra en Mensa: De plaats van de preekstoel en avondmaalstafel in het oudchristelijke kerkgebouw volgens de opgravingen in Noord Afrika*. Franeker, 1955.

Lumieres franches sur la question libanaise. Vol. 3. Beirut, 1976.

Lyko, D. *Gründung, Wachstum und Leben der evangelischen Kirchen in Iran*. Leiden, 1964.

Macererian, J. *Le génocide du peuple arménien*. Beirut, 1965.

Makarius, R. and L. Makarius. *Anthologie de la literature arabe contemporaine (le roman en ta louvelle)*. Paris, 1964.

Malik, C. "The Orthodox Church." *Religion in the Middle East*. Vol. 1. Ed. A.J. Arberry. Cambridge, 1969. Pp. 297-346.

Maqdissi, Antoine. "Les chrétiens et la renaissance arabe." *Islamochristia* XIV (1988): 107-126.

Mardiganian, A. *Verkochte zielen.* Haarlem, 1957; Eng. tr. *Ravished Armenia, or, 'The Auction of Souls'.* New York, 1919.

Martin, H. *Journals and Letters.* Vol. 1-2. London, 1837.

Mazawi, A.E. "Palestinian Local Theology and the Issue of Islamo-Christian Dialogue: an Appraisal." *Islamochristiana* XIX ((1993): 93-115.

MECC News Reports. Limassol, Cyprus: Middle East Council of Churches, Liaison Office, since 1987.

Meinardus, O.F.A. *Christian Egypt Faith and Life.* Cairo, 1970.

————. "The Coptic Church in Egypt." *Religion in the Middle East.* Ed. A.J. Arberry. Vol. I. Cambridge, 1970. Pp.450f.

————. "Drie Aspekte der Erneuerung in der koptische Kirche." *Oriens Christianus* LXXVI (1992): 101-22.

————. *Die Wüstenväter des 20. Jahrhunderts: Gespräche und Erlebnisse.* Würzburg, 1983.

Memmi, A. *The Colonizer and the Colonized.* Boston, 1969.

————. *Le Francais et le racisme.* Paris, 1965.

————. *Portrait du colonisateur: La liberation de juif.* Paris, 1966.

————. *Le Statue de sel.* Paris, 1957.

Meno, J. *A Brief History of the Syrinan Orthodox Church of Antioch and Her Faith.* (Unpublished).

Meyendorff, J. *De orthodoxe kerk: verleden en heden.* Roermond, 1964; Eng. tr. *The Orthodox Church: Its Past and its Role in the World Today.* Crestwood, NY: 1981.

Miskotte, K.H. *Om het levende woord.* 's-Gravenhage, 1948.

Mitchell, R.P. *The Society of the Muslim Brothers.* London, 1969.

Mönnich, C.W. *Geding der vrijheid: De betrekkingen der oosterse en westerse kerken tot de val van Constantinopel (1453).* Zwolle, 1967.

Moore, E. *Some Soldier Martyrs of the Early Christian Churvch in East Jordan and Syria.* Beirut, 1964

Moorehead, A. *The Blue Nile.* London, 1972.

Moosa, Matti. *The Maronites in History.* New York, 1986.

Moreh, S. (tr. and ed.). *Al-Jabarti Chronicle of the First seven Months of the French Occupation of Egypt.* Leiden, 1975.

Mott, J.R. *The Moslem World Today.* New York, 1926.

Moubarac, Y. *Islam et Christianisme en dialogue.* Eds. J.B. Gabus and A. Merad. Paris, 1982.

Moukheiber, H. *Les apports du Liban á la civilisation mondiale.* Beirut, 1980.

Müller, C.D.G. *Gründzuge des christlich-islamischen ägypten.* Darmstadt, 1969.

Nasrallah, J. "L'église melchite en Iraq, en Perse et dans l'Asie central." *Proche Orient Chrétien* 25 (1975): 133-175, and 26 (1976): 16-33.

Nazir-Ali, M. *Islam: A Christian Perspectives.* Exeter, 1983.

Neill, S.C. *Colonialism and Christian Missions*. London, 1966.
——. *A History of Christians Missions*. New York, 1977.
Niesel, L. *Die Liturgien der Ostkirche*. Freiburg, 1960.
Nobecourt, J. "L'Arménie du paradis au génocide." *Le Monde*, 30 and 31 January 1983.
Norton, Q.R. "Shi'is, and Social Protest in Lebanon." *Shi'is, and Social Protest*. Eds. R.S. Cole and N.R. Keddie. New Haven/London, 1986.

O'Leary, De Lacy. *How Greek Science Passed to the Arabs*. 4th ed. London, 1964.
——. *The Saints of Egypt*. London, 1975.
Ouspensky, L. *Theology of the Icon*. New York, 1978.
Owen, R. *Essays on the Crisis in Lebanon*. London, 1976.

Padwick, C.E. *Temple Gairdner of Cairo*. London, 1929.
Patlagean, E. "Le triomphe des icones." *Le Monde Dimanche*, 11 January 1981.
Pelikan, J. *The Christian Tradition: A History of the Development of Doctrine*. Vol. 2. *The Spirit of Eastern Christendom (600-1700)*. 2nd ed. Chicago/London, 1975.
Perham, M. *The Government of Ethiopia*. London, 1969.
Péroncel-Hugoz, J.P. *Une croix sur le Liban*. Paris, 1984.
——. *Le radeau de Mahomet*. Paris, 1983.
Pfander, K.G. *Mizan ul-Haqq: Balance of Truth*. 2nd ed. London, 1969.
Polo, Marco. *Travels*. New York, 1958.
Proche Orient Chrétien 18 (1968): 185-198.

Rabbath, E. *Unité syrienne er devenir arabe*. Paris, 1937.
Rabinovich, I. *The War for Lebanon*. New York, 1984.
Rapport analytique sur l'attitude des musulmans du Liban depuis le 13 avril 1975. October 1976.
Reed, G.S. "La Mission de l'archêveque de canterbury au prés des assyriens." *Le Monde non chrétien* 75 (October 1967): 4.
Religious Life and Communities. Jerusalem, 1974.
Renault, Francois. *Le Cardinal Lavigerie, 1828-1892, L'Eglise, l'Afrique, la France*. Paris, 1992.
Report of the Oriental Orthodox Churches. Addis Abeba Conference, 1965.
R.G.G., or, *Die Religion in Geschichte und Gegenwart*. 3rd ed. Tübingen, 1965.
Richter, J. *A History of the Protestants Missions in the near East*. Edinburgh/London 1910.
Ritter, J. "Algerian: Christliche Minderheit in einer islamischen Gesellschaft." *Renaissance des Islams*. Eds. M. Fitgerald *et al*. Cologne, 1980.
Robertson, R.G. *The Eastern Christian Churches: A Brief Survey*. Rome, 1988.
Roccasalva, J.L. *The Eastern Catholic Churches: An Introduction to their Worship and Spirituality*. Collegeville, Minn., 1992.

241

Ronart, S. and N. Ronart. *Concise Encyclopaedia of Arabic Civilization.* Amsterdam, 1959.

Roncaglia, M. *Histoire de l'église Copte.* Vol. 1-4. 1966-1968.

Rosenthal, E.I.J. *Judaism and Islam.* London/New York, 1961.

Runciman, S. *The Fall of Constantinople, 1453.* Cambridge, 1969.

———. *The Great Church in Captivity: A Study of the Patriarch of Constantinople from the Eve of the Turkish Conquest to the Greek War of Independence.* Cambridge, 1968.

———. *A History of the Crusades.* Vol. 1-3. Cambridge, 1965.

Rushdy, S. *Imaginary Homelands.* London, 1991.

Ryan, J. "Kafr Bir'am and Iqrit." *Journal of Palestine Studies* 2 (1973): 55-81.

Sabra, G. "Protestantism in the Middle East; a Colonial Phenomenon, Western Transplanter...?" *The Near East School of Theology: Theological Review.* XIV/1 (1993): 22-39.

Sahas, D.J. *John of Damascus on Islam: The Sect of the Ishmaelites.* Leiden, 1972.

Salibi, K.S. *Crossroads to Civil War: Lebanon, 1958-1976.* Beirut, 1976.

———. "The Maronite Church in the Middle Ages and Its Union with Rome." *Oriens Christianus* 42 (1958): 92-104.

———. *Maronite Historians of Medieval Lebanon.* Beirut, 1959, 1976.

———. *The Modern History of Lebanon.* London, 1965.

Sanjian, A.K. *The Armenian Communities in Syria under Ottoman Dominion.* Cambridge, Mass., 1965.

Sarkissian, A. *The Witness of the Oriental Orthodox Churches: Rediscovering Renewal.* Antelias, 1970.

Sartorius, B. *Die Orthodoxe Kirche.* Geneva, 1973.

Schacht, J., (ed.). *The Legacy of Islam.* London, 1974.

Schoen, U. "The Death of the Church." *Near East School of Theology Review* II (1979): 3-20.

———. *Determination und Freiheit in arabischen Denken heute.* Göttingen, 1976.

Schwarz-Bart, A. *Le dernier des justes.* Paris, 1959.

Sélis, C. *Les Syriens Orthodoxes et catholiques.* Brepols, 1988.

Sema'an, W.A. *Aliens at Home: A Socio-religious Analysis of the Protestant Church in Lebanon and Its Backgrounds.* Beirut, 1986.

Shaw, C. *American Contacts with the Eastern Churches, 1820-1870.* Chicago, 1937.

Shaw, S.J. *History of the Ottoman Emopire and Modern Turkey.* Vol. I. Cambridge, 1976.

——— and Ezel Kural Shaw. *History of the Ottoman Empire and Modern Turkey.* Vol. II. Cambridge, 1977.

Shipler, D.K. *Arab and Jew: Wounded Spirits in a Promised Land.* Penguin: 1986.

242

Sivan, E. *Religious Racialism and Politics in the Middle East*. New York, 1990.

Smith, E.M. *The Way of the Mystics: The Early Christian Mystics and the Rise of the Sufis*. Baarn, 1982.

Snouck Hurgronje, C. "The Holy War 'Made in Germany'." *Verspreide geschriften*. Vol. III. Bonn, 1918, 1923. Pp.259-84.

Speyer, H. *Die bibischen Erzählungen im Qoran*. Darmstadt, 1962.

Spuler, B. *Geschichte der Mongolen nach östlichen und europäischen Zeugnissen des 13. und 14. Jahrhunderts*. Stuttgart, 1981.

———. "Die West Syrische (Monophysitische) Kirche unter dem Islam." *Saeculum* 10 (1958).

Steck, F.X. *Die Liturgie der katholischen Armenier*. Tübingen, 1845.

Stevenson, W.B. *The Crusaders of the East*. Beirut, 1968.

Stewart, J. *Nestorian Missionary Enterprise: The Story of a Church on Fire*. Edinburgh, 1928.

Stillman, N.A. *The Jews of the Arab Lands: A History and Source Book*. Philadelphia, 1979.

Strothmann, R. "Heutiges Orientchristentum und Schicksal der Assyrier." *Zeitschrift für Kirchengeschichte* LV (1930): 17-82.

Suleiman, M.W. *Political Parties in Lebanon: The Challenge of a Fragmented Political Culture*. New York, 1967.

Taft, R.F. *The Liturgy of the Hours in East and West*. Collegeville, Minn., 1985.

Teissier, H. "L'Entourage de l'émir 'Abd al-Qâdir et le dialogue islamo-chrétien." *Islamo-christiana* (1975): 41-69.

Thubron, C. *Mirror to Damascus*. London, 1967.

Tibi, Bassam. *Conflict and War in the Middle East, 1967-91: Regional Dynamic and the Superpowers*. New York, 1993.

Timmerman, J. *The Longest War: Israel in Lebanon*. New York, 1982.

Tlass, M. *H. Kapoutchi: Le pasteur de Jérusalem*.

Trimingham, J. Spencer. *Christianity Among the Arabs in Pre-islamic Times*. London, 1979.

———. "Mawiyya, the First Christian Arab Queen." *The Near East School of Theology Review* I (1978): 3-10.

Tritton, A.S. *The Caliphs and Their Non-Muslim Subjects*. Oxford, 1930.

Tueni, G. *Une guerre pour les autres*.

Valognes, Jean-Pierre. *Vie en Mort des chrétiens d'orient. Des origines à nos jours*. Fayard, 1994.

Van der Aalst, A.J. *Byzantinisme en orientalisme in de oosterse theologie*. Nijmegen/Utrecht, 1967.

Van der Meer, F. *Augustinus de zielzorger*. Vol. 2. 3rd ed. Utrecht, 1957; Germ. tr. *Augustinus der Seelsorger: Leben und Wirken eines Kirchenvaters*. Cologne, 1958; Fr. tr. *Saint Augustin: Pasteur d'âme*. Colmar, 1959.

Van der Ploeg, J. *Oud-Syrisch monniksleven*. Leiden, 1942.

Van der Werff, L.L. *Christian Mission to Muslims*. South Pasadena, CA, 1977.
Van Erp, A.H. *Gesta Francorum: Gesta Dei? Motivering en rechtvaardiging van de eerste kruistochten door tijdgenoten en moslimse reactie*. Amsterdam 1982.
Vatikiotis, P.J. *The Modern History of Egypt*. London, 1919.
Vaziri, C. *Comprendre* 81/1 (January 1981).

Waddell, H. *The Desert Fathers*. 2nd ed. London, 1965.
Wagenaar, G. *Woestijnvaders: een speurtocht door de Vadersgreuken*. Nijmegen, 1981.
Ward, B., (tr.). *Harlots of the Desert: A Study of Repentance in Early Monastic Sources*. Oxford, 1987.
———. *The Sayings of the Desert Fathers*. London, 1981.
Ware, T. *The Orthodox Church*. New York, 1975.
Waterfield, R.E. *Christians in Persia*. London, 1973.
Watson, C. *The American Missions in Egypt*. Pittsburgh, 1904.
Watt, W.M. *A History of Islamic Spain*. Edinburgh, 1965.
———. *The Influence of Islam on Medieval Europe*. Edinburgh, 1965.
———. "Religion and Anti-religion." *Religion in the Middle East*. Ed. A.J. Arberry. Vol. 2. Cambridge, 1969. Pp. 605-39.
Wensinck, A.J. *Mohammed en de joden in Medina*. Leiden, 1908.
Wigram, W.A. *The Assyrians and their Neighbours*. London, 1929.
Wilms, F.E. *Al-Ghazali's Schrift wider die Gottheit Jesu*. Leiden, 1966.
Woolfson, M. *Prophets in Babylon: Jews in the Arab World*. London/Boston, 1980.
Wybrew, Hugh *The Orthodox Liturgy: The Development of the Eucharistic Liturgy in the Byzantine Rite*. London, 1990.

Yamak, L.Z. *The Syrian Nationalist Party: An Ideological Analysis*. Cambridge, 1966.
Young, W.G. *Patriarch, Shah and Caliph: A Study of the Relationships of the Church of the East with the Sassanid Empire and the Early Caliphates up to 820 A.D. with Special Reference to Available Translated Syriac Sources*. Rawalpindi, 1974.

Zamir, M. *The Formation of Modern Lebanon*. London, 1985.
Zwemer, S.M. "The Evangelization of the Mohammedan World." Ed. Annie van Sommer. *Blessed Be Egypt*. Tunbridge Wells, 1906. P. 82.
———. *The Unoccupied Missionfields of Africa and Asia*. New York, 1911.

INDEX

183, 221, 226
Arsenius 129
Ashura 11
Assad, M. 106
Assemani 107
Assisi 134
Assiut 125, 140, 141, 145-47, 220
Assyria 80, 97, 124
Assyrians 7, 81, 89, 94, 96-98, 171, 179, 180
Ataturk, Mustafa Kemal 40, 64, 65, 159
Ateek, Naim 203
Athanasius 124, 126, 127, 139, 144
Athenagoras 62, 63
Athos 80
Atiya 21-26, 30-35, 48, 51, 52, 54, 55, 57, 80-83, 85-87, 90-93, 95, 96, 104, 126, 133, 134, 139, 142, 143, 152-55, 157-59, 216
Augustine 190-94
Autocephalous 6, 63, 70, 90
Aws 11
'Awwad, Tawqif Yusuf 111, 116, 118, 119
Ayyubids 26, 28, 133
Azhar 138, 143, 199
Aziz, Abdul 38
Aziz, Tareq 224
Aznavour 163
Azuri 76, 111, 207
Baalbek 66, 102
Badger, G. 95, 96
Baghdad 7, 18, 19, 21-24, 29-33, 66, 89-91, 94, 97, 98, 153, 155, 161, 204, 205, 224
Baibar 217
Balamand 72, 73, 75
Baldwin 77, 83
Balta 219, 228
Baptists 20, 125
Baradaeus, J. 80, 81, 84, 85

Barbarossa 5
Bar Hebraeus 31, 87
Barlett, S.C. 158, 166, 168
Bartholomeus 151
Barton, J.L. 156
Basetti-Sani, G. 29
Basil 55, 63
Basler 156, 167
Basra 89, 98
Beirut 5, 36, 40, 66, 73, 76, 77, 88, 89, 102, 106, 107, 113, 116-18, 155, 159, 161, 172, 177, 178, 183, 184, 201, 206
Begin, M. 117, 202
Behrens, A.D. 131, 135-38, 142, 143, 146, 147
Bell, R. 14, 55, 132, 213
Benjamin 131
Benz, E. 32, 37, 90, 92
Berkouwer, G.C. 51
Berlin 38, 169
Berron, Dr. 160
Bethlehem 19, 29, 225
Betts, R.B. 3, 20, 28, 35, 68, 70, 73-75, 88, 98, 104, 112, 139, 188
Bidawid 98
Bird, Isaac 172, 177, 178
Bishara al-Khoury 113, 114
Bishoy 140
Bkirki 7, 102
Blunt, W.S. 136
Board 94, 156, 157, 168, 170-74
Bokhara 91
Borrmans, M. 16, 194
Bosnia 38, 207
Boyajian, D. 159
British 4, 34, 36, 37, 40, 71, 94, 96, 112, 136-38, 147, 157, 167-70, 173, 178-82, 194, 219, 226
Browne, E.G. 3, 14, 22, 30-32, 46, 51, 57, 83, 87, 92, 93, 133, 217

84, 87, 93
Mesrob 152
Metropolitan 38, 47, 52, 69, 72, 73, 84, 87, 90, 92, 120, 218
Meyendorff, J. 64, 70, 73
Michael I 21
Miller, Milroie 223
Millet 14, 34, 40, 64, 88, 97, 155, 157
Minority 1, 10, 25, 36, 92, 97, 103, 119, 134, 137, 140, 190, 196, 225
Minyah 140, 145, 146, 220
Mira'j 15
Mission 8, 36, 38, 39, 48, 69, 83, 92-95, 145-47, 151, 156, 157, 159, 160, 165-68, 170, 171, 173-84, 189, 194, 195, 208, 227
Missionaries 31, 35, 36, 39, 57, 68, 77, 80, 81, 93-95, 126, 137, 145, 146, 156-58, 194, 219
Missionary 36, 39, 48, 80, 85, 92, 93, 145, 156, 165-73, 175, 180, 181, 183
Mithaq al-watani 113
Mitri, Tareq 19, 227
Mohammed 2, 5, 10-17, 67, 68, 71, 91, 111, 113, 124, 130, 138, 160, 167, 168, 177, 188, 200, 209, 210, 212, 214, 219
Mongols 29-33, 80, 87, 93, 205, 221
Monophysites 8, 52, 54, 82, 84, 90, 91, 131, 152
Monotheletism 104
Moorehead, A. 134
Moosa, Matti 105, 121
Moreh, S. 134
Morocco 1, 189, 190
Moslem Brothers 120, 200, 220
Mossaddegh 181
Mosul 32, 87-89, 96

Mott, J.R. 39
Moubarac, Y. 86, 120
Mönnich, C.W. 64, 171, 190, 191
Muhammad 71, 135, 137, 180, 193, 217, 220, 225
Mundhir 85
Muqaffa 142
Muqawqis 130, 131
Mutawakkil 22, 23
Mu'awiyya ibn Abu Sufyan 16, 19
Müller, C.D.G. 22, 26, 85, 130, 131, 133, 134, 142, 147
Al-Muqtadir 16, 19, 211
Nablus 228
Naccache, G. 114
Nadir 11, 158
Nahda 70, 205, 214, 227
Naipaul, V.S. 221, 222
Najran 2, 14, 91,
Napoleon 107, 125, 134, 135, 217, 218
Nasrallah, J. 102
Nasser, G.A. 66, 139, 141, 212, 220
Natrun, Wadi 84, 128, 130, 136, 140
Neill, S.C. 31, 32, 168, 192, 217, 222
Nestorians 7, 8, 19, 21, 23, 31, 34, 52, 57, 67, 82, 83, 87-98, 171, 175, 179, 221
Nestorius 50, 51, 81, 90, 127
New Julfa 155, 161, 178
Nicea 24, 49, 50, 53, 55, 57, 127
Nicephorus 22
Nicosia 7, 96, 106, 160
Nikion 19
Nineveh 60, 90, 94
Nisibis 80, 82, 83, 87
Nizar al-Aziz 26
Nobecourt, J. 158, 159, 162
Notaras, Lucas 64
Nubian 217
O'Leary, De Lacy 23, 46, 47, 92,

252

Tunisia 38, 189, 190, 193, 194, 197, 220, 228

Turkey 1, 6, 32, 34-38, 40, 47, 57, 66, 80, 86, 88, 89, 96-98, 111, 153, 155, 156, 158-62, 169-171, 183, 207, 218, 219, 223, 226

Turks 27, 33-37, 40, 64, 65, 71, 77, 88, 89, 92, 95, 97, 103, 106-12, 134, 137, 154-56, 158-60, 166, 174, 212, 216, 218, 224

Tyre 29, 102, 104, 107, 144, 192

'Ubayd, Makram 137

'Umar ibn al-Khattab 2, 91

'Umar II 2, 3, 14, 20, 21, 105, 153

Umayyads 19-21, 76, 105, 196

Umma 115, 116

'uraba 71

Urabi 39, 136

Valognes, J.P. 70, 72-74, 88, 89, 97, 98, 102, 121, 145, 201

Van der Werff, L.L. 95, 96, 171

Van der Meer, F. 190, 191, 195

Vartan 221

Vatican 1, 31, 37, 74, 77, 88, 107, 201

Venice 35, 64, 139, 145, 155, 216

Versailles, Treaty of 96

Von Bismarck, O. 38, 39

Waddell, H. 129

Wakil 34

Al-Walid 19, 20

Ward, B. 129, 130

Ware, T. 34, 35, 56-59, 64, 67, 73

Wardapet, G. 178

Waterfield, R.E. 179, 180

Watt, W.M. 23, 26, 205, 210, 211, 216

Wensinck, A.J. 11, 13

Werfel, Franz 159, 160

West 1, 4, 6, 7, 11, 21, 22, 27, 29, 32-35, 39, 46, 47, 52, 54-56, 59, 63, 64, 67, 69, 76, 80, 81, 83, 87, 88, 92, 94, 104, 117, 118, 137, 144, 153, 165-67, 174-76, 178, 188, 189, 191, 199, 201-05, 209, 210, 214, 215, 217, 219, 220, 221-25, 227,

White Fathers 194

Whitefield, G. 184

William of Tyre 104, 107

Wilms, F.E. 14

Würtz, F. 167

Yamak, L.Z. 4

Yeshuyab 93

Yom Kippur 124, 200

Young, W.G. 5, 130, 140, 145, 147, 158, 159, 212

Yuhanna Sulaqa 97, 103

Zaglul, S. 138

Zakka, Moran Ignatius 88

Zeno 82, 86

Zionism 196, 198-01, 205

Zurayq, C. 73

Zwemer, S.M. 167, 169